1 MONTH OF FREE READING

at

www.ForgottenBooks.com

By purchasing this book you are eligible for one month membership to ForgottenBooks.com, giving you unlimited access to our entire collection of over 1,000,000 titles via our web site and mobile apps.

To claim your free month visit:
www.forgottenbooks.com/free882884

* Offer is valid for 45 days from date of purchase. Terms and conditions apply.

ISBN 978-0-265-74130-6
PIBN 10882884

This book is a reproduction of an important historical work. Forgotten Books uses state-of-the-art technology to digitally reconstruct the work, preserving the original format whilst repairing imperfections present in the aged copy. In rare cases, an imperfection in the original, such as a blemish or missing page, may be replicated in our edition. We do, however, repair the vast majority of imperfections successfully; any imperfections that remain are intentionally left to preserve the state of such historical works.

Forgotten Books is a registered trademark of FB &c Ltd.
Copyright © 2018 FB &c Ltd.
FB &c Ltd, Dalton House, 60 Windsor Avenue, London, SW19 2RR.
Company number 08720141. Registered in England and Wales.

For support please visit www.forgottenbooks.com

Technical and Bibliographic Notes / Notes techniques

The Institute has attempted to obtain the best original copy available for filming. Features of this copy which may be bibliographically unique, which may alter any of the images in the reproduction, or which may significantly change the usual method of filming are checked below.

- [ ] Coloured covers / Couverture de couleur
- [ ] Covers damaged / Couverture endommagée
- [ ] Covers restored and/or laminated / Couverture restaurée et/ou pelliculée
- [ ] Cover title missing / Le titre de couverture manque
- [ ] Coloured maps / Cartes géographiques en couleur
- [ ] Coloured ink (i.e. other than blue or black) / Encre de couleur (i.e. autre que bleue ou noire)
- [ ] Coloured plates and/or illustrations / Planches et/ou illustrations en couleur
- [ ] Bound with other material / Relié avec d'autres documents
- [ ] Only edition available / Seule édition disponible
- [ ] Tight binding may cause shadows or distortion along interior margin / La reliure serrée peut causer de l'ombre ou de la distorsion le long de la marge intérieure.
- [ ] Blank leaves added during restorations may appear within the text. Whenever possible, these have been omitted from filming / Il se peut que certaines pages blanches ajoutées lors d'une restauration apparaissent dans le texte, mais, lorsque cela était possible, ces pages n'ont pas été filmées.
- [x] Additional comments / Commentaires supplémentaires:

L'Institut a microfilm été possible de se plaire qui sont peut-ographique, qui peu ou qui peuvent exig de normale de filmag

- [ ] Coloured page
- [ ] Pages damage
- [ ] Pages restorec Pages restauré
- [x] Pages discolou Pages décolor
- [ ] Pages detache
- [x] Showthrough /
- [ ] Quality of print Qualité inégale
- [ ] Includes suppl Comprend du
- [ ] Pages wholly tissues, etc., h possible ima partiellement o pelure, etc., or obtenir la meill
- [ ] Opposing pa discolourations possible image colorations va filmées deux fc possible.

Pagination is as follows: [1]-viii, [1

s been reproduced thanks

of Canada

are are the best quality
condition and legibility
in keeping with the

paper covers are filmed
cover and ending on
ted or illustrated impres-
hen appropriate. All
filmed beginning on the
or illustrated impres-
last page with a printed

on each microfiche
— (meaning "CON-
▼ (meaning "END"),

, may be filmed at
. Those too large to be
xposure are filmed
ft hand corner, left to
as many frames as
iagrams illustrate the

L'exemplaire filmé fut reproduit grâce à la
générosité de:

Bibliothèque nationale du Canada

Les images suivantes ont été reproduites avec l
plus grand soin, compte tenu de la condition et
de la netteté de l'exemplaire filmé, et en
conformité avec les conditions du contrat de
filmage.

Les exemplaires originaux dont la couverture en
papier est imprimée sont filmés en commençan
par le premier plat et en terminant soit par la
dernière page qui comporte une empreinte
d'impression ou d'illustration, soit par le second
plat, selon le cas. Tous les autres exemplaires
originaux sont filmés en commençant par la
première page qui comporte une empreinte
d'impression ou d'illustration et en terminant pa
la dernière page qui comporte une telle
empreinte.

Un des symboles suivants apparaîtra sur la
dernière image de chaque microfiche, selon le
cas: le symbole — signifie "A SUIVRE", le
symbole ▼ signifie "FIN".

Les cartes, planches, tableaux, etc., peuvent êtr
filmés à des taux de réduction différents.
Lorsque le document est trop grand pour être
reproduit en un seul cliché, il est filmé à partir
de l'angle supérieur gauche, de gauche à droite
et de haut en bas, en prenant le nombre
d'images nécessaire. Les diagrammes suivants
illustrent la méthode.

2	3		1
			2

(ANSI and ISO TEST CHART No. 2)

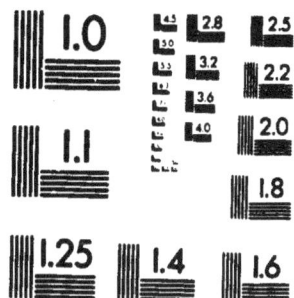

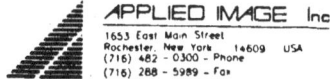

APPLIED IMAGE Inc
1653 East Main Street
Rochester, New York 14609 USA
(716) 482 - 0300 - Phone
(716) 288 - 5989 - Fax

Department of Education, Ontario

EDUCATIONAL PAMPHLETS, No. 9
1915

Laboratory Accommodation

IN

Continuation and High Schools and Collegiate Institutes

BY

GEORGE A. CORNISH, B.A.

Lecturer in Science, Faculty of Education, University of Toronto

---

PRINTED BY ORDER OF
THE LEGISLATIVE ASSEMBLY OF ONTARIO

TORONTO:
Printed by L. K. CAMERON, Printer to the King's Most Excellent Majesty
1915

Printed by
WILLIAM BRIGGS
Corner Queen and John Streets
TORONTO

PREFATORY NOTE

This Pamphlet is the ninth of a series which the Department of Education publishes from time to time. The other Pamphlets are:

The Montessori Method, 1912.
Industrial, Technical, and Art Education, 1912.
Reports of Visits to Schools in the United States, 1913.
Visual Aids in the Teaching of History, 1913.
List of Reproductions of Works of Art, 1914.
Report of Visits to Schools in the United States, 1914.
Organization and Management of Auxiliary Classes, 1914.
Medical School Inspection, 1914.

CONTENTS

CHAPTER I   PAGE

GENERAL ARRANGEMENT, EQUIPMENT, POSITION, LIGHTING, AND SIZE OF LABORATORIES 1
    Walls and Floor of Science Rooms 5
    Arrangement, Size, and Material of Work Benches 6
    Bench Tops, Finishes 10
    Laboratory Stools 13
    Laboratory Water Supply—tanks, sinks, taps, pipes, hot-water supply 15
    Burners and Gas Supplies 22
    Acetylene Gas Plants 24
    Gasolene Plant 26
    Mansfield Gas Generator 27
    Coal-gas for Laboratories 28
    Electricity for the Laboratory 30
        The Daniell Cell 30
        Edison Primary Cell 32
        Storage Cells 33
        Electrolytic Rectifier 36
        Mercury-arc Rectifier 39
        Motor-generator 40
    Electrical Equipment for a Large School 41

CHAPTER II

COMBINED CLASS-ROOM AND LABORATORY 43
    Arrangement of Furniture 43
        Pupils' bench, finishes 43
        Uses of the parts of the bench 48
        Water and gas 48
        Arrangement of benches 49
        Modifications 49

CHAPTER III

COMBINED PHYSICAL AND CHEMICAL LABORATORY 51
    Advantages and Disadvantages 51
    The Pupils' Bench 52
    Arrangement of Furniture 61

CHAPTER IV

CHEMICAL LABORATORY 65
    Lighting 65
    Furniture 65
        Pupils' bench; possible modifications 66
        Demonstration bench 71
        Reagent cabinets 76
        Reagent shelves 79
        Apparatus cabinet 79
        Balance shelf 81
        Draught closets 83
        Blast lamp table ....
        Keyboard ....
    Arrangement of Furniture ....

CONTENTS.

CHAPTER V

	PAGE
PHYSICAL LABORATORY	94
Situation	94
Lighting	94
Furniture	94
Pupils' bench	95
Demonstration bench	101
Apparatus cabinet	101
Shelves	104
Balance shelves	106
Sinks	106
Miscellaneous furnishings	106
Arrangement of Furniture	108
Electrical Wiring of Laboratory	110

CHAPTER VI

BIOLOGICAL LABORATORY	113
Situation	113
Size	113
Lighting	113
Furniture	113
Pupils' bench, multiple bench	114
Demonstration bench	116
Plant House	117
Bay Window	117
Conservatory	117
Wardian case, museum case, herbarium cabinet, aquarium table	120
Situation of Room	126
Arrangement of Furniture	128

CHAPTER VII

LECTURE-ROOM	131
Uses and Advantages	131
Situation	131
Lighting	131
Dark blinds	132
Demonstration Bench	134
Pupils' Seats—Arrangement, height of platforms	136
The Black-board	138
Demonstration Galvanometer	140
Combined Air-pump and Air-blast	140
A Chart Hanger	142
Suspensions	143
Arrangement of Laboratories	143

ILLUSTRATIONS

FIG.		PAGE
1.	Vertical Section through Window	3
2.	Laboratory Stools	14
3.	Section to show Arrangement of Gravity Tank	16
4.	Pneumatic Tank	18
5.	Water-tap with Swan-neck	19
6.	Outlet of Sink	20
7.	Outlet showing Standing Waste	20
8.	Hot-water Heater	22
9.	Bunsen Burner for Methylated Spirits	23
10.	Section through same	23
11.	Bunsen Burner for Methylated Spirits	24
12.	Kerosene Blast Lamp	24
13.	Acetylene Generator, external appearance	26
14.	Acetylene Generator, internal structure	26
15.	Gasolene Installation	27
16.	Generator for Gas from Oil	28
17.	Rose-top Burner	29
18.	Teclu Burner	29
19.	Compound Blow-pipe	29
20.	Bat's-wing Burner	29
21.	Flame Spreader	29
22.	Gravity Battery for Demonstration Bench	31
23.	Storage Cells with Charging Battery	35
24.	Aluminium Rectifier	37
25.	Diagram of Aluminium Rectifier	38
26 and 27.	Mercury-arc Rectifier	39
28.	Plan of Combined Laboratory and Class-room	44
29.	Wall Bench	46
29a.	Plan of Combined Laboratory and Class-room	a50
29b.	Front Elevation and Section of Pupils' Bench	b50
30.	Combined Science Bench (for Chemistry)	53
31.	Combined Science Bench (for Physics)	54
32.	Combined Science Bench (front elevation)	55
33.	Combined Science Bench (vertical long section)	56
34.	Combined Science Bench (end elevation and section)	57
35.	Combined Science Bench (plan)	58
36.	Plan of Combined Physical and Chemical Laboratory	60
37.	Plan of Combined Science and Lecture-room	62
38.	Combined Laboratory and Lecture-room	64
39.	Pupils' Chemistry Bench (elevations and sections)	67
40.	Pupils' Chemistry Bench (plan and section)	68
41.	Reagent Drawer	69
42.	Demonstration Bench for Chemistry	72
43.	Demonstration Bench for Chemistry	73
44.	Water-tap for Demonstration Bench	74
45.	Reagent Cabinet (elevations)	77
46.	Reagent Cabinet (plan and section)	78
47.	Cabinet for Chemical Apparatus (front elevation)	79
48.	Cabinet for Chemical Apparatus (sections)	80

ILLUSTRATIONS.

	PAGE
49. Balance Shelf	81
50. Balance Shelf (front and end elevations)	82
51. Draught Closet	84
52. Draught Closet (elevation and section)	85
53. Keyboard for Chemical Laboratory	89
54. Plan of Chemical Laboratory	92
55. Pupils' Physics Bench (plan and elevation)	96
56. Pupils' Physics Bench (elevation and section)	98
57. End of Horizontal Swing Arm with Clamp	99
58. Electrical Terminals on Physics Bench	100
59. Demonstration Bench for Physics	102
60. Demonstration Bench for Physics	103
61. Collar on Cross-beam of Demonstration Bench	104
62. Cabinet for Physical Apparatus	105
63. Sink for Physical Laboratory	107
64. Plan of Physical Laboratory	109
65. Plan of Physical Laboratory showing Electrical Wiring	111
66. Pupils' Individual Bench for Biology	113
67. Pupils' Multiple Bench for Biology	115
68. Pupils' Multiple Bench for Biology (section)	116
69. Wardian Case (plan and front elevation)	119
70. Wardian Case (side elevation and section)	120
71. Museum Case	122
72. Section through Sash of Museum Case	123
73. Herbarium Cabinet	124
74. Aquarium Table	125
75. Plan of Biological Laboratory	127
76. Plan of Small Biological Laboratory	129
77. Laboratory Dark Blinds	133
78. Plan of Science Lecture-room	137
79. Section through Science Lecture-room	139
80. Science Lecture-room (view of front)	141
81. Plan of Science Rooms for Medium-sized School	143

LABORATORY ACCOMMODATION

CHAPTER I

INTRODUCTION

GENERAL ARRANGEMENT AND EQUIPMENT

THE science of the secondary schools in Ontario has now taken so prominent a place and necessitates the expenditure of such large sums of money for both equipment and maintenance that it has become a matter of importance to have this money utilized to the greatest advantage. In planning school buildings architects and principals are seldom sufficiently informed as to the best position, arrangement, size, and equipment of science rooms, and even the science men of the Province have given these matters little thought. As a result, the positions of the science rooms are frequently unsuitable, and their size and lighting inadequate for the best work. Much has been written regarding the science laboratories of colleges and universities, but the laboratories of the secondary schools have hitherto received little attention, although the methods of experimental work in these schools are so different as to require different laboratory equipment.

Indeed, some of the chief defects of the school laboratories in this Province are due to the fact that their plans have been copied from those of the universities. In the college and the university the students are more mature, are thrown largely on their own resources, have greater freedom in communicating with one another, and are not so likely to abuse their privileges. In the high school the teacher is in the laboratory all the time; he must have an unobstructed view of the whole class, and he must be able to move about among the pupils, assisting them if necessary. Frequently he asks them to cease practical work for a few minutes in order that he may make some explanation or discuss some questions. In the college the periods for practical work are two or three hours long, in the high school they are never more than an hour, and they are frequently much less. As a result of these differences there should be considerable difference both in the construction and in the arrangement of the benches in the laboratory.

It is intended in this *Educational Pamphlet* to state briefly the conditions to be considered in selecting rooms for laboratories, to describe the laboratory furniture and equipment, and to supply some details of a technical nature that will assist the science master to perform his work with greater success and enthusiasm.

POSITION OF SCIENCE ROOMS

The rooms for science work should be isolated as much as possible from the rest of the school. It is better to place them in one corner or at the end of a wing, than among the class-rooms. During the class period there is always a certain amount of noise in the laboratory; when it may be necessary, for example, to hammer or grind rocks in a mortar, to blow on organ pipes, or to ring an electric bell. As the pupils are standing at the benches or moving about for their material there is bound to be much other unavoidable noise not heard in the ordinary class-room. As these noises disturb the adjoining classes the more isolated the laboratory is the better for all concerned. Then, too, offensive gases are frequently produced, which escape from the room and very quickly penetrate the corridors and adjacent class-rooms, much to the disgust of the occupants. Moreover, if the laboratory is situated between class-rooms, it is more likely to be visited during recess by pupils who have no right there, and who may tamper with materials and apparatus.

The different science rooms should all be together in the same part of the building. A good many pieces of apparatus are needed in common in the different laboratories, and the science teacher should not be obliged to carry these long distances or up and down the stairs.

The rooms should be as free as possible from vibration and should be well away from the boilers or from any other large mass of iron, as iron has a disturbing effect on experiments in magnetism and electricity. Needless to say the rooms should be adequately lighted, for the success of the work in science depends on accuracy of observation, generally with the eyes, and such observation is quite impossible in a badly lighted room.

The ground floor is too public and does not give the proper isolation. The basement is generally unsuitable unless it is quite dry and well lighted. If largely underground, as it usually is, it is sure to be damp, and this condition is ruinous to the delicate apparatus as well as to the furniture of the laboratory. Basement lighting, too, is generally poor. Altogether, the top flat has a good deal to recommend it. The lighting there is usually good, and can be made good by the use of skylights. It is isolated, and not likely to be visited by passers-by. Evil-smelling, noxious, or offensive gases are more likely to be confined to a limited area and, as there are usually drafts from below upward, the corridors and class-rooms below are not likely to be polluted. But the top flat has certain disadvantages. It is very warm in the summer. The plumbing has to be carried a long distance at an increased cost. The taps may sometimes be left running, or a water-pipe may break during the winter, and may lead to a flooding of all the lower stories. The ideal position would be a separate wing, one story high, connected with the main corridor by a hall.

LIGHTING OF SCIENCE ROOMS

It would be difficult to find an example of a laboratory that is too well lighted, but the badly lighted laboratories are altogether too numerous. When the delicate graduations of the pieces of apparatus used in physics and chemistry and the minute objects under observation in biology are considered, the paramount necessity of numerous large windows is evident. One of the reasons for devoting part of the top flat to science is that the side lights may be supplemented by skylights. Where the skylights are large the number of side windows may be diminished. This arrangement has the additional advantage that it permits more wall space for cup-boards and black-boards. In the chemical laboratory the light from above is suitable for looking into crucibles and evaporating dishes, but side light is necessary for observing test-tubes and other transparent objects. In the biological laboratory the light from above is good for aquaria and germination experiments, while side light is necessary for microscopic work. Under no conditions is it advisable to have a skylight entirely replace the side windows, because the entire absence of the latter gives the room a gloomy aspect and creates the atmosphere of a prison. There is a difference of opinion as to which exposure is most suitable. Some teachers of biology prefer the windows on the south side, while others object to direct sunlight and favour them being placed on the north side. If a conservatory is attached to the biology room it must have south or east windows. In teaching chemistry and physics the direct sunlight is useful for some of the experimental work, and in teaching optics the direct sunlight is almost a necessity for experiments where a lantern is lacking. While a northern aspect is recommended by many science teachers in the United States it is not the best in Ontario for any of the laboratories. In this Province during the winter months the sun rises so late and sets so early that northern windows leave the rooms too dark during the first hour of the morning and the last hour of the afternoon. The too great heat and the too intense light are objections to a southern exposure, but both of these can be overcome by suitable blinds. On the whole, then, better results are obtained for all the laboratories with a southern exposure where it is possible.

It is recommended by school architects that the lighting area for an ordinary class-room should be from one fourth to one sixth of the floor space. In a laboratory it should not be less than one fourth, and even one third will not make the room too bright. The illumination of the working space farthest from the windows must be kept in mind in deciding the shape of the room and the position of the windows. A long, narrow room is easiest to light, and has much to be said in its favour. When the ratio of window to floor space is made one to four, it is the actual light-transmitting area that is considered, and hence the part of the window occupied by sashes and frames is eliminated. The front eight feet of the side wall should contain no windows, but the rest of the side wall should be as completely occupied by windows as the construction of the wall will permit. The sill is placed about 3 ft. 6 in. above the floor; this makes the base of the window a little higher than the tops of the laboratory benches. The window tops extend right to the ceiling, or as near to it as the construction of the building allows. This latter point cannot be emphasized too strongly. The darkest part of the room receives most of its light from the upper half of the windows, and the higher the windows extend the more adequately lighted will this part be. The window blinds should be white or light green and very translucent, so that they may scatter the direct sunlight without darkening the room to any great extent. The blinds need not extend right to the top of the window, as the outer wall, projecting over the window, always cuts off the direct rays from the upper foot or more, and, with a blind covering this part, it throws the farther side of the room in double shade. Figure 1 illustrates this point. The parallel rays of the sun pass in the direction MN. All above CD are cut off by the projecting thickness of the wall at E. A blind, the top of which is placed at B, will cut off all the direct light, while the space between A and B is always open, even when the blind is drawn, and diffused light passes through this space to brighten especially the parts of the room farthest from the window.

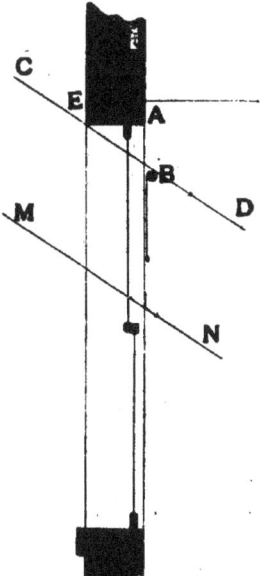

Fig. 1. — Vertical section through a window to show the proper position for the attachment of the blind. CD and MN, the direction of the direct rays of light. B, the point at which the blind is attached.

LABORATORY ACCOMMODATION

Suppose the laboratory is a room 30 ft. long and 24 ft. wide, then the area of the floor space is 720 square feet. If the ratio of window area to floor space is as one to four, the area of the effective window space is 180 square feet. Probably one tenth of the window space is not efficient, as it is occupied by the sash partitions separating the panes of glass; thus the area devoted to windows should be 200 square feet. If the wall is 14 ft. high and the window begins 3½ ft. from the floor and extends to within 6 in. of the ceiling (as it should), it will be 10 ft. high. Five windows, each 4 ft. wide, give just the required area, and this number of windows is about the right minimum for a room of the above proportions. For wide rooms the proportion of four to one should be increased; for long and narrow rooms it may be diminished. Where skylights are present the number and size of the side windows may be proportionally diminished. Frequently it is possible to have windows on two sides, and this arrangement gives a more even distribution of light. It has, however, the drawback of diminishing the amount of wall space available for shelves and black-boards. If skylights are present, the window sashes in the roof should not be horizontal, but should have a slope steep enough to shed the rain and snow. They should not slope toward the south, as this tends to make the room excessively hot, but a north or east slope is satisfactory. Of course no coloured, ground, or painted glass should be used in any of the windows. All the window sashes, both bottom and top, are hung with counterbalance weights so that they slide easily. Everybody who has worked in a laboratory knows what a great advantage it is to be able to throw up all the windows and get a complete change of air after some accident by which the room has become contaminated with irritating fumes.

The sills of the windows in laboratories should slope outward as little as possible, and be as wide as is consistent with appearances. Much use can be made of such sills in experimental work, as, for example, where exposure to sunlight is required in physiological work in botany. They can also be utilized to hold germinating boxes. Moreover, chemical experiments, in which an explosion is possible, or in which irritating fumes are produced, can be best performed on the window-sill in the open air.

SIZE OF LABORATORIES

In estimating the size of the laboratory a good many factors have to be considered. It should be of such size and shape that the pupils will be able to do their work with the minimum amount of movement and with the maximum amount of convenience. It should be of sufficient size to accommodate at one time the largest number of pupils who are to do practical work. This number is limited in high schools in Ontario by the size of the class that one instructor can efficiently manage at practical work. In England the number is usually placed at twenty; the tendency in the United States is to diminish this to fifteen, or even twelve. The Department of Education in this Province fixes the maximum number at twenty-four, and calculations had best be made for this number. Each pupil should have a bench space 3 ft. 6 in. long and 2 ft. wide; behind each bench should be a working space of at least 3 ft., in which the pupil stands, and which also permits the instructor to pass along freely to superintend and assist in the work. This makes a floor area of 3½ ft. by 5 ft., or 17½ square feet for each pupil. This does not include the space necessary for aisles, sinks, the instructor's bench, and storage cases of different kinds. Professor Minot, of Harvard University, places the extra amount of floor space per student at 11 square feet. He, however, is

SIZE OF LABORATORIES

estimating for the college student and chiefly for biological laboratories where the number of sinks and cabinets is not so great as it is in a high school laboratory. This extra space may be placed at 12½ square feet per pupil; so that the total area of floor space per pupil is 30 square feet. This is the amount recommended for elementary science laboratories by the Board of Education in England. Twenty-four pupils require a room 720 square feet in area. A well-proportioned room would be 30 ft. long by 24 ft. wide. Where a store-room is lacking or where extra furniture is placed in the laboratory, such as balance tables, additional space is required. If chairs or desks are grouped together where the pupils sit for lectures or demonstrations, a good deal more accommodation is necessary. These factors alone do not determine the size of the room. Each pupil requires a certain volume of air space, and when the ceiling is low the floor area must be still further increased. A great deal also depends on the method of ventilation. Where artificial blowers or fans of sufficient size are used, the volume of air per pupil may be considerably diminished. In the chemical laboratories, the Bunsen burners consume large quantities of oxygen and pollute the air with carbon dioxide, and the irritating fumes require much air to dilute them, so that this laboratory requires lofty ceilings, large floor area, and quick and effective ventilation.

WALLS OF THE SCIENCE ROOMS

The colour of the walls of the laboratory is of much importance. A colour must be used that, while destroying the unpleasant glare of a bare white wall, does not allow too much absorption of light. It is also necessary to select a colour that is restful to the eye. Light yellow and buff are frequently used, but it has been proven that all yellows are fatiguing and produce nervousness in a marked degree. Some shade of green seems the most satisfactory to use, as it is restful to the eye, it does not absorb greatly, and light reflected from it resembles the reflected light out-of-doors. Many architects recommend a green or grayish-green as most suitable. The ceiling should be left perfectly white, as this colour is the best reflector of light. The walls should always be painted so that they may be washed. The paint should be flatted to eliminate any gloss or glare, and should be free from white lead or other pigment that will tarnish from fumes produced during experiments. Clay, in his book, *Modern School Buildings*, recommends a light greenish-gray made from Antwerp blue, raw sienna, and zinc white. A wooden wainscotting or a toe-board and chair-rail should be placed around the room, and into the chair-rail screws or nails may be fastened. The severe plainness of the wall might be broken by touc' s of colour and a little detail. Such attractive refinements, together with pict . undoubtedly have an unconsciously elevating influence. Scientific pictures, d especially portraits of eminent scientists, are particularly appropriate.

THE FLOOR

In America the floor is almost always of wood. Tiling and square wooden blocks are frequently used in England, but are too expensive to be generally utilized. Tile or concrete floors are incombustible, and only slightly affected by chemicals, but they are cold and somewhat noisy. If the floor is of wood, it should be of some hard, durable kind. Pine floors wear rapidly in the aisles and in the standing places behind the benches, and soon become rough and splintery, so that they appear unsightly and are difficult to keep clean. Maple and birch are probably the best materials to use for this purpose. The floor should be finished either with wax or with hard oil, so that any chemicals spilled will not corrode it deeply. If the floors are made of maple or birch, scrubbed frequently, and then oiled or waxed, in about a year a fine hard surface will be produced that will require little attention. Stains should be scratched or planed off as soon after their discovery as possible. Clay gives the following as a good wax finish:

Yellow wax	20 parts
Yellow ozocerite	20 parts
Linseed oil (boiled)	1 part
Turpentine	25 parts
Raw sienna	5 parts

Mix the two waxes over a slow fire, add the colouring previously mixed with the oil, and when cold add the turpentine.

ARRANGEMENT OF WORKING BENCHES

The working benches should be so arranged that the pupil may obtain material and apparatus with as little inconvenience and waste of time as possible. He should have sufficient space to move about without being crowded. The light from the windows should adequately illuminate his working place. When standing or sitting at his working place, he should not be in his own or in any other pupil's light. The benches should be so constructed and arranged that the instructor can readily reach any pupil in order to assist him with his work. The benches should be so placed that the pupils find little opportunity either to talk to one another or to interfere with one another's apparatus. In what style of bench do all these conditions obtain to the greatest extent? Before answering the question finally, let us consider the kinds of benches that are most frequently used in physical and chemical laboratories.

A long bench with working places on one or both sides is common in our laboratories at the present time. These benches are arranged in one of the following ways:

1. They form a rectangle around the room, with working places on both the inside and the outside of the rectangle.
2. Single benches extend across the room, with side aisles, and with or without a central aisle.
3. Single benches run lengthwise along the walls of the room and a double bench runs lengthwise down the middle.
4. Double benches run lengthwise down the room.
5. Double benches run across the room, with side aisles, and with or without a central one.

The first of these methods is very bad, as the teacher can reach a pupil only by walking around to the opening in the rectangle. The second method is good, especially if there is a central aisle, as all pupils are facing in the same direction, and so are in a good position to receive instructions or explanations from the teacher. As they are not facing one another, there is not the same inducement to irrelevant conversation, and all receive light from the same direction. Three, four, and five involve the use of double benches, which are advantageous only in economizing space, sinks, and reagent bottles. From a disciplinary standpoint they are distinctly disadvantageous, as the inducement to talk across the bench is great, and the apparatus is liable to become mixed, often intentionally, across the middle line. If the double benches run lengthwise, half of the pupils work with their backs to the windows and the other half work in the shadow of the pupils opposite to them. If the benches run across the room, half the class have their backs to the instructor's bench and require to turn around to attend to him, while he is giving instructions or conducting lessons. These long benches, either double or single, are imitations of those in the college laboratory, where the conditions of instruction and discipline are quite different from those in the high school, as has been mentioned already (page 1).

What kind of bench is better than any of these? The ideal to be aimed at in all the laboratories is *a separate bench for each pupil*. All the conditions mentioned above as conducive to good discipline and to economy of effort are obtained to a maximum extent by such a bench. All the pupils face in one direction; each has his own bench top exclusively for his own use; there is no excuse for any conversation; pieces of apparatus will not be transferred by the pupils; no dispute will arise as to whose duty it is to clear the sinks or bench tops; all the benches can be arranged with the same relation to the windows; and the teacher can easily reach any pupil, as aisles pass between the rows. The only serious objections to such benches are their greater initial cost and the larger floor space they require. Neither of these is serious, as the increased cost is not large and the additional space required is not great. When the advantages of such an arrangement are placed against the extra pecuniary outlay, no educational board which has high ideals of the purpose and value of education will hesitate to contribute the additional amount.

The benches in the physical laboratory alone will be of a different kind. In physical experiments large pieces of apparatus are frequently used, such as sonometers, Wheatstone sliding bridges, and Kundt's tubes. These require a long bench; experiments with lenses and mirrors also usually require a long bench top. Therefore it is better, in the physical laboratory, to have benches long enough to supply working places for two pupils, and when experiments like those mentioned above are being performed, two pupils can work together and have a stretch of bench top about seven feet in length.

Physical and chemical benches should be placed across the room opposite the windows, so that the full light of the window shines directly on the bench top. It is preferable to have the benches face in such a manner that the light comes in from the left. For biology, where lenses and microscopes are much used, it is preferable to have the light come from the front, but side light is permissible, if wedge-shaped benches are used, so that one pupil sitting at such a bench will not cut off the light from the pupil next to him.

SIZE OF PUPILS' WORK BENCHES

The benches for experimental physics and chemistry are usually made so high that they are convenient for a pupil to work at while he is standing. Stools may be supplied, but they will not be used to any great extent. The biology benches, on the other hand, will be of a height suitable for working at while sitting, and will be made so low that a high school pupil can look down into a microscope while sitting on his stool with his feet resting on the floor. A pupil standing at work should have the bench top so high that he can have his forearm horizontal while working with apparatus on the top. Therefore, the height will depend on the size of the pupils. In an elementary laboratory, which is used only by the pupils of the lower Forms, from fourteen to sixteen years of age, a height of 2 ft. 9 in. or 2 ft. 10 in. is best, but in a room used mostly by pupils over sixteen years of age the tops should be 3 ft. high. A biology bench should be as low as 28 in., in order that dissections and examinations through lenses and microscopes may be made with ease and comfort to the pupil.

The length and width of a bench top will depend, to some extent, on the amount of disposable floor space. A top 3½ ft. long is generally sufficient for any pupil for any kind of bench, whether in physics, chemistry, or biology. But occasionally, in physics, a greater amount of space is needed, and for that reason double benches are recommended. A pupil standing behind the bench should be able to reach apparatus without bending his body over the bench. A top 30 in. wide is as great as can be comfortably utilized and gives ample area; where space needs to be economized, even less width can be given to the tops without losing much in efficiency.

As has been stated, the benches used for physics and chemistry should have the ends opposite the windows, so that the light will all come from the left if the benches are single; if the benches are back to back, it will come from the left for those facing the front and from the right for those facing in the opposite direction. The particular arrangement will depend on the shape and size of the room, but some general rules may be stated for the guidance of those planning laboratories. The aisles should run up and down the room and not across. These aisles should be 3 ft. wide, if possible. There should be aisles 4 ft. wide on each side of the room; and these should be still wider, if apparatus cabinets are placed against the walls. The spaces between the benches, from front to back, should be sufficiently wide to give the worker ample room and also to allow the teacher to move across the room behind the pupils. This will require at least 3 ft. space between the successive benches in a row. It is better not to have the ends of the benches against the walls; such an arrangement diminishes the number of aisles, and decreases the amount of wall space available for apparatus, cabinets, or black-boards. Where the necessities of a limited floor space require that the benches should be placed against the walls, it is preferable to put them against the wall between, rather than opposite, the windows; for if they are opposite, the accessibility of the windows is too restricted.

In the biology room the arrangement of the benches will be different. Here the light should come from the front, to be most convenient for dissecting and for using the lens and microscope. If it comes from the sides, the pupil will be continually working in the shadow of his hands. In order that he should not be in the shadow of the pupil in front of him the benches should be arranged so that in succeeding rows across the room they occupy alternate positions. If they are of the individual type, as they should be, this means that they should be arranged in quincunx order, the benches in one row across the room occupying a position in a line with the spaces between the benches in the adjacent rows in front and behind. See Figure 75 as an example of this arrangement. As this eliminates all the aisles between the rows from front to rear, the side aisles should be wider than usual, and the spaces between the benches from front to rear should be broader than the dimensions already given.

The old practice of having reagent shelves raised above the top of the chemistry bench was borrowed from the college, where the conditions are different, and where it is not so necessary for disciplinary purposes that nothing should obstruct the view between teacher and pupil. The consensus of opinion among secondary science teachers is that the fewer the number of such objects raised above the bench top the better; and in the best laboratories other places are being found for the reagent bottles.

MATERIAL OF BENCHES

Several factors determine the material of which the laboratory furniture is constructed. There should be a certain amount of harmony between the laboratory fittings, the woodwork of the room, and the other furniture. Some kinds of wood in some sections of the Province may be more readily available and cheaper than others. The amount available for expenditure will be an important determining factor. One point is worth noting regarding the cost. The price of the furniture is not determined chiefly by the price of the material from which it is constructed. A much more important factor in determining the cost is the ease or difficulty with which the wood can be worked, for, in the case of most laboratory furniture, the largest item of expense is the payment of the labour rather than the cost of material. There is not much difference in the price of white pine, birch, and maple at the present time. Yet a piece of furniture built of birch or maple will cost more than one made of pine, because pine is an easy wood to work, being soft and even-grained, while birch and maple are hard and require much more time in the working.

The body of the benches and the various cabinets require certain qualities in the wood used. The material should not be likely to shrink, warp, crack, or splinter. Shrinkage causes the parts to separate, so that openings form into which dust penetrates, and also causes the parts to fall to pieces or, at least, to fit loosely. As the shrinking will be unequal, drawers and doors will bind, and will require to be continually eased by planing. Warping produces similar defects, and cracks and splintering spoil the appearance and cause rapid deterioration in the furniture. Thorough seasoning is absolutely necessary. Care should be taken that the furniture be not placed in the building while it is still damp from the newly plastered walls, but only after the fires have been lighted to lessen the humidity of the air.

White pine makes a satisfactory material for the body of the benches and other furniture. It is easily worked, fine, and straight-grained, usually sound, and free from knots. It warps and shrinks very little, and when properly finished it has a good appearance. True, it is soft and lacks strength, but, for the body of the bench, these qualities are not necessarily objectionable. White pine formerly was cheap, but the price has advanced considerably, so that it is now as high as most of the hardwoods. Georgia, or pitch pine, is also good. It is much harder and heavier than white pine, but shrinks and cracks more, and is more difficult to work. Maple and birch are also good materials, as they are quite hard, shrink and warp to a small extent only, are moderate in price, have a close, even grain, and take a good finish. Ash is also a suitable material, as it is fairly easily worked; if properly seasoned it will not warp or shrink much, and it has a coarse grain of considerable beauty. Elm is entirely unsatisfactory and should not be used. It shrinks and warps very greatly, and is sure to crack and splinter; it is also difficult to work. Oak is not to be recommended generally. Unless it is very carefully selected, it shrinks very unevenly and warps badly; and it is also very difficult to work. Where expense is not a consideration, the ideal wood is teak. It is moderately hard and, when once seasoned, does not split, crack, warp, or alter its shape in any way. No mistake will be made if pine, beech, birch, maple, ash, or teak is used.

The drawers are fronted with the same material as the body, and the unexposed parts are usually of pine or bass-wood, but the sliding sides should always be of birch, as it has a smooth, satiny surface which slides well. The drawers should be made so that they do not pull out completely, otherwise careless pupils are certain to spill their contents occasionally, with resultant loss of fragile apparatus. This can be arranged by having a wooden button screwed to the back, which catches before the drawer is completely withdrawn. By turning this button the drawer can be wholly withdrawn for cleaning. The drawers should have turned pulls of wood rather than metal, as the latter material is liable to tarnish, and if they are made of iron, they may interfere with experiments in magnetism. A flush pull is preferable, as a projecting knob is liable to be in the way, particularly when the drawer is partially open. If the flush pull is used, the front of the drawer must be made rather thick. Cupboard doors underneath benches should fasten with a ball catch.

There should be as little moulding as possible on the furniture, so that there will be no resting-place for dust, and if there are panels, they should be almost flush. Under the bench tops there should be recesses for the knees when the pupils are sitting down. All along the base of the benches at which pupils stand there should be toe-spaces about 4 in. high. These will allow the pupils to stand close to the benches with comfort while they are at work, and prevent the unsightly appearance produced along the base by the continual contact of the pupils' toes with the lower part of the bench.

The finish will be largely determined by that of the surroundings. No paint of any kind should be used. The nearer the finish is to the natural wood in appearance the better is the result. All the exposed parts may be covered by a silica filler and then finished with one coat of white shellac and one of Johnson's wax—the latter being thoroughly rubbed. The inside of the drawers and cupboards may be given one coat of orange shellac.

BENCH TOPS

The bench tops in all the laboratories have to resist the action of chemicals, including the strongest acids and alkalis. They have also to resist the heat of the Bunsen burners, hot beakers, flasks, and crucibles. Many hot solids and liquids will continually be spilled upon them. In order that they may effectively withstand these, the selection of material for the top requires much more careful consideration than the selection of material for the body. The bench top requires also to be perfectly level and free from chinks or crevices that might give lodgement to dust or to chemicals spilled on its surface. Warping is fatal to its usefulness. Too much care cannot be bestowed on the material and structure of the top. The chief materials used in its construction are wood, lead, glass, slate, lava slabs, and alberene stone. The best wood by far is teak. It is fairly hard, tough, shows no warping or cracking, and is non-porous. It is filled with resins that prevent the entrance of water or chemicals. Georgia, or pitch pine, is more likely to warp, crack, or splinter, but it is hard and non-porous also on account of it being permeated by resin, and makes a very fair top. Maple forms a good hard top, but warps considerably. A material that up to the present has not been much used but has much to recommend it, is American white-wood. By this name is meant the wood of the tulip-tree which is a native of south-western Ontario. It is not liable to warp or shrink, is durable in contact with water, and is easily worked. It is less expensive than any of the other woods mentioned. Its chief defect consists in its great softness, but with a proper finish this is not a serious defect. For any school that wishes to keep down the expense, there is no better material to select for tops than white-wood. It will, however, be understood that it is not so suitable as are the other higher priced woods mentioned. If any of the above woods, with the exception of teak, are selected, the tops should not be made of wide boards, as under the severe conditions of the laboratory, wide pieces are bound to crack, warp, and pull apart. The tops must be built up of narrow strips about 1 in. wide, alternate pieces having opposite sides up, and all being placed on edge. These pieces must be glued firmly together, and should also have dowels running through them at regular intervals. These dowels should be started at different depths from different positions and put in in such numbers that all parts of the top are traversed by them. Fig. 3.5 shows the arrangement of them. As water lies on the tops of all the benches and sometimes for considerable periods, so that it has time to penetrate, it is important that a waterproof glue be used to fasten together the strips, for moisture is sure in time to penetrate and soften ordinary glue. The following are recipes for such a glue. All of them are easily prepared, inexpensive, and quite impervious to water.

1. Ordinary glue is swollen by soaking in water and then is dissolved in four fifths weight of linseed oil.

2. One part glue is dissolved in one and one-half parts water; then add one-fiftieth part of potassium dichromate (prussia potash).

3. Boil two ounces of isinglass in a pint of skim

4. Marine glue. Equal parts of shellac and caoutchouc are dissolved in separate portions of naphtha and then mixed.

If the bench top is made of wood, it should be about 2 in. thick. A small groove should run around it on the under side about ½ in. from the edge. This prevents the water drip from running in on the under side.

When bench tops are made of wood, as described above, it is necessary that they receive a finish that will make them as impervious as possible to the chemicals that are liable to be spilled upon them. There is no finish that is absolutely impenetrable by chemicals, but several have been used that are only slightly affected and prevent the wood from being rapidly corroded, and it is only when chemicals are allowed to remain on them for long periods that even a stain is produced. Several such finishes are here given, all of which have been tried with successful results. They are all easily prepared and applied, and the cost is relatively small.

FINISHES

1. A solution is made by boiling logwood chips in an iron kettle. A strong solution of this is applied to the clean wood with a brush, a second coat is applied when this is dry. This is followed by a coat of a strong solution of copperas in hot water. When dry the top is well rubbed with sand-paper. Then a coat of hot melted paraffin is applied. This paraffin should be hard and of a

high melting point, not less than 55°C-60°C. By means of a hot flat-iron the paraffin is thoroughly rubbed into the pores of the wood, and when cool the surplus amount is scraped off with a thin piece of steel with a smooth, straight edge.

2.

Solution No. 1

Copper sulphate	125 grammes
Potassium chlorate	125 grammes
Water	1,000 grammes

Boil until the salts are dissolved.

Solution No. 2

Aniline oil	120 grammes
Hydrochloric acid	180 grammes
Water	1,000 grammes

By means of a brush apply two coats of solution No. 1 while hot, the second coat being applied as soon as the first is dry. Then apply two coats of No. 2 and allow the wood to dry thoroughly. Next apply a coat of raw linseed oil with a cloth rather than with a brush, so as to get it very thin. Then the top is thoroughly washed with soap-suds. The finish is ebony black and permanent. Old benches can be treated in this way if they are first scraped and planed. This is a method used largely in Denmark and Germany and also used much, within recent years, in America.

3. By means of a woollen cloth apply to the clean surface of the bench a mixture of equal parts of turpentine and linseed oil, using it freely and rubbing it in evenly and well. Let it dry for two or three days. Dissolve in turpentine shavings of yellow bees'-wax until the mixture forms a jelly which at ordinary temperatures is about the consistency of vaseline, becoming a clear liquid when slightly warmed. Apply this warm, by means of a woollen cloth, rubbing it in as in the case of the first mixture, and let it dry over night. Polish by rubbing first with a brick or flat-iron covered with a woollen cloth and then with a piece of dry cloth held in the hand. A reapplication of the wax is advisable occasionally.

For chemical bench tops other materials are sometimes used. Wood, treated as mentioned above, will in time become stained and corroded, and more resistant materials are found necessary. Slate one inch thick laid on a wooden base is resistant enough. It is, however, quite porous, and absorbs the chemicals and stains badly. A bench top that has much to recommend it and is pleasant to the eye is one of plate glass. The plate should have corrugated rubber fillets under it, so that it may lie quite firmly. It is easily kept clean, not attacked by any ordinary chemicals, and has a fine appearance; on the other hand it is costly, occasionally breaks, and is very hard on glassware. The thin beakers and flasks have to be placed on it with great care, or they will crack, and it is unsafe to place hot vessels of glass or iron on it, as the sudden heating may produce a crack. Undoubtedly the best material for the tops of chemical benches is a form of soapstone that goes, in America, under the trade name of alberene stone. It is not porous and so will not stain deeply, it is so soft that it is easily worked, and is as easy on glassware as is wood; it is attacked by none of the ordinary reagents; strong acids, when left in contact with it for prolonged periods, produce no apparent effect. It is very durable and by proper oversight on the part of the teacher can be kept free from mutilation for years. While these materials are preferable to wood for tops for chemistry benches, they are not to be recommended for biological and physical bench tops. They are cold and unpleasant to the touch and are not suitable for clamping apparatus to. It should be scarcely necessary to say that marble tops for chemistry benches are as unsuitable as anything it is possible to imagine, for every novice in chemistry knows that marble is vigorously corroded by all acids and by many other chemicals as well.

LABORATORY STOOLS

Stools are necessary in the biology laboratory, as the pupil does practically all the work while he is sitting down. They are not so essential for pupils while performing experimental work in physics or chemistry, as usually they prefer to stand; but when instructions are being given by the teacher, they will require to sit at the benches to take notes. Of course, where the laboratory is also used as a demonstration and recitation room, stools must be supplied. The stool should be of such a height that the pupil, when seated at the bench, will be in such a position that his forearm rests horizontally on the top without pushing up the shoulders. For biology the stools should be slightly higher than this, so that young pupils can look comfortably through the microscope. In order to obtain the above conditions, the top of the stool should be 11 in. lower than the top of the bench in physical and chemical laboratories, and about 10 in. lower in biological laboratories. To go with physics and chemistry benches, which are built 3 ft. high, in order to be suitable for the pupils to work at while standing, these stools will require to be over 2 ft. high. With stools so high, the pupils' feet will not touch the floor, and some resting-place for the feet must be supplied, either as a cross-piece running between two legs of the stool or a foot-rest under the bench. Two illustrations of stools are given in Figure 2, both of which are suitable. Sometimes chairs with backs are used; these are more comfortable, but take up so much room that they are frequently in the way. A stool with three legs always rests with its legs on the floor, but it is rather weak and easily tips over. A four-legged stool with either a circular or a rectangular top is to be preferred. A rectangular slit in the top of the seat makes a convenient opening through which the hand may be thrust for lifting the stool. Otherwise it is very awkward to carry if only one hand is disengaged. These stools should be made quite solid. The legs and cross-pieces are made of rectangular pieces rather than of thin turned rungs, which are much too weak. It is doubtful if the advantages of a revolving top are not more than counterbalanced by the increased weakness, greater noise, and a strong tendency on the part of the boys to treat them as whirling-machines for amusement purposes. In girls' schools a chair with a back is to be preferred. The bottom of the legs should always be covered by a rubber pad to diminish the noise due to the moving of them about, which is very likely to disturb the work of the room directly below.

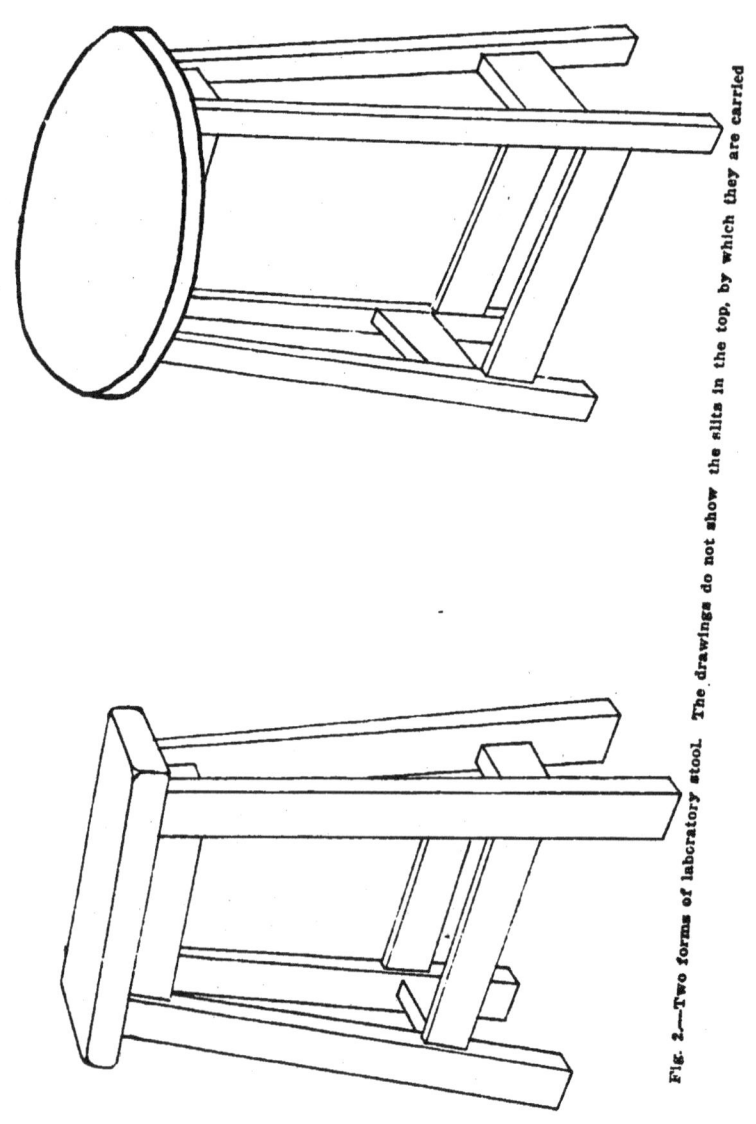

Fig. 2.—Two forms of laboratory stool. The drawings do not show the slits in the top, by which they are carried

LABORATORY WATER SUPPLY

A supply of water is a necessity in the science room, and the only satisfactory provision for supplying it is to have it flowing through pipes from taps. In the chemical laboratory a tap and a sink should be supplied to each working place, while in the physical laboratory only a few taps and sinks are required. Running water is also needed in the biological laboratory for supplying aquaria, watering plants, washing dissecting pans, etc.

In towns supplied with water-works there is no difficulty whatever in the source of supply. But in the towns and villages, where a good many of the smaller schools are located, there is no system of waterworks and a real difficulty presents itself. All sorts of inconvenient and cheap arrangements are to be found. Sometimes the caretaker carries water in pails to be ladled out by the pupils as required, the waste being caught in a barrel below the sink if such a convenience is present. The solution of the problem is a very simple one, and it is surprising that school boards have not more frequently fitted the schools in an adequate manner to supply this need. The progressive farmers in the country now have running water in their houses and stables; and what can be done by the individual as a convenience for himself and his stock is surely not too expensive to be supplied by the community for their children in the schools.

There are two methods of producing a supply of flowing water for buildings, namely, by means of the gravity tank and the pneumatic tank. In each case the source of supply is either a well or a cistern. If the water is used for laboratory purposes only, rain-water collected in a cistern is by far the most suitable. Well-water is usually hard, having varying amounts of salts dissolved in it. These will give some very puzzling reactions in chemical experiments, and will be a source of great confusion to both pupils and teacher. If such water, or that from the waterworks, is utilized, much of the accurate work in chemistry will require a supply of distilled water. Cistern water is so free from salts that will interfere with chemical reactions that it is almost as good as distilled water. It is proposed to describe the method of utilizing rain-water for laboratory purposes and then to show what modifications are necessary when a well is used instead.

The gravity tank method is considered first. Some schools have a tank in the attic connected with the eaves troughs, but this is not sufficient provision unless the tank be large enough to store a supply that will last throughout the winter, when there is little or no rainfall. A tank of such weight would be unsafe in an attic. The proper method, as illustrated in Figure 3, is to have a cistern dug in the basement to accumulate the rain-water during the rainy weather, and to pump it to a small attic tank from time to time, as required.

The size of the cistern will vary with the size of the school. In most parts of Ontario there is little rainfall in the winter and very little water can be obtained by melting snow. The cistern should be made large enough to hold two months' supply at least. The cistern should be located in the basement, preferably in a room partitioned off from the rest. It may be either round or rectangular. The former is stronger, but is more difficult to construct. Its walls may be made of concrete or brick. If they are made of brick, these should be hard and of good quality. The walls should be about 8 in. thick, laid in Portland cement mortar. The bottom should be laid with two courses of brick well bedded in the cement mortar. The whole inside should be plastered with a coat of cement mortar also. The cement mortar is composed of one part of

16 LABORATORY ACCOMMODATION

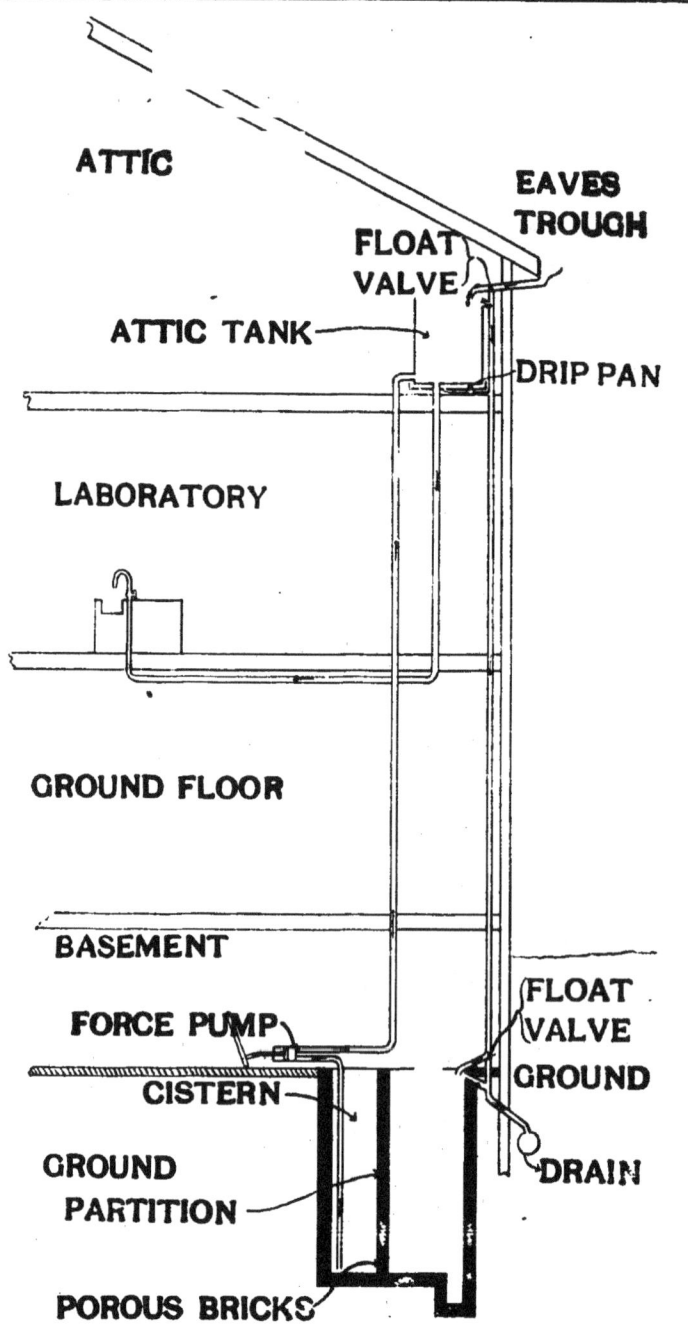

Fig. 3.—Vertical section through a part of the school building to show the arrangement pipes, etc., for a supply of running water in the laboratory

good Portland cement and two parts of clean, sharp sand. A vertical partition should separate the cistern into two compartments. The partition is also made of brick and all of it, except the lower 15 in. is treated exactly as the sides. This lower part is composed of six or seven courses of porous brick laid together without cement, and its surface is not covered with mortar. It acts as a filter. The water enters one chamber and filters through this porous partition into the other, from which it is used for laboratory purposes. Attached to the compartment into which the water enters first is an overflow. This is situated at a lower level than the top of the partition and is connected with the drain. A force-pump, just above the cistern, pumps the water from the compartment containing the filtered water into the attic tank. In the bottom of the cistern there is a depression at one corner, which will be useful in baling out the last of the water when the cistern requires to be cleaned. As all the sediment washed from the roof is retained in the cistern, it should be thoroughly cleaned out once or twice a year.

The tank from which the water is immediately used is placed in the attic. The higher its situation the greater the pressure at which the water will be delivered. This tank must be located at a part where it will not get below the freezing-point during the winter. It may be made of wood, iron, or steel. If it is made of metal, the outside of it will condense much moisture during humid weather, and this moisture will drip on the ceiling below and ruin the plaster. This can be avoided by having a galvanized drip pan beneath the tank, which catches this water; this can be made to drain into the water-pipe carrying the rain-water from the roof above to the cistern (Fig. 3). This tank may be open above or closed; in the latter case it must have a water-seal valve. The water from the roof caught in the eaves troughs is led inside the building by a pipe of large size. A vertical pipe carries it directly to the drain below (Fig. 3). From this vertical pipe lateral branches lead into the attic tank and into the cistern. At the juncture of these lateral pipes with the vertical one are located automatic float valves. These close the vertical pipe below the juncture, until the tank or the cistern is full, but, when these are filled, the valves so act as to close the lateral pipe and to open the vertical one. It is not safe to depend on these valves alone, therefore overflows are placed so as to drain both tank and cistern into the vertical pipe which, as stated above, is connected with the drain. These overflows should be larger than the inlets so that there will never be any danger of either tank or cistern overflowing. If these overflows were always certain in their action, the float valves might be entirely discarded, but the double precaution is to be recommended. A cut-off should be placed on the rain-water pipe so that the water can be diverted outside when it is thought necessary, as, for instance, at the beginning of a shower, when the water is liable to be dirty, as the roof and troughs become covered with dust. The attic tank is connected with the laboratory taps by pipes, thus ensuring a flow of clean, soft water.

The second method is by means of a pneumatic tank. One manufactured by W. & B. Douglas, Middletown, Connecticut, is shown in Figure 4. This tank is located in the basement near the cistern. It is a steel cylinder and, as the water is pumped in, the confined air is compressed and exerts a pressure. If a pipe is connected with this and led up to the laboratory, the water will be forced along it. This, though more expensive, has certain advantages over the gravity tank. It is placed in the basement and is completely protected from frost. It is also more accessible, and, if it springs a leak, only a little water will run out on the cellar floor, while such an accident happening to the attic tank might prove disastrous.

A force-pump is utilized both in raising the water to the gravity tank and in forcing it into the pneumatic tank. A windmill is not to be recommended in connection with a school, as it is noisy and liable to get out of order. A small gasolene or oil engine might also be used to work the pump in larger schools; but usually a willing caretaker is all that is required.

The custom, almost without exception, is to run the water-pipes within the walls and under the floor. This is not a method to be recommended, particularly with the waste-pipes. All should be exposed so that they can be examined without difficulty. The vertical pipes should run close to the wall but not within it,

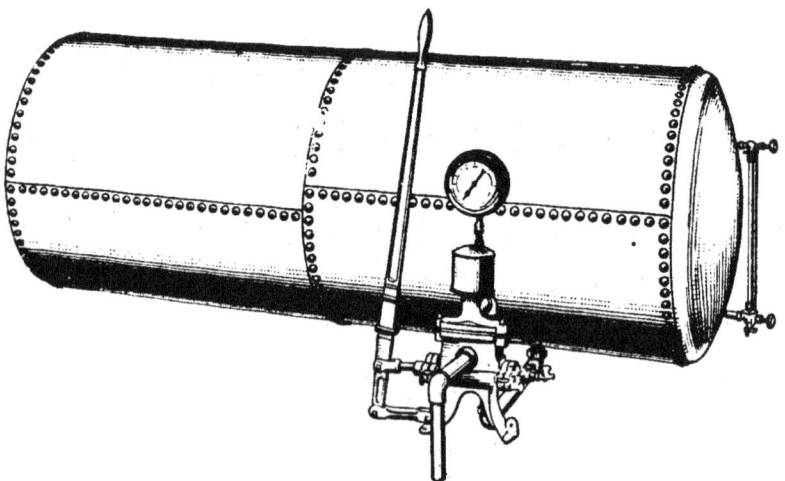

Fig. 4.—A pneumatic tank and force-pump

and all pipes running horizontally should pass just below the ceiling. The inlet pipes and waste-pipes of the laboratory should pass directly through the floor to the ceiling of the room below and should run along it. By painting them of the same colour as the ceiling they become quite inconspicuous.

The size of both the water-pipes and the waste-pipes depends on the number of working places in the laboratory. A water-pipe should be chosen sufficiently large to give a free flow of water from all the taps of the laboratory even when they are all running at the same time. All inlet pipes are made of iron and should be galvanized both inside and out. If they are made of ordinary black iron, the water standing in them will cause the formation of rust, and this discolours the water and makes it unfit for chemical experiments. Such rapid rusting also diminishes the life of the pipe by one half. The waste-pipes are made preferably of heavy lead, as the acids would eat through iron piping very quickly.

Laboratory Sinks and Taps

It is altogether too common to fit up laboratory sinks with ordinary kitchen taps, located low down, so that it is impossible to get a bottle under one. The taps should be of the swan-neck style as illustrated in Figure 5. The distance from the opening of the tap to the bottom of the sink should be from 12 in. to 15 in., so that all ordinary vessels can be placed below the tap. The valve of the water-tap should have a wheel cut-off, but the valve of the gas tap should have the lever style of cut-off. The mouth of the tap should be small, tapering, and corrugated, so that rubber tubing of various sizes can be pushed over it and remain firmly in this position. The style of corrugation illustrated in Figure 5 is recommended by the W. & J. George Company of Birmingham, as well as by others. The taps should be of gun-metal, as the corroding fumes will not tarnish this material. Brass or nickel are sure to lose their bright lustre very quickly, and will not look well. Various special taps can now be procured, as may be seen by consulting the catalogues of scientific apparatus issued by the English and continental dealers.

Only sinks specially prepared for science laboratories should be used. Generally, these cannot be procured locally. Sinks made of enamelled iron, such as are used in bath-rooms and kitchens, are unsuitable for laboratory purposes. The enamel chips off and then the iron is exposed, which rust and acids soon eat through. The sink should be made of vitrified stone-ware or enamelled fireclay, with a white glaze on the inside and a cane glaze on the outside. The depth should not be more than 6 in., and 5 in. would be still better; but such shallow ones seem difficult to procure unless they are made to order, which greatly increases the cost. The bottoms should be flat and should have a slight slope toward the outlet, so that pools of water will not remain in the bottom to stain the sink or give off foul odours. On no condition should the bottom be rounded

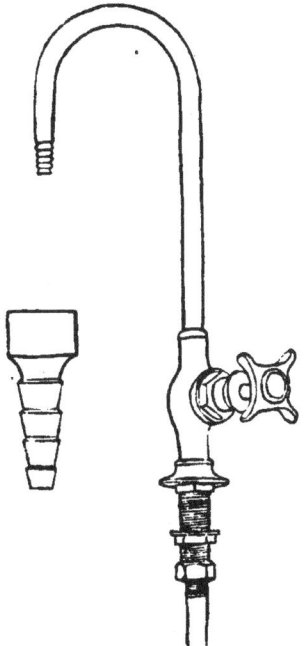

Fig. 5.—Swan-necked water-tap, suitable for a laboratory sink. To the left is shown the corrugated nozzle enlarged.

as it is in ordinary bath-room sinks. These sinks are frequently used as pneumatic troughs and for standing glass-ware in, and with a curving bottom they are useless for both these purposes. There are two ways of placing sinks in the bench. Either they have rims and a projecting flange and are set flush with the bench top, or they are set entirely under the top, the latter projecting slightly over them. When they are placed in the latter position, they are held in place by iron brackets screwed to the bottom of the bench top. The latter method is always to be preferred, as the projecting bench top prevents splashing from the sink, and the leakage between the sink and the top, which is common when the former method is used, is entirely avoided. At pupils' benches only a small-sized sink is necessary; one 12 in. by 10 in. by 5 in. is a suitable size. For the teacher's bench a larger one is necessary. One of large dimensions in some part of the laboratory is convenient for washing large glass vessels. The bench top should project about ½ in. over the opening of the sink all around in order to prevent splashing. A slight furrow on the under side of the projecting top all around prevents the drip from running in on the under side of the top. The sinks should always be placed close to one end of the bench and toward the back, so that a surface as large as possible will be left free. The sinks are not placed in the benches at all in some laboratories, but on brackets at the ends; but this is not to be recommended, as in this position they occupy too much valuable space and cause a good deal of spilling of water on the floor around them. The outlet of the sink may be closed in various ways. A porcelain grating is sometimes placed in the opening, and there is much to be said for this arrangement. The grating is just as durable as the sink, and when it is necessary to use it for a pneumatic trough a piece of sheet rubber can be placed over it. Brass sockets with grids are sometimes fixed in the openings with putty, and a brass plug fits into these. The brass, however, is easily attacked by acids and soon becomes corroded. A

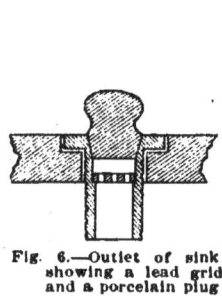

Fig. 6.—Outlet of sink showing a lead grid and a porcelain plug

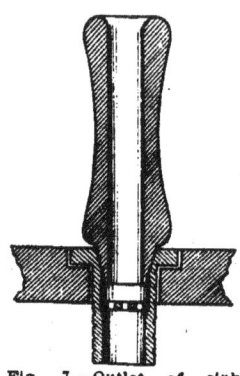

Fig. 7.—Outlet of sink, showing the standing waste

lead grid with a porcelain plug (Fig. 6) makes an outfit that can be highly recommended. The plug should always have a chain attached, so that it can be removed from the opening without putting the hands into the water. All sinks should be furnished with an overflow, which is connected with the outlet through the wall of the stone-ware itself. An arrangement very frequently met with in sinks in English laboratories is a standing waste (Fig. 7). This is a hollow plug that fits into the outlet and is open above, so that the water when it rises to the top of the plug overflows through it. This plug is usually of lignum vitæ or ebonite, the latter being the better. With such a plug a lateral overflow is unnecessary. The only objection experienced in using such plugs is that in small sinks they require so much space that they are somewhat in the way.

WATER-PIPES AND WASTE-PIPES

The water-pipes coming to each tap should have a screw down cut-off just above where they pierce the floor. Then if one tap needs to be repaired, the water can be cut off from it without affecting the others. A main cut-off should also control the water supply to all the taps. As in many schools fires are not kept burning during the Christmas holidays, there should be placed in the basement a cut-off of such a kind that when the water is turned off the pipes are drained.

The waste-pipes from the sinks should be made invariably of the best quality of drawn lead. This should be quite heavy. If the pipe is 1½ in. in diameter, it should weigh 3 lb. to the foot; if 2 in., 4 lb.; and if 3 in., 6 lb. Iron pipes for waste are unsuited to laboratories, where the corrosive fluids would prove destructive to them in a very short time. The lead wastes from each sink may pass directly into the main waste without having a trap on each, one large trap being located on the main at its lowest point before it passes to the basement. The vertical wastes from the sink should never connect with the main at right angles but always obliquely in the direction of the flow. The horizontal waste should nowhere have a drop of less than one-fourth inch per foot and should have clean-outs at the ends, at each horizontal bend, and every fifteen feet apart where it runs in a straight line. Between where the last sink waste enters the main pipe and where the latter leaves the room there should be situated a trap in which all sediments and coarse solids will be deposited; this should be accessible and should be cleaned from time to time. As all the traps contain standing water, they must be placed where they will not freeze during the winter. All connections between lead pipes should be wiped; all connections between lead and iron pipes should be made by means of heavy brass ferrules of the same size as the lead and caulked with lead. Connections between cast-iron pipes are to be made tight with oakum and lead well caulked. The lead waste is to be connected with the outlet of the sink by means of a brass ferrule. This brass ferrule is connected to the stone-ware by a gaskin followed by cement, and the former is connected to the lead by a wiped joint. The waste-pipes from medium-sized sinks should be 2 in. in diameter. The size of the horizontal waste will depend on the number of sinks connected with it.

In England an entirely different method of carrying off the waste is used. The work benches there run the length of the room. Under the sinks runs an open trough of wood or porcelain, which slopes in one direction. All the waste pipes from the sinks terminate above this trough, so that the water runs out of the waste and falls into the trough. This trough at its lowest end empties into a receiver in the form of a small tank, and an overflow from this forms the waste-pipe that carries the water from the room. All solids and sediments sink to the bottom of the tank and can be removed from time to time. In such an arrangement the waste is certainly handy and not likely to be blocked up. On the other hand evil-smelling liquids continue to vitiate the air while passing along the trough; besides such an arrangement is only suitable for long benches and, as has been already explained, such benches are not to be recommended for high school purposes.

HOT-WATER SUPPLY

It is of great convenience to have a hot-water supply coming from at least one tap in each room. In the larger schools a hot-water tank, heated by a coal fire, is kept in the boiler room to supply the wash basins and to furnish water for the use of the charwomen in cleaning the floors and woodwork. If such a convenience exists, pipes connecting it to the demonstrator's bench should be installed. Where no such arrangement exists, a small water heater can be easily installed in any science room that has running water and a gas supply. The Ruud and Vulcan heaters, manufactured in Toronto, require a water tank such as is used for the hot-water supply in kitchens. A very handy form of water heater (Fig. 8) is manufactured by Fletcher, Russell & Co., Warrington, England, which can be fastened directly to the wall. There is no storage tank required with this heater, the water being heated while it is passing through the metal coils. It will deliver almost two quarts per minute at about 100° Fahrenheit.

Fig. 8.—A hot-water heater suitable for the laboratory. It is screwed directly to the Wall

BURNERS AND GAS SUPPLIES

The most frequent operation of the laboratory is the application of heat to different bodies. Various sources of heat are used according to the circumstances of the school. Wood alcohol, gasolene, kerosene, coal-gas, and acetylene are the substances most frequently used. Coal-gas is always the fuel used wherever it is available. Unfortunately it is only available in the larger towns and cities of the Province. There is no doubt that it is the most suitable of all fuels for the laboratory. In almost all the smaller schools throughout the Province the ordinary glass or brass alcohol lamp is the chief means of heating, but it is very unsatisfactory. The heat from it is very feeble and quite incapable of producing the requisite temperature for the successful performance of many of the experiments in physics and chemistry. It also wastes much time on the part of the pupil, as an operation that could be performed with gas in a few minutes will take three or four times as long when performed with the alcohol lamp. Besides it has been abundantly proven by government tests that it is much more expensive than kerosene or gasolene, and that it is not to be compared with coal-gas for cheapness. Last of all, the ordinary laboratory alcohol lamp is a dangerous thing, as has been proved again and again by accidents that have happened through its use.

BURNERS AND GAS SUPPLIES 23

If alcohol lamps are used, some of a special structure are necessary—in order that a flame may be produced of sufficient temperature to make possible the performance of the most common experiments in chemistry. To convince one of this it is only necessary to state that an ordinary alcohol lamp does not give sufficient heat to burn magnesium in a crucible, to calcine limestone, or to melt a piece of medium-sized glass tubing sufficiently to bend it or to draw it out to a pointed tube. Several alcohol lamps are now on the market that give a very powerful flame, and a supply of these should be present in all schools where this substance is used as a fuel. Figure 9 represents one of the best of these lamps. It is listed in all English catalogues and is called the Automatic Bunsen Burner for Methylated Spirits. It costs about five dollars. In Figure 10 is given a section of it. As the instructions that come with the lamp are usually in German, it may be useful to give an abstract of them here, especially of those that have reference to the cleaning of the apparatus. Deposits from the methylated spirits

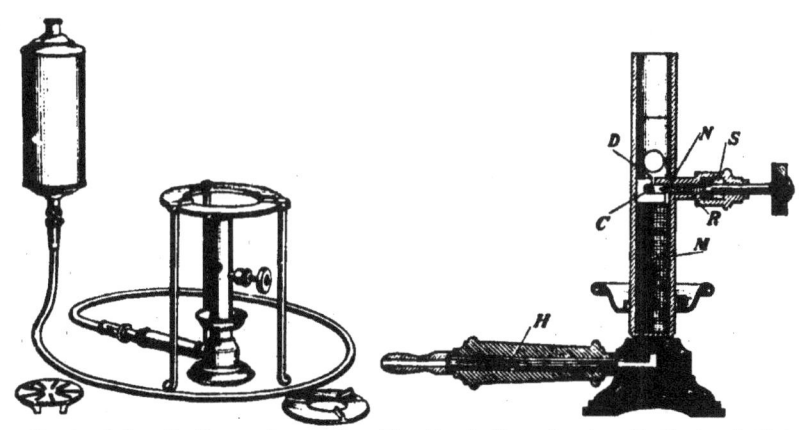

Fig. 9.—Automatic Bunsen burner for methylated spirits

Fig. 10.—Section of automatic Bunsen burner for methylated spirits

in time clog the passage in the handle (H) and the body (M), also occasionally the nozzle of the burner (D) and the valve (C). The flame will then burn one-sided or irregularly and too short. Use the pricker which accompanies each burner, for pricking out the nozzle; but never use other instruments, such as pins, needles, etc., for if the hole in the nozzle is enlarged the burner cannot act properly. It will be necessary occasionally to unscrew the burner, to clean the valve (C), and to take out, clean, and replace the wires in the passages (H) and (M), as these wires serve to collect the impurities contained in the methylated spirits. When cleaning, it is necessary to take care that none of the wires are lost and that the whole number of the wires are replaced in their original positions, the thick piece of wire in the centre. The asbestos packing (S) of the valve must be renewed when worn. All parts must be screwed up vapour-tight, so that vapour cannot escape except at the nozzle of the burner. With this burner all ordinary combustion experiments can be performed, limestone can be calcined, and all other operations of the secondary school physical and chemical laboratory can be successfully carried out.

There is now a Bunsen burner on the market which burns methylated spirits, and which is almost as effective as the regular Bunsen, and is certainly a great improvement on the old form of spirit-lamp. It is illustrated in Figure 11. It is necessary with all these burners, whether for alcohol, gasolene, or kerosene, to get a tube so hot that the liquid is vaporized in passing through it and comes to the top of the tube mixed with the required amount of air for complete combustion. This combustion keeps the tube at the proper temperature, when once it has been raised to that point. A special method of heating the tube is at first required. In the Bunsen burner for methylated spirits this is done by saturating the asbestos ring with spirits and putting it around the tube containing the wick of the lamp. In about half a minute vapours arise from the nozzle and are ignited. The size of the flame can be adjusted by raising or lowering the wick.

The best and safest kind of blast lamp for the laboratory not supplied with gas is one that burns kerosene (Fig. 12). It works very simply, is not in the least dangerous, and gives a very powerful flame.

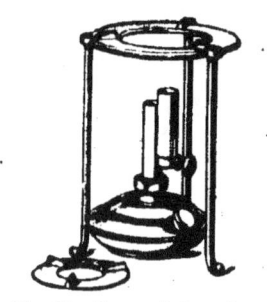

Fig. 11.—Bunsen burner for methylated spirits

In fact the flame is as efficient as that of a powerful blast lamp utilizing coal-gas. One or more of them should be in every laboratory. In order to start it, a little methylated spirits must be poured into the ring surrounding the tube and ignited. When this is all burned, the valve is opened, and the kerosene passes out as a vapour which ignites on mixing with the air.

The gasolene blast lamp in several forms is commonly used already in the high schools and with fair results. The chief objection to it is that gasolene is very explosive and its use is somewhat dangerous. These objections cannot be offered to the same extent to the alcohol and kerosene blast lamps.

ACETYLENE GAS PLANTS

It is intended here to advocate, as a substitute for the use of alcohol lamps, the installation of an acetylene plant. It is a somewhat remarkable circumstance that very little progress has yet been made in the direction of installing such plants in the schools of Ontario. Many private houses, churches, hotels, and public buildings have installed acetylene lighting plants during the last ten years, and many laboratories in schools and colleges in the United States have been using it for laboratory purposes; but as far as is known not a single high school laboratory in the Province of Ontario has yet installed one. Bunsen burners are now on the market that burn acetylene with absolutely no smoke and produce a temperature higher than that of the ordinary Bunsens which use coal-gas. Its value for illumin-

Fig. 12.—Kerosene blast lamp

ating purposes is also unexcelled, as it gives a light more nearly approaching that of the sun than any other illuminant. As has been said, the heat is very intense; the oxy-acetylene flame is much more powerful than that of the oxy-hydrogen blast lamp.

The cost of installation is not excessive; a machine that would be satisfactory could be installed for about three hundred dollars. This does not include the cost of distributing the pipes to the various rooms, which would vary greatly in different schools. It is not too expensive to be installed in the private home, in the hotel, or in the village church, and hence it ought not to be too expensive for the school, where it is still more necessary. After the installation, the cost of the gas compares very favourably with that of coal-gas at ninety cents a thousand cubic feet.

The generator is simple to manipulate and not likely to get out of working order if attended to with reasonable care. If the farmer, the church janitor, and the general servant-man of the village hotel can operate successfully an acetylene plant, a school with an intelligent science master should have no difficulty in the management of the generator.

Finally, acetylene is not more dangerous than kerosene or ordinary coal-gas. Acetylene is still in its infancy. In some of the earlier machines there were explosions. Now the properties of the gas are thoroughly understood, and the generating machines are so constructed and automatically protected against all danger that they are quite as safe as any other means of lighting. The early prejudice against them has not entirely vanished among those who do not know; but the insurance companies recognize that there is no great fire risk in acetylene installations, as they levy no extra premium on buildings containing this means of lighting.

The generators are of two kinds, those in which water falls on carbide, and those in which carbide falls into water. The latter is always to be preferred. Where water and calcium carbide meet, heat is produced, and when the point of contact becomes very hot gummy substances are produced instead of acetylene, and these being carried to the burners tend to clog and carbonize them. If the carbide drops into the water, the temperature can never become higher than 100°C. and, in reality, never does become more than a few degrees higher than the temperature of the surrounding atmosphere. But where water drops on carbide, the temperature may become too high and cause the gummy materials to be produced.

The generator should be placed in a dry part of the basement on a brick or cement floor. It must be placed in a well-lighted room, so that all manipulations can be carried on without artificial light; and good ventilation should always be maintained. The generator should be located where it can never be reached by the pupils. Of course a room should be selected that is always above the freezing temperature of water.

The following are some of the qualifications of a good generator: (1) It must be "fool-proof", (2) it must ensure cool generation, (3) it must be simple in construction, (4) no considerable pressure should ever be produced in any of its parts, (5) it should need little attention, (6) it should indicate at all times how low the charge of carbide is, (7) the charge should be introduced and the residue removed with ease. One feature mentioned above should be stressed. Acetylene at low pressure cannot explode but, when subjected to a pressure greater than two atmospheres, it becomes highly explosive if ignited at one point; hence the importance of keeping the pressure low. Every reputable generator in the market at the present time has safety-valves connected with the outside that open long before the pressure reaches the danger point. Figures 13 and 14 show a generator suitable for a school, manufactured by the Davis Acetylene Company of Niagara Falls, Ontario. This is a machine that allows carbide to drop into water.

The calcium carbide itself is also not a dangerous material to handle provided it is kept in a dry place. It always comes in sheet-iron, air-tight packages, and only one should be opened at a time.

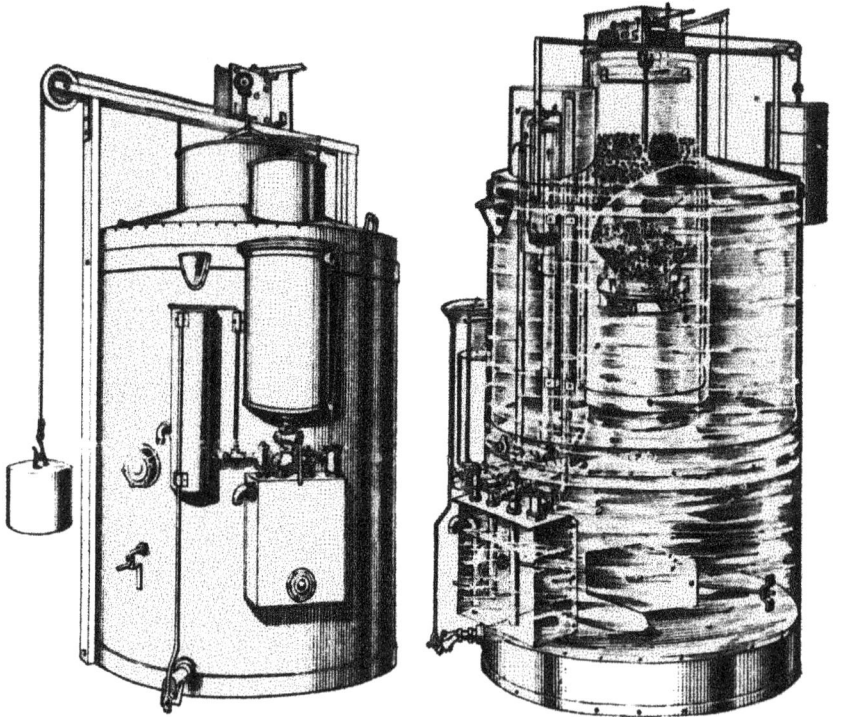

Fig. 13.—External appearance of acetylene generator

Fig. 14.—Internal structure of acetylene generator

Such installations are to be found in many high school and college laboratories in the United States; the bacteriological laboratory at the Experimental Farm in Ottawa contains one; the Biological Station at St. Andrews, New Brunswick, has used one with great satisfaction for a number of years; and many institutions in the Canadian West are using acetylene.

GASOLENE PLANT

Gasolene is also used as a fuel for laboratories in many secondary schools in the United States. The danger is no greater than with coal-gas or acetylene, the first cost is moderate, and the expense of the fuel compares very well with that of coal-gas. In order to get satisfactory results, a machine of established repute should be purchased, and it must be installed by an expert. The principle on which it works is that air is forced through or over the gasolene and the mixed gases are forced to the burners, where they are kindled. There are usually three parts to the machine—the pump, the carburettor, and the mixer (Fig. 15). The pump is used for forcing the air through the gasolene and is worked by a heavy weight attached by a wire cable over a pulley. The weight, when wound up, will run the pump for a week or longer, depending, of course, on the extent to which the gas is used, for the pump only runs when the gas is being used. The carburettor is a chamber, or series of chambers, in which the gasolene vapour becomes intimately mixed with the air; in the mixer a still further admixture takes place, and the proportions of the two are adjusted to make combustion more perfect. The pump and the mixer are usually installed in the basement, while the carburettor, which is a tank, is buried underneath the ground at least thirty feet from the building. This latter

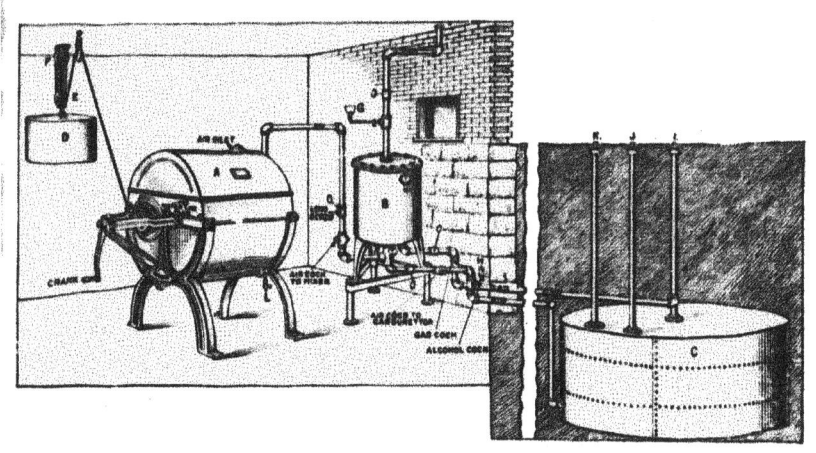

Fig. 15.—Installation for generating gasolene for laboratory

precaution is necessary, in order to meet the demands of insurance companies respecting the storage of gasolene. The institutions using this method of heating speak in the highest terms of its efficiency. Figure 15 is an illustration of a complete outfit manufactured by the Matthews Gas Machine Company of Chicago, one of the largest manufacturers of this type of apparatus.

MANSFIELD GAS GENERATOR

There is still another method of getting a supply of gas for the laboratory or for illuminating purposes. The machine (Fig. 16) is manufactured by Mansfield & Sons, Limited, Birk... ...d, England. It is really a small gas-producing plant consisting of a generator and a gas tank. Instead of coal any heavy oil is utilized. The oil is run slowly into a chamber which is strongly heated, and it is immediately broken up into inflammable gases which pass to the gas tank to be stored until required. Any ordinary oil will do. Kerosene, which is the product available in Ontario, is quite satisfactory. About 11 gal. of oil and 225 lb. of coal will generate

1,000 cu. ft. of gas, and 1,000 cu. ft. of this gas is equivalent in heating capacity to 3,000 cu. ft. of ordinary coal-gas. This would make it slightly more expensive than coal-gas. No skilled workman is required to operate the plant, as all that is necessary to do is to throw in a shovelful of coal every twenty minutes while the gas is being generated, and it is necessary to generate gas only once a week, or even less frequently.

The first cost of this installation is higher than that of an acetylene plant, as about $1,000 would be required. Such an installation would be excellent for some of our larger schools where coal-gas is not available. This generator is very extensively used schools and colleges throughout the British Empire. It is found in dozens of schools and colleges of British India, and is also commonly used in South Africa. One is now in operation in the University of Alberta, at Edmonton. Figure 16 is an illustration of the oil-gas producer complete. The tank and generator are usually erected outside the main building, the generator being inclosed in a small building.

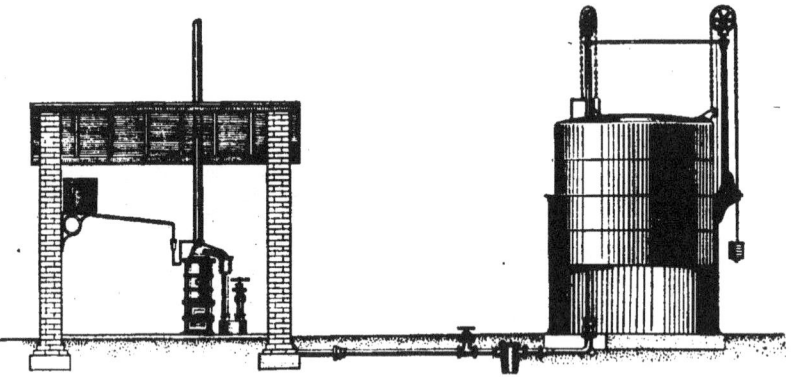

Fig. 16.—Installation for manufacturing gas from oils

COAL-GAS FOR LABORATORIES

A school situated in a town or city which has a supply of coal-gas is fortunate, as there is no fuel that is as satisfactory for laboratory purposes. An acetylene or oil-gas generator is a convenience, but there is always a certain amount of trouble in looking after it, and this is entirely absent when coal-gas is used, as it is always generated at a central gas-house and distributed by pipes to the users.

The supply pipe must be large enough to give a sufficient supply of gas to all the Bunsens in a laboratory, burning at once. Of course, its size will depend on the kind, of burners and the number of gas taps. In a chemical laboratory there will usually be from 25 to 30 gas taps and about the same number in the physical laboratory. Each of the burners connected with a tap will consume five cubic feet per hour, so a pipe to each laboratory, large enough to deliver at least 150 cu. ft. per hour, should be used. A 1¼-inch pipe will be of ample size to supply each laboratory.

There are such a variety of Bunsen burners now on the market that a word might be said regarding which to select and which to avoid. For ordinary class work the erect form with a side opening near the bottom for admitting air is most satisfactory. The size of the opening in the side is regulated by means of a cylindrical ring which neatly fits the tube. The size of the hole is diminished or increased by turning the cylindrical ring so that the hole in it no longer coincides with the opening in the tube. Bunsens, where the adjustment is made by a lever underneath, do not give a powerful flame, and the air is not fully cut off even when

Fig. 17.—Rose-top burner

Fig. 18.—Teclu burner

the lever is pushed over to its limit, so they are not to be recommended. Besides these two kinds of burners there are others used for special purposes. The rose-top burner (Fig. 17) is especially adapted for spreading the flame out and is used for heating Florence flasks, as they are not so likely to break under the more

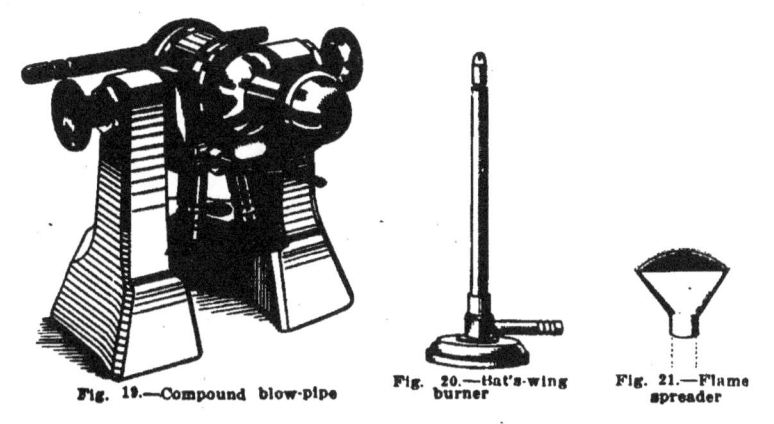

Fig. 19.—Compound blow-pipe

Fig. 20.—Bat's-wing burner

Fig. 21.—Flame spreader

even distribution of heat. There are several forms of burners that give much more powerful flames than does the ordinary Bunsen; indeed, the heat produced by some of them compares very favourably with that of a blast lamp. These have different trade names. The Teclu burner (Fig. 18) is perhaps the best known; one of these instruments of large size will do almost all the work of a blow-pipe, and every laboratory supplied with gas should have at least one of them. The most useful blow-pipe is one listed by the well-known makers, Fletcher, Russell & Co., Warrington, England, called the Compound Blow-pipe (Fig. 19). It is listed in all the English scientific catalogues. By means of it a flame of almost any shape or size can be produced. For glass-blowing it is almost indispensable. A supply of bat's-wing burners (Fig. 20) is necessary for bending glass tubing, as the work cannot be done properly with the ordinary Bunsen burner. As a substitute for bat's-wing burners, flame-spreaders (Fig. 21) can be obtained, which fit over the opening at the top of the ordinary Bunsen burner. These, when operated with the air-hole of the burner closed, can be used to advantage for bending glass tubing. If they are not well cared for, the width of the opening becomes uneven in different sections, and the flame is hotter in some parts than in others, so that the glass will not bend evenly.

ELECTRICITY FOR THE LABORATORY

The supply of electricity for the laboratory will next be considered. Electricity is used for lighting, for the lantern, and for experimental work. Nothing will be said about the first, but the last two are of great importance. Nothing is more convenient and more necessary for experimental work than a steady, well-controlled electric current at the teacher's and pupils' benches; yet in very few schools are adequate arrangements made in this respect. A very usual source of supply is a few dry cells. These are certainly better than nothing, but are quite unsuited to a good deal of the experimental work, except where an instantaneous or interrupted current is required. They are short-lived, unreliable, and, worst of all, the current strength rapidly deteriorates owing to polarization, and, where steady work is required, they fail entirely. For electrolysis, electro-plating, work with voltameters, measurement of current strengths, etc., one cannot imagine a source more unsuitable than the dry cell. The bichromate cell was a favourite source of electricity twenty years ago, but has now almost passed out of use. It is quite uncertain, dirty, easily exhausted, and altogether an unreliable source that frequently failed at inopportune times. We will consider the sources that are to be recommended, commencing with the simplest and cheapest and passing on to describe the more expensive, but also more efficient, sources. They will be considered in the following order:

1, The Daniell cell; 2, the Edison cell; 3, Storage cells; 4, Rectifiers; 5, Motor-generators.

THE DANIELL CELL

1. In a small school, where the pupils perform individual experiments at their places, a small Daniell cell will usually give the required current. The voltage is low, but the current is absolutely steady for several hours. Of course for electrolysis several such cells in series would be necessary. Such a Daniell cell can be put together by a handy science teacher. The copper sulphate should be saturated, and an excess of the crystals should be present. The sulphuric acid in the porous cup is composed of one volume of concentrated sulphuric acid and 20 volumes of water; the acid must always be poured into the water and not the water into the acid, for, as much heat is produced, the acid sinking through the lighter water distributes the heat to the water, which, being in such large quantity, only gradually

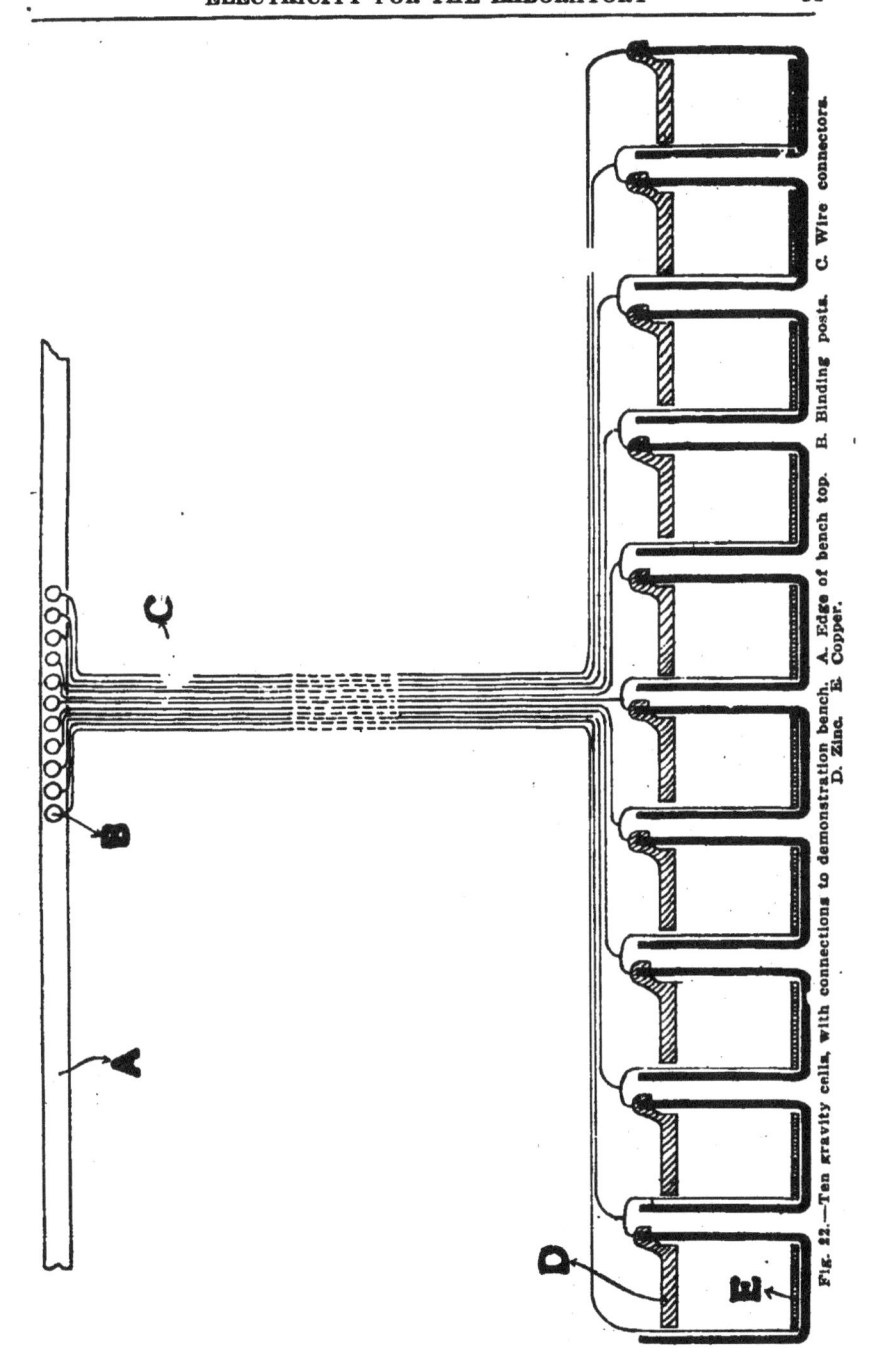

Fig. 22.—Ten gravity cells, with connections to demonstration bench. A. Edge of bench top. B. Binding posts. C. Wire connectors. D. Zinc. E. Copper.

rises in temperature. A stout stick of zinc should be used and it should be kept well amalgamated. To set up the cell, the zinc element is placed in a porous cup containing the diluted acid or a weak solution of zinc sulphate, and the copper is placed in a saturated solution of copper sulphate with lumps of sulphate in the bottom or on the shelf. A few cubic centimetres of sulphuric acid in the copper sulphate makes it more effective. Another way to set up the cell is to put the elements in their places, copper sulphate on the shelf, and fill it up with water. Short circuit it for a few hours and it will then be in good condition.

For the demonstrator's bench the gravity form of a Daniell cell should be used, as this gets rid of the porous cup, which is always a disturbing factor in batteries. A solution of zinc sulphate is used for the upper layer of the liquid in which the zinc is suspended. The demonstrator should have eight or ten of these (Fig. 22) stowed away in a cupboard under his bench. These should be connected in series by wires soldered from the zinc (D) in one to the copper (E) in the next. From these connecting wires, and also from the unconnected zinc at one end of the series and from the unconnected copper at the other end of the series, wires (C) pass to the terminals on the teacher's bench. With this arrangement the teacher has a variety of voltages at his disposal. Suppose the voltage of each cell is one volt and there are ten cells. By using the first and last terminals, a steady current with a pressure of 10 volts is generated. By connecting an instrument to any two alternate terminals, 2 volts pressure is generated. In using these cells the work can be distributed between the different cells so that some will not become exhausted sooner than others. If several currents are required for different pieces of apparatus, the latter may be connected up to different terminals. For pupils' work a 3-pint Daniell cell will be of good size, and for the demonstration bench a 3-quart gravity cell will be best. The resistance of a good cell of the former size will be about 2 ohms and of the latter about 1.6 ohms.

The gravity cell is set up as follows: Place the copper strips on the bottom of the jar and suspend the zinc near the top of the jar. Pour distilled or rain-water into the jar until it is well above the zinc. Then drop in the blue vitriol in small lumps until the copper is well covered. No sulphuric acid or zinc sulphate need be added unless the cell is required for use almost at once; then one ounce of zinc sulphate powdered fine may be added gradually. The solution must be kept saturated. If the blue colour begins to fade, more vitriol must at once be added. The blue colour should always reach at least half-way up to the surface of the liquid. The cells should be kept covered to prevent excessive evaporation, and water must be added from time to time so as to keep the liquid always well above the zinc.

Edison Primary Cell

2. Another cell that may be used in the same way as the Daniell and gravity cells is the Edison primary cell; this was formerly called the Edison-Lalande cell. It does not need description, as full details of its construction are given in *The Ontario High School Physics*. It is a cell of low voltage, but the resistance is also very low. There is absolutely no action during open circuit, and the current from it is steady. There is little weakening of the current strength with age. The different parts can be removed when exhausted. The voltage is almost .7 volts and the internal resistance is only .025 ohms, so that for instruments of low resistance this cell gives a powerful current. No fumes are produced and it does not freeze during the coldest weather. In setting up the cell the caustic soda is dissolved in

the water and, as much heat is produced, great care is necessary not to crack the jar. As oil is placed over its surface there is no evaporation. This cell is not so suitable for pupil's work as for demonstration purposes; for this latter purpose it is placed under the teacher's demonstration bench. It cannot well be carried about, as the liquid is liable to splash out and corrode whatever it comes in contact with. Five or six of these cells placed under the teacher's bench will give a satisfactory source of electricity for all the experiments of an ordinary course in physics. Wires pass from the cells to the terminals on the bench in the same way as they do from the gravity cells illustrated in Figure 22.

Storage Cells

3. The most satisfactory of all sources of electricity for experimental work are storage cells, or accumulators. As these cells are easily injured or entirely spoiled, and as definite practical information as to their management is difficult to obtain, the care of them will be discussed at length. They have a long life, need little attention, and none of the parts require renewal for years if they are given proper attention. They have a very high voltage—over 2 volts—and give a steady current throughout the discharge. No irritating fumes are produced, as only oxygen and hydrogen are given off and, if covered loosely, no spray of acid will pass out into the room. Of course, during normal discharge there are no fumes whatever produced. It is not necessary to describe the structure of the storage cell. The plates are made in different forms and of different materials. The one most frequently used for laboratories and, on the whole, most suitable for that purpose, is what is called the chloride cell. The Electric Storage Battery Company, of Philadelphia, manufactures this cell, and their goods are listed by all the American dealers in scientific apparatus. These cells can be purchased with plates of various sizes and of differently numbers to a cell. They should be sufficiently large to allow without injury a current of three amperes during discharge. It is better to have five or six cells each with only two plates than to have one or two cells each with several plates, as the former combination will give a greater variety of voltages to select from. If five cells, each of two plates, are chosen as the outfit, then the demonstrator is able to use 2, 4, 6, 8, or 10 volts for experiments, but if only two cells, each with five or six plates are chosen, he is able to use only 2 or 4 volts; yet the price of the two outfits will not differ greatly. The PT. chloride cell, manufactured by the Electric Storage Battery Co., of Philadelphia, can be recommended for laboratory purposes. It is a 2-plate cell, each plate of which is 8¾ in. x 5 in. The positive and negative plates of adjacent cells are burned together in a single piece. The positive of the first cell and the negative of the last are separate. Five of these cells make a good equipment for demonstration work, and ten of them are all that any school could possibly require.

After the jars have been cleaned, they should be set in place on a suitable platform. This platform should be made of a wooden block. Slats nailed around it project one inch above the block, forming a shallow inclosure; this is filled with fine, clean sand. This platform rests on insulator legs made of glass. The battery is set upon the sand on the platform. The outfit is placed in a part of the room where it can be easily inspected, and should, therefore, be located where it will be well lighted. It must be placed where the temperature will not fall to freezing-point, and where no lights or burning matches will be brought near it; because at times the cells give off mixed hydrogen and oxygen, which is highly explosive. Great care should be taken that the plates are all connected up in the proper order. When they are placed in their jars, all arrangements for charging must be ready before the electrolyte is added.

The electrolyte is prepared by mixing pure sulphuric acid (specific gravity 1.840) and distilled or rain-water in the proportions of one part of acid to 5¼ parts of water by volume; the specific gravity of the mixture should be 1.18. When mixing, pour the acid in a thin stream into the water, keeping the latter vigorously stirred during the operation. Allow the electrolyte to cool before pouring it into the cells. Cells, when new, are always in a discharged condition. As soon as the electrolyte is added, the charging should at once begin and continue uninterruptedly, until the cells are fully charged and are giving off gas freely.

Each storage cell has certain descriptive features that the science teacher should understand. For example, a catalogue describes the cell PT, that has been already recommended, as follows:

Type	No. of Plates	Size of Plates	Normal charging rate	Normal discharging rate		
				8 hours	5 hours	3 hours
PT	2	8¾ in. x 5 in	3	3	4¼	6

The number of plates means the total number, both positive and negative; so in this cell there would be only a single positive and a single negative plate. The meaning of the next column is evident. Normal charging rate means the number of amperes that should be passed through the cell when charging it. Discharging rate refers to the capacity of the cell, which is usually expressed in ampere hours. This cell, giving a current of 3 amperes, is discharged in 8 hours, if giving a current of 4¼ amperes it is discharged in 5 hours, and if a current is 6 amperes it is discharged in 3 hours. It will be noticed that the more rapid the discharge the less electricity can be got from a cell; or, as it is usually expressed, its capacity is decreased.

As has been said, the initial charging should begin as soon as the electrolyte is added, after the cells have been set up. The positive pole of the charging current should be connected with the positive pole of the storage cell. The latter is always marked, and the former can be easily found by dipping the copper terminals in a solution of salt, the one from which bubbles of gas rise more freely is the negative pole. It is always best to charge at the normal rate, and better to charge below than above it. The initial charge must be continued until complete. It is best to continue the charge beyond completion rather than run any risk of any cell being incompletely charged. The signs of complete charging are: (1) Specific gravity of electrolyte is 1.21; (2) the electro-motive force of each cell is just over 2 volts in open circuit; (3) the positive pole is dark brown in colour, the negative is slate blue; (4) gas should rise freely from both plates during the latter part of the charge.

Under no circumstances should the cells be discharged below 1.85 volts, as very great permanent injury will be done if complete discharge is permitted. The cells must never be left in a discharged condition. They might well be charged every two weeks or oftener, and an overcharge should be given once a month. The plates should be watched for growths (see page 35) and, when one appears, it is to be dislodged with a rubber or wooden stick, but not with any kind of metal, as that would introduce foreign salts and exhaust part of the acid. The plates must never extend closer to the bottom than one inch, as a free space must be left below into which scales, etc., that drop from the plates may lodge without any danger of short-circuiting the cell. The liquid will continually evaporate, and water must be added from time to time, so that the liquid always stands above the tops of the plates. As in the course of time much water will be added to the liquid, it is of great importance that distilled water be used to replenish that lost by evaporation. If it is difficult to procure distilled water, then rain-water may be used. The different cells should be discharged as evenly as possible. Suppose that there are 10 in the set, and that frequently only 2 are to be used, let the two

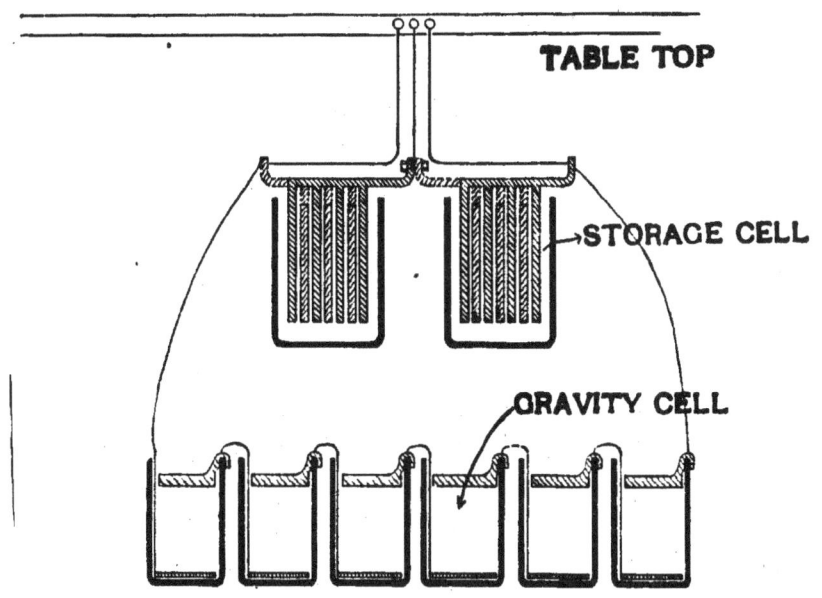

Fig. 23.—Two storage cells connected up with six gravity cells to produce current for experimental purposes

used vary from time to time, so that there will be no danger of any being discharged long before the others. Under no circumstances should the load be above the normal discharging amperage. If the cells are short-circuited or connected with a resistance so small that the current becomes high the plates may buckle, and a white, inactive coat may form over the plates, which is difficult to remove.

The chief injuries to storage cells are buckling, growth, sulphating, and disintegration. Buckling is due to too rapid discharge, which causes the plates to become bent, or distorted. Growth is the formation of projections on the plates; these must be removed as mentioned above, or they may cause short-circuiting. Sulphating is a serious defect. It is due to the formation of a white, inactive layer on the outside of the plates, and is caused by too heavy a current or by neglect of the cell. This white layer prevents the normal chemical reactions from taking place and it has a high resistance. A cell in this condition can never be restored entirely to its former efficiency. Sulphate of soda added to the solution will sometimes clear it up. Disintegration of the plates is indicated by an accumulation of scales in the bottom of the cell, and cannot be entirely avoided, but it is hastened by too rapid discharge.

The storage cells can only be used when there is a source by which they can be charged. This source may be: (1) A set of gravity cells; (2) a street-lighting direct current; (3) an alternating current. Too much stress cannot be placed on the use in the schools of Ontario of storage cells. Almost every town and village in Ontario will soon have alternating current; and, while this is almost useless for experimental purposes, it can be utilized for charging storage cells in a manner that will be discussed immediately

A very good arrangement in a school laboratory where there is neither alternating nor direct current available is that represented by Figure 23. There are six gravity cells, and above are two storage cells. These are permanently connected in the manner shown in the illustration. They are all placed in a recess under the demonstrator's bench. The positive of the gravity cell is connected with the positive of the storage cell and the eight cells are connected in a single series. The gravity cells are continually charging the storage cells. Three terminals from the storage cells are connected to binding posts on the demonstration bench. The demonstrator can then use either one storage cell or two for the experiments, as is necessary. Three storage cells might be connected up with eight gravity cells, or more in proportion. The advantage of using the two storage cells instead of the six gravity cells with their higher voltage consists in the fact that the internal resistance of the former is so much less than that of the latter that, in most experiments, it more than makes up for the difference in voltage.

Where an alternating current is available, as it is sure to be in most parts of this Province within a short time, this will be the source from which the direct current is to be derived, whether to charge a storage battery, to run a lantern, or to use for experimental work.

If it is required merely to charge storage cells from an alternating current, an aluminium rectifier is the simplest means of converting an alternating to a direct current. This rectifier is so simple that it can easily be made by any science teacher.

A RECTIFIER FOR ALTERNATING ELECTRIC CURRENTS

4. The principle of the device is this: A current will not flow in a cell from an aluminium electrode to an iron electrode, if the electrolyte be a saturated solution of common sodium phosphate or potassium bichromate. It will, however, flow freely from the iron to the aluminium in such a cell. One such cell, therefore, put into an alternating circuit, would cut out one phase of the current and give a direct current, which would however be an interrupted one.

The above arrangement of four such cells (Fig. 25) gives a direct current which is not interrupted, but continuous.

M_1 and M_2 are the alternating current terminals. C_1 and C_2 deliver the direct current.

Al is an aluminium electrode in the form of a cylinder surrounding an iron electrode Fe. When M_1 is positive, the path of the current is as shown by the solid arrow. Note that the current will not go from Al_1 to Fe_4, nor from Al_3 to Fe_2; but goes as shown through the external circuit even against high resistance in

RECTIFIER FOR ALTERNATING CURRENTS

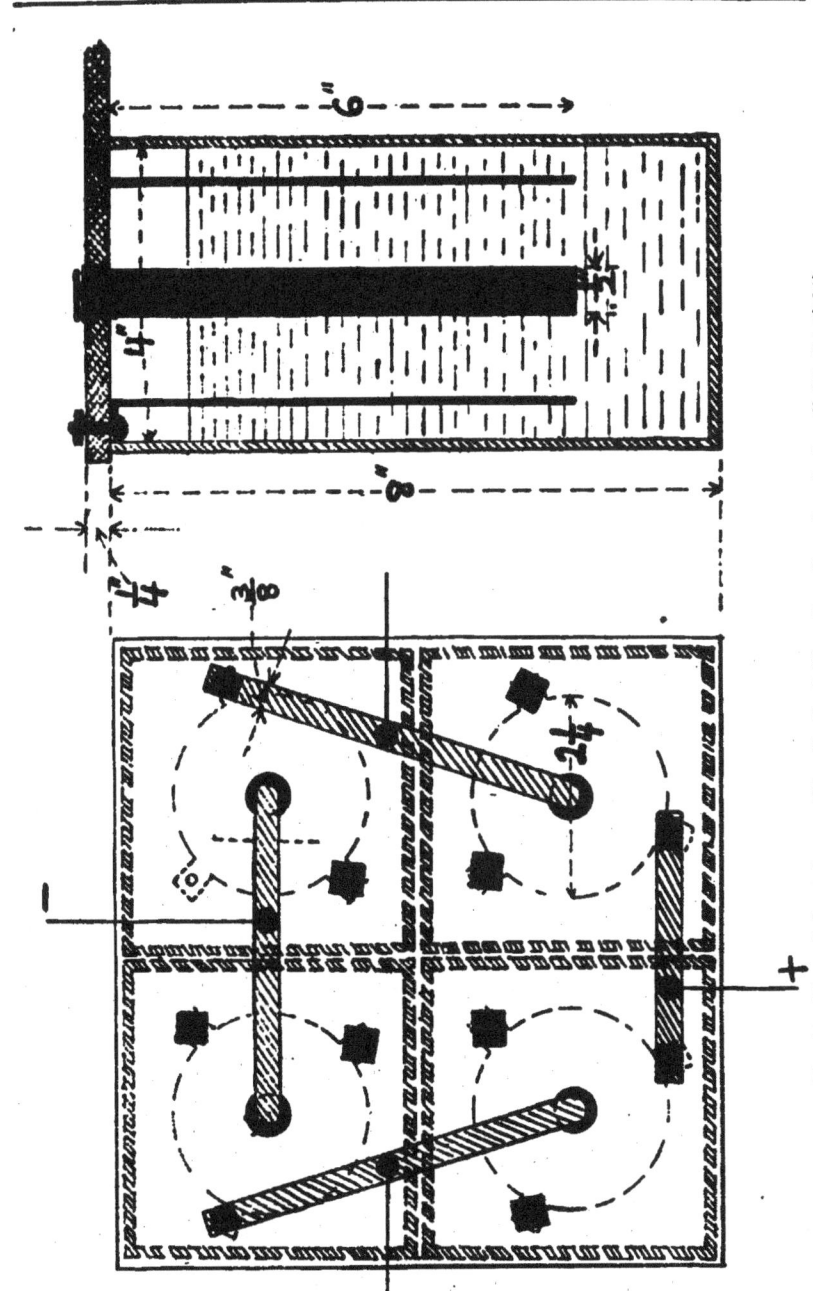

Fig. 24.—Plan of aluminium rectifier (to the left) and section of a single cell (to the right)

that circuit. When M₂ is positive (other phase) the current goes as shown by the broken arrow. Thus the terminal C₁ is always the positive terminal of the working circuit.

The construction of the cells is shown in Figure 24. The cells are four prismatic glass jars; fruit jars would do very well. The aluminium electrode is a piece of thin sheet aluminium bent in the form of a cylinder to surround the iron electrode. The four vessels are covered by one cover, which must be a good insulator; slate is quite suitable, as it is easy to drill and is a non-conductor. Wood well soaked in paraffin would do quite well also. To this slate or wood top all the electrodes are fastened, so that the top and the electrodes all lift out together; there is thus less danger of short-circuiting. The aluminium electrode has ears cut on it and is bolted to the top. The top end of the iron electrode is pounded out a little so that it cannot slip through the hole in the slate. Connections are made on top of the slate with copper strips, which

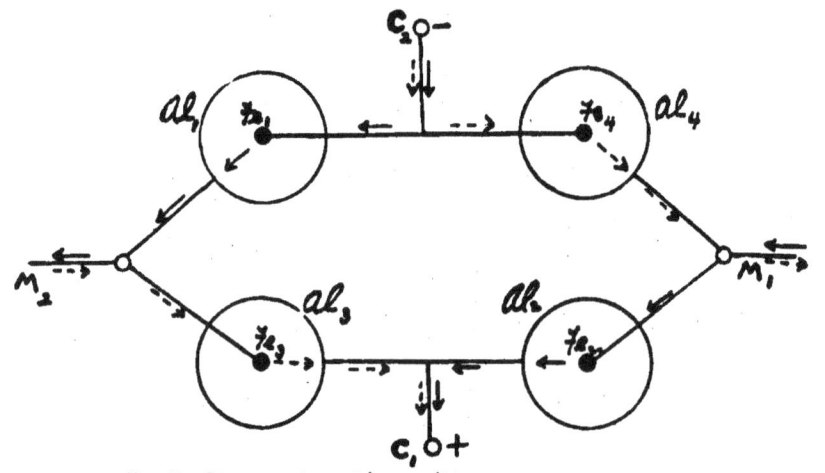

Fig. 25.—Diagram of aluminium rectifier, showing the connections

are soldered to the top of the iron electrodes, and placed under the nut to act as a washer where these strips are joined to the aluminium electrode. Binding posts may be soldered or screwed to the copper strips. The electrolytes giving equal success are saturated potassium bichromate solution and saturated di-sodium phosphate (common sodium phosphate) solution.

Solubility of potassium bichromate .... 10 parts in 100 at 15°C.
Solubility of sodium phosphate .... 15 parts in 100 at 15°C.

Both salts are much more soluble in hot water and, therefore, saturation is easily attained by dissolving the salt in warm water and then allowing it to cool.

Always use a rheostat in the circuit M₁, M₂. A good form of rheostat consists of a vessel containing very dilute sulphuric acid with two copper electrodes. This vessel is a glass trough 15 in. by 8 in. by 6 in., with electrodes which can be raised, or lowered, or slid along a rod, so as to vary the resistance. It is well, whenever possible, to regulate the current by the rheostat in M₁ M₂ and use as little resistance in the circuit C₁ C₂ as the experiment will permit.

This rectifier must be used to charge storage cells only when the alternating current is reduced either by the water resistance just described or, better, by a lamp resistance. This rectified current is unidirectional but is pulsating, so that it is not as satisfactory for experimental work in the laboratory as is the storage battery. It is much better to use it for charging storage cells, and then to use these for sources of electricity. However, this rectified current can be used for almost all the experimental work except that of induced current, where its pulsating character makes it entirely unsuitable.

The storage cell has been highly recommended as a source of electricity for experimental work. In one important respect it breaks down; it cannot be used for running the lantern unless thirty or forty cells are in series; and not many schools can hope to have such a supply. The alternating current can be used for this pur-

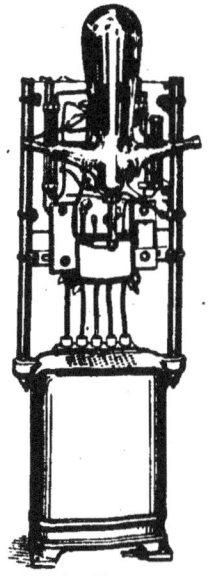

Fig. 26.—Mercury - arc rectifier installation from the front

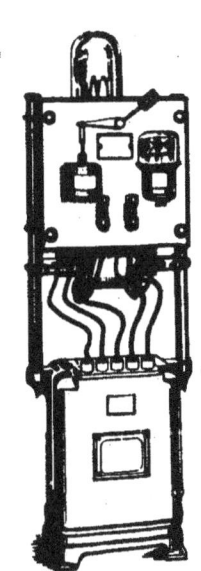

Fig. 27.—Mercury - arc rectifier installation from behind

pose, but it is not nearly so efficient as is the direct current. The illumination is not more than one half as great, there is an unavoidable humming sound which proves very disagreeable and, if the cycle is slow, there may be an unsteadiness in the illumination which is very fatiguing to the eyes. The alternating current can be converted into a direct current of 110 volts by several kinds of transformers; such a transformed current is suitable for all laboratory purposes—experimenting, running a lantern, and charging storage cells. The only two transformers that are likely to be used in high schools are: (1) The mercury-arc rectifier; (2) the motor-generator.

MERCURY-ARC RECTIFIER

The mercury-arc rectifier is a comparatively new form of transformer for converting an alternating into a direct current. The actual transforming instrument is a highly exhausted bulb with two graphite anodes and a mercury cathode. A current can pass from the graphite to mercury, but not in the opposite direction. It is not necessary to go into details regarding the working of this tube, but it is enough to say that at the present time outfits can be purchased which will supply loads up to 50 amperes, at from 10 to 175 volts pressure. The necessary outfit consists of a good deal more than the bare tube. Figures 26 and 27 illustrate a complete outfit from the front and from the back respectively. The one illustrated is specially prepared by The General Electric Co. of Schenectady, New York, for moving-picture lanterns. The rectifier tubes have a life of from 500 to 2,000 hours, but can be replaced at small expense.

MOTOR-GENERATOR

5. The best method, however, for converting either the alternating current or the high-voltage direct current to a low-voltage direct current, suitable for all purposes of the laboratory, is by means of a motor-generator set. A motor-generator set consists of a motor and a dynamo fitted to one shaft so that they rotate at the same rate. The motor is connected to the main alternating current circuit, and by its rotation causes the dynamo to rotate also, thus generating a current whose voltage and output depend or its construction. The generator usually delivers a current at 110 volts, as this is most suitable for laboratory purposes. The motor-generator is more expensive than the mercury-arc rectifier outfit, but it is also more satisfactory and has a longer life, and as the difference in cost is not great it is generally to be preferred.

In ordering a mercury-arc rectifier or a motor-generator, what must first be decided is the most suitable voltage for the purposes of the laboratory. In the laboratory it will be used for experimental purposes and also for running the lantern. Lanterns usually have rheostats made for 110 volts to go with them, and this is probably the most suitable voltage for the generated current. This voltage is too high for most experiments, but with a lamp resistance it can be brought down to any required voltage. It must be remembered, however, that the voltage goes wherever the resistance is great. If 110 volts is connected to an electric bell in series with a lamp resistance, at the make and break there will be bright sparking at the tip on the bell, tending to injure the points. The next point to consider is what output of current is required. This will depend on all the uses the current may be put to at any one time. All the circuits in the laboratories will be in parallel, so in order to get the total output, all the currents in use at one time must be added together. Suppose two rooms are wired for lanterns which may be used together and that the physical laboratory has a pair of binding posts at each pupil's place, and that there are twenty-four places, then the output of the generator should be great enough to feed all these circuits at the same time. Each lantern requires 15 amperes, and if one is used for opaque projection it will require 25 amperes. Say each pupil uses $\frac{1}{2}$ ampere in experimenting, then the total output required is $15 + 15 + 12$ amperes if no opaque projection is used, or $15 + 25 + 12$ amperes if one lantern is replaced by an opaque projector. Generally a generator with an output of 30 or 40 amperes at 110 volts will prove adequate for all schools except the largest, where an output of 50 amperes at 110 volts will be required.

Up to the present the current delivered to the pupils' benches has not been discussed, but only that delivered to the demonstrator's bench. It has been mentioned that Daniell cells can be used for the former purpose. The cells are carried to the benches when required for work, and when not in use are placed in the store-room. When the electrical supply comes from a group of storage cells, a mercury-arc rectifier, or a motor-generator, it will be best to have the physics benches equipped with terminals at each pupil's working place. In large schools terminals should be placed in each room in the science department, on all the pupils' benches in the physical laboratory, on the demonstration benches, and at the back of all the rooms in which a lantern is to be used. In large schools, and even in small ones, it cannot be too strongly recommended to have every class-room wired for the use of the lantern.

In distributing the current to the pupils' benches, the terminals for each place will come off the mains always in parallel, so that each circuit may be opened or closed quite independently of the others. It is absolutely necessary to have some protection for the wires and for the storage cells against short-circuiting. Pupils will be sure either thoughtlessly, ignorantly, or wilfully, to produce a short circuit, so that it is not enough merely to protect it by fuses, as these will be continually blown, causing a good deal of irritation, delay, and expense; therefore a socket is placed below each pupil's terminal, and into each of these either a bulb lamp or a fuse can be screwed. In one of these sockets always screw a bulb lamp when pupils are going to use the current. A 16-candle-power carbon-film lamp will allow one half ampere to pass from a 110 volt circuit, and this is ample for most work. If there are 24 places the circuits at which are all closed at once, then there will be a flow of 12 amperes from the mains. Where storage cells are used to deliver such a current, it would be best to have them joined in parallel, as 12 amperes would be a too rapid discharge for any ordinary storage cell. Figure 65 represents diagrammatically the wiring for distributing the current to the students' benches in a physical laboratory. This is more fully discussed under that topic on page 110.

ELECTRICAL EQUIPMENT FOR A SCHOOL

A short description might be given of the electrical arrangements in a fairly complete school. In such a school there will be electrical connections on the teacher's benches, in the science lecture-rooms, and in each laboratory. The physical laboratory, and perhaps the chemical laboratory also, will have terminals on the pupils' benches. Besides these there will be terminals for the lantern at the backs of the lecture-rooms and at the backs of some of the laboratories. It is strongly recommended that lantern terminals be placed also at the backs of some or all of the class-rooms. The high school of the future will most assuredly use the lantern, not merely for teaching science, but also for geography, history, literature, and languages.

Each set of wires will lead from the terminals to the general switchboard, which will be placed in close proximity to the electrical generator. It is not necessary that every terminal should have its wires run independently to the switchboard. In the case of the lantern terminals several rooms might be connected in parallel along a single set of wires. It is preferable in such a case to connect rooms that are not likely to be using the lantern at the same time. All the terminals to the pupils' benches in one laboratory are connected in parallel to a single pair of wires coming from the switchboard. It is an advantage, but not a necessity, to have the wiring to the teacher's bench independent of the wiring to the pupils' benches in the physical and the chemical laboratory.

The switchboard is usually a marble slab fastened on metal brackets and placed far enough from the wall to allow the back of it to be quite accessible for repairs or changes of any kind. Each set of wires will terminate in a knife-switch. In a row on the switchboard are as many knife-switches as there are sets of wires ramifying to different terminals. The two mains leading from the electrical source pass along the back of the switchboard, and pass through a knife-switch, also attached to the switchboard. These mains, after passing through the knife-switch, are connected in series with the ammeter and in parallel with the voltmeter and with each of the line switches. The voltmeter and ammeter are, of course, placed on the switchboard. If the current is produced by a motor-generator, a starting rheostat, a field rheostat, and a switch will be placed either on this common switchboard or on a separate one. We will suppose that the current is produced by a motor-generator which converts alternating into direct current. It is an advantage to have an arrangement by which the alternating current can also be thrown into any of the lines. For this purpose it is only necessary to have this current brought to two terminals on the switchboard. If two wires have metal clips soldered to one end of each, then by connecting the other ends of the wires to the alternating-current binding posts and attaching the clips to the two arms of any knife-switch the alternating current can be fed to any terminal.

For the most perfect equipment in such a school a set of storage cells will also be installed and the terminals brought to the switchboard in a row of binding posts as already described, and illustrated in Figure 22. Connection is made from these storage terminals to any knife-switch by the same wires as are used for connecting the alternating current to the line current.

By such an electrical arrangement as this, every set of terminals can be fed, (1) with the alternating current, (2) with the generator current—generally a 110-volt direct current, (3) with the storage-cell current; and from this latter source any voltage desired up to a maximum determined by the number of cells can be obtained. One of these currents can be sent to any number of lines, and either of the other two currents can be used on any of the other lines. Thus as complete a variety of currents can be obtained as is at all necessary for scientific work.

CHAPTER II

COMBINED CLASS-ROOM AND LABORATORY

OWING to lack of accommodation the practical work in science must frequently be conducted in a room which is also utilized as a regular class-room. This condition also arises when the number of pupils taking science is so small that it does not seem necessary to set apart a whole room for the purpose. Such an arrangement has serious disadvantages, both for the pupils who are conducting experiments, and for those who are studying at their desks. Where science benches and school desks occupy the same room, conditions are almost sure to be cramped and inconvenient for both, and the experimental work will distract the attention of those who are supposed to be studying or having a lesson with the teacher. This distraction will make the enforcement of discipline much more difficult. In chemical experiments there are sure to be evil-smelling and irritating gases formed which, although tolerated by those performing the experiments, are exceedingly annoying to others. The apparatus is much more likely to be tampered with when in a common class-room, which must be accessible at times when a regular science room would be locked. There is perhaps a certain advantage in such a combination of class-room and laboratory for a school that is under-staffed with teachers; for under such circumstances the pupils can perform experimental work while the teacher is busy with other classes, and he can give them a certain amount of assistance and advice during spare moments. However, the aim of every teacher should be to have a special room devoted exclusively to the teaching of science.

ARRANGEMENT OF FURNITURE

What is considered the best form and the best arrangement of furniture for such a combined class-room and science laboratory will now be described and illustrated by drawings. Much in the arrangement must depend upon the size and the shape of the room as well as upon the position of the windows, so that the best that can be attempted is to show the most suitable arrangement for a typical room, which each science teacher can modify to suit conditions. A room 30 ft. by 24 ft. has been selected, and it is lighted on one side by four windows (Fig. 28). Thirty seats for pupils are arranged in the ordinary method, occupying the middle of the room and so facing that the light enters from the left. The laboratory benches are placed around the wall and most of them at the back of the room or along the sides toward the back. They thus occupy the minimum amount of available floor space and are in such a position that the pupils experimenting at them cause as little distraction as possible to the pupils seated at their desks. As the benches are placed between the windows, the light coming to the pupils at their desks will not be interfered with nor will any pupil at the laboratory bench have the light full in his face.

THE PUPIL'S BENCH

The laboratory benches themselves (Fig. 29) are constructed so as to economize floor space. Each has a cupboard beneath with two doors in front. The bench top is folded up when not in use, and when thus folded, forms a front to

[43]

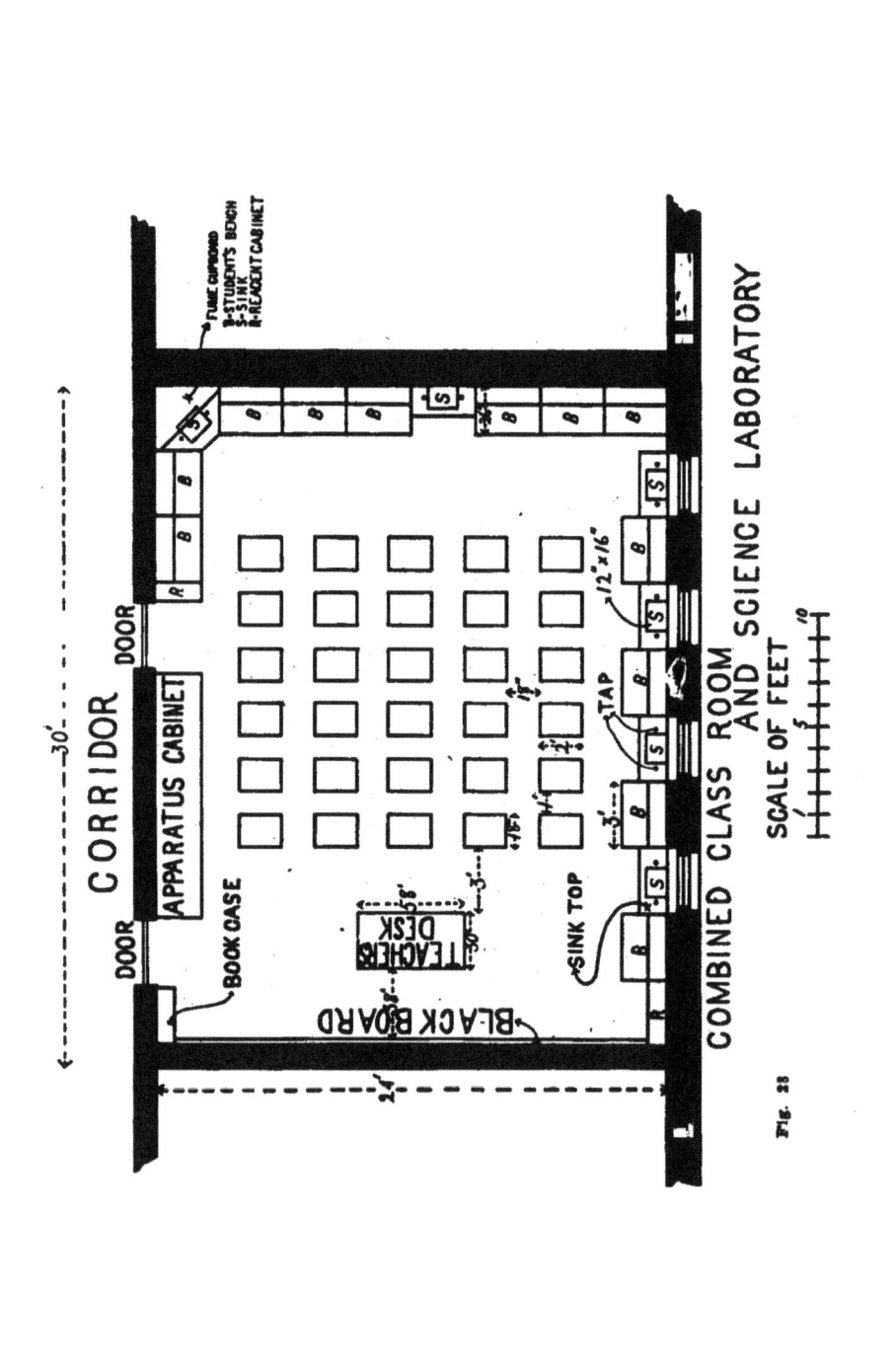

FIG. 25. COMBINED CLASS ROOM AND SCIENCE LABORATORY

inclose the two shelves above the bench. It thus shuts in the apparatus on the shelves from dust and prevents it from being tampered with. Above all runs a beam along the whole front with hooks for suspension. This beam projects out so far that, when the top is folded, a suspended pendulum will clear the edge. A gas-tap comes through the top of each bench equally distant from either end and well toward the back. The main gas conduit runs around the room just above the floor and is thus quite accessible.

These benches are 3 ft. long, 2 ft. 2 in. wide when open, and 4 ft. 7 in. high over all. The top of the bench is 3 ft. above the floor, and experience shows that this is the most convenient height for a chemical or physical bench for the average high school pupil when he is standing at work. Stools whose tops are 11 in. lower than the top of the bench may be supplied if desired, but they will not be much used. The working space on the top of the bench is 2 ft. 1 in. deep, which is ample. A length of 3 ft. is sufficient for physics and more than is necessary for chemistry. The top is 1½ in. thick. Beneath the folding top is a secondary top projecting 1 ft. 4 in., and this is none too wide to support the heavy top on which a careless pupil may occasionally sit. Indeed the bench would be better if the top were further supported by brackets on hinges, which could be folded in against the front when the top was raised.

The cupboard beneath is 11 in. deep, and the shelf in it can be placed at any desired height. It will be preferable to have in it one space for apparatus that stands high, and a shallower space above. The shelves above are about 9 in. wide and 11½ in. high; this will be sufficient for most purposes. The beam above is 2 in. square, supported on 2 in. x 4 in. scantlings. It may be made of birch or beech; and the hooks attached may be similar to those used to fasten to the under side of shelves in clothes closets. The ends, shelves, back, and bottom are made of inch material. The nature of the material and finish are partly determined by the surroundings, the taste of the teacher, and the amount of money that can be expended.

The body of the bench may be made of white pine, ash, birch, or maple. These are all suitable if well seasoned. The unexposed parts may be made of basswood. Elm is unsuitable, as it warps and cracks and splinters very greatly. Oak, unless old and well seasoned, will shrink greatly, leaving unsightly spaces between the boards; it is also liable to crack greatly in drying. While the material of the sides, front, and shelves is of secondary importance, the structure and material of the working top cannot be given too much attention. It requires to be perfectly flat and horizontal and quite *impervious to liquids of any kind.* Cracks, warping, or porosity in the wood must be carefully avoided. The top should be made of narrow strips, say one inch in width, glued firmly together. To add to its strength, dowels may be run across the strips, and if these are introduced at different depths along the strips as the top is being built up, the constituents will be firmly bound together. Fig. 35 shows the proper arrangement for the dowels.

Ordinary glue is quite unsuitable for uniting the strips that make the bench tops, as the moisture gradually softens it. A good waterproof glue must be used for this purpose. Such a glue can be made in a variety of ways. The following are two good recipes: No. 1. Boil two ounces of isinglass in a pint of skim milk; No. 2. Mix together one part glue, and one and one-half parts water; then add one-fiftieth part of potassium bichromate; and keep in a dark place. On page 11 will be found more complete directions for making a waterproof glue.

46 LABORATORY ACCOMMODATION

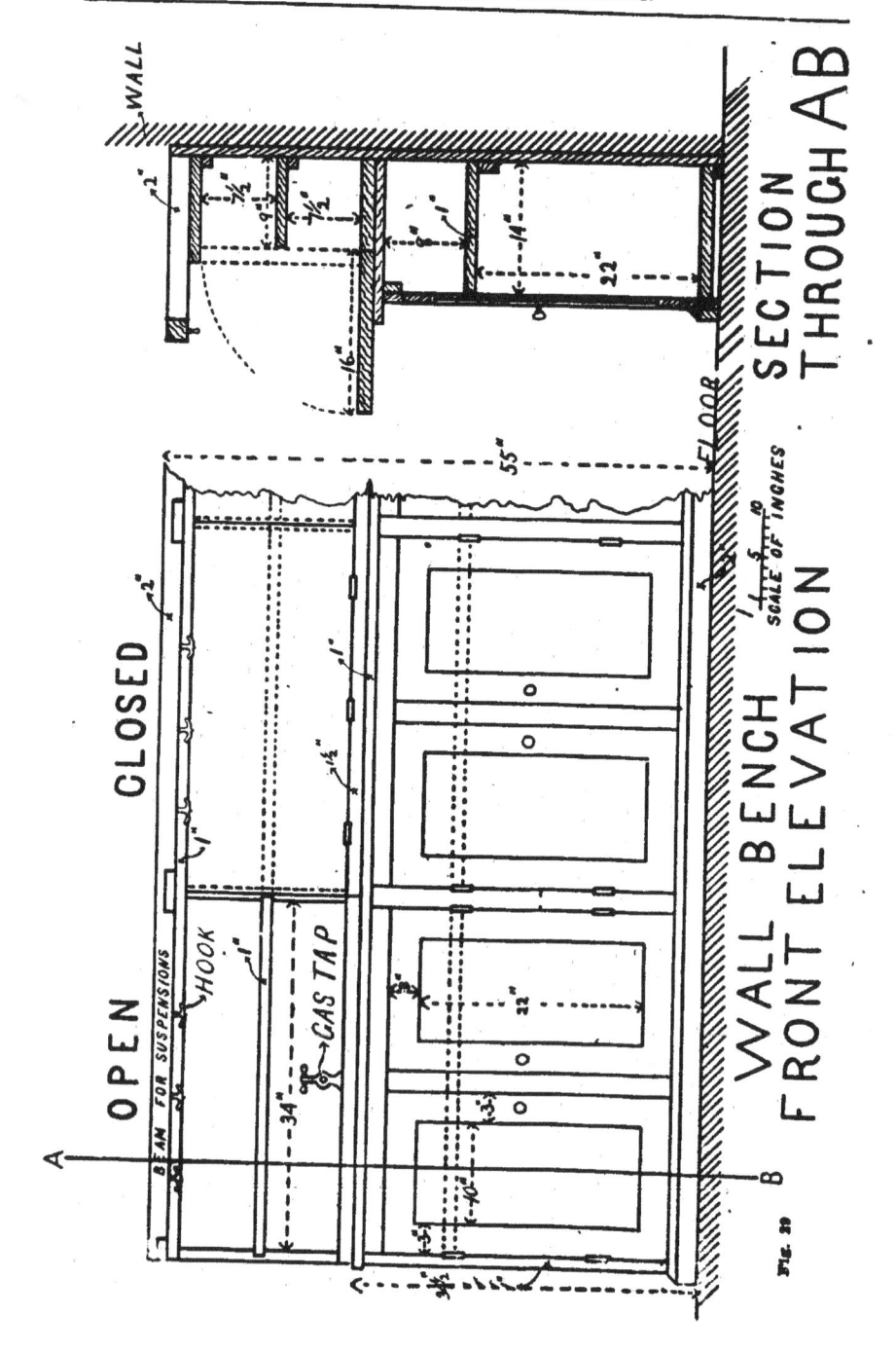

FINISHES

The best material from which to make this composite top is teak, and this is almost exclusively used in England. If made of this wood the top hardly needs to be built up of strips, as teak scarcely warps, splinters, or cracks in drying. This wood is not commonly used on this continent on account of its expensiveness, and maple and birch are the most suitable substitutes. Ash is too porous and inclined to splinter; oak is also porous and too much inclined to warp and crack. White pine answers well, except that it is much too soft for such hard wear as a bench top receives. White-wood serves the purpose very well where a cheaper material than any of these is demanded. It stands water well and does not warp or crack easily. Its chief defect is that it is quite soft. The top should be fastened in place by three strong, brass, fast-pin butt hinges, and the doors of the cupboards should be attached similarly, except that the butts will be lighter; only brass screws should be used. Iron hinges will rust quickly, not look well, and wear out quickly. The hinged top, when closed, may be fastened by flush ring catches attached to the underside, and the cupboard doors by flush bolts. The doors should also have knobs of wood or porcelain. Brass pulls will rapidly tarnish, owing to the corrosive vapours produced in experiments in chemistry.

The finish is for two purposes—to preserve the wood and to add to the appearance of the furniture; it must be in keeping with that of the remainder of the room. All exposed parts may be filled with silica paste-filler, then finished with one coat of white shellac and one or more coats of Johnston's wax. The latter should be thoroughly rubbed and polished. The inside unexposed parts should be given one coat of orange shellac. The bench top and the top of the shelf that holds the reagent bottles must receive a different treatment, as they must be resistant to acids and strong alkalis. Many recipes have been given for the treatment of bench tops in order to make them acid proof. Two of the best are given here.

FINISHES FOR BENCH TOPS

No. 1. Apply with a brush the liquid made by boiling logwood chips in an iron kettle. When dry give a second coat. This second coat, when dry, is followed by a coat of a solution of copperas in hot water. When the bench is dry, rub it down with sand-paper. Next pour on melted paraffin at a high melting point (55° to 60°). By means of a hot flat iron the paraffin is thoroughly rubbed into the wood in order to impregnate the pores. When cool, the superfluous wax is removed by scraping the surface with a piece of thin steel having a smooth, straight edge.

No. 2.

Solution No. 1

Copper Sulphate ....1 part
Potassium Chlorate ....1 part
Water ....8 parts
Boil until salts are dissolved.

Solution No. 2

Water ....50 parts
Aniline .... 6 parts
Hydrochloric Acid............................. 9 parts

By means of a brush apply two coats of Solution No. 1 while it is still hot, and allow the first coat to dry before applying the second. Then apply two coats of Solution No. 2, and allow the wood to dry thoroughly. Later, a coat of raw linseed oil is applied by means of a cloth instead of a brush, in order to get a thinner coat of oil. Then thoroughly wash the top with soap-suds, and an ebony appearance is the result. Either ¨ these solutions should be applied to the bench top and also to the shelf above it on which the reagent bottles are kept. More complete instructions for finishing bench tops are found on page 11.

Uses of Parts of Bench

The opened top is the part used for all experimental work in both physics and chemistry; it can also be used for biological work, but the lighting is not very suitable for such a purpose. This top must be rubbed dry after use and always left folded up.

The ideal method is to have one pupil at a bench in experimental work, both in physics and in chemistry, and under these conditions there is accommodation for twelve in the room (see Fig. 28); if two work together, then twenty-four can work at once. No sets of lockers have been provided in the benches, as it is taken for granted that in a school with such limited accommodation there will not be more than one set of pupils working in chemistry and, hence, one set of apparatus for each bench is all that is required. It will be advisable to have separate locks on each cupboard. The cupboards below are to hold the larger and rougher pieces of apparatus, such as retort stands, burners, pneumatic troughs, test-tube stands, wire gauze, dusters, mop-cloths, and all metal apparatus that will corrode if placed above with the reagent bottles, from which some fumes are sure to escape. On the shelves above are placed the reagent bottles and glass beakers, funnels, Florence flasks, etc., which the fumes will not injure. As the reagent bottles are closed in, they will be kept free from dust, which is sure to accumulate on them if they are left exposed. The beam above will be found very useful for a number of purposes, such as the suspension of pulleys, levers, magnetic needles, spring balances, etc.

Water and Gas

The ordinary kitchen or bath-room sinks are not at all suitable for science laboratories, as the enamel soon becomes chipped off, exposing the iron, which rapidly becomes a prey to the corroding liquids so frequently used in chemistry. The sinks should be rectangular, and shallow, so that they can be easily kept clean. The bench top above should project slightly over the edge of the sink, in order to prevent the water from splashing over. The sinks themselves should be made of thick enamelled vitrified stone-ware, white-glazed inside and cane-glazed outside, with overflows and plugs attached by chains to a ring in the top. A good size is 16 in. by 12 in. by 6 in. For more details regarding laboratory sinks see page 19. These sinks should be surrounded by a draining-board with a raised apron at the margin, in order to prevent the water from being splashed upon the floor. The draining-board and apron are preferably of slate, but this will be too expensive for most schools, and white-wood may be substituted, as it stands the water well. In Canada, this name is frequently given to varieties of poplar or cucumber trees, but both these are quite unsuitable for this purpose, the real white-wood being the product of the tulip-tree.

The taps should be of the swan-neck type, and the mouth should be high enough to allow a tall jar to be placed beneath it. They should be made of gun-metal with a tapering corrugated nozzle, so that rubber tubing can be easily pushed over them (see Fig. 5). Brass and nickel-plated ware should be avoided, as both rapidly tarnish owing to the corrosive gases (see pages 19, 20, and Figure 5, for particulars regarding the taps). The water-pipes should be placed around the room in the bottoms of the cupboards against the wall, but above the floor, and each branch leading to a tap should have a cut-off, in order that the whcle water supply need not be shut off when it is necessary to repair a single tap. Two taps, one on each side of a sink, will be useful, where several pupils require to use the same sink simultaneously. An adequate supply of running water is very important even in small schools, and the method of obtaining it is fully described on pages 15-18. One or two gas-taps are placed at the middle of each bench well toward the back. While water-taps are regulated by a wheel valve, the gas-taps are regulated by means of a lever valve. The gas-mains are placed along the floor under the benches and close against the wall, the branches for each tap rising vertically through the back of the cupboard. A gas supply for schools is discussed fully on pages 22-30.

ARRANGEMENT OF BENCHES

The benches (Fig. 28) are placed between the windows and along the back of the room, while the sinks are placed opposite the windows and at the corner, and one also at the back of the room. By this arrangement no pupil is far from a sink. As the sinks are lower than the bench tops they do not prevent access to the windows.

In order to have the minimum amount of distraction, most of the pupils experimenting are well behind the pupils at the desks. There is also a sufficiently wide aisle between the science benches and the desks, as the space between them is twenty-two inches wide when the bench tops are down, and thirty-one inches when they are closed.

The other furniture must be placed according to the wall space remaining. A large apparatus cabinet is placed against the wall opposite the windows (Fig. 28), and two reagent cabinets are placed one on each side of the room. These contain the stock liquids and solids that are only occasionally used, and hence are not placed on each pupil's bench. A draught closet placed in one corner should have a pipe above leading into a flue, and must have a strong draught, either natural or by an electric or hydraulic fan. A full description of each of these pieces of furniture is given in other parts of this book, as follows: Apparatus cabinets on pages 79 and 101, reagent cabinets on page 76, and draught closets on page 83. The custom of having a single cabinet in which all the apparatus and reagents are kept is very objectionable indeed and should be discontinued. The reagents must be kept quite separate from the apparatus, as there are always corrosive gases escaping from the bottles, which rapidly destroy the metallic and wooden parts of the apparatus. The reagent cabinet should be placed as far as possible from the apparatus cabinet.

MODIFICATIONS

The benches just described are placed between the windows, and are not suitable for a room in which one side has the windows close together, which is the usual arrangement in the best lighted school-rooms of the present time. If it is necessary to place science benches in front of such windows (Fig. 29a) there are several features in their construction which will require modification. No shelves can be placed above the top at the back, as they would stand directly in front of the windows and cut off the light; moreover, the hinged part of the bench top cannot be raised. To overcome these difficulties the shelves must be omitted altogether, and the part of the bench top projecting beyond the edge of the cupboard will be hinged and drop down like the leaf of a table (Fig. 29b). The leaf is held in a horizontal position by a bracket turning on a pivot in exactly the same manner as the leaf of a table is supported. The hinged part of the bench top in this case will be much narrower than in the case described above, where it folds up. A modification of the cupboard in such a bench might also be made to advantage. A shelf might be placed in the space beneath the top at such a height that the space above it is shut in by the movable part of the top when it is down, and so this latter acts as a front for the upper compartment of the cupboard, the lower compartment having a cupboard door as in the original bench. The leaf should have arrangements for bolting or locking it when down, so as to make the space behind it safe from interference. All the benches in such a room might be of this latter pattern, though it is probably better in most cases to place this type of bench in front of the window, and to place those represented by Fig. 29 at the back of the room as in Fig. 29a.

The above gives a description of the complete furniture, but the arrangement and furniture lend themselves to much variation, according to the shape of the room, the number of pupils, the amount of money to be spent, etc. The cost may be reduced in various ways. Cheap materials for the furniture may be used, the number of benches or sinks diminished, and the quality of the finish may be lowered. It would be possible, but not advisable, to put in another row of pupils' desks if the number of the pupils demanded it. There is a possible objection to such a laboratory bench as is here described. Frequently a new laboratory is added, or a special room is set aside for use as a laboratory exclusively, and the old laboratory benches are required for use in the new room. These wall benches are built primarily for use only against a wall, and are not the best for an ordinary laboratory. They are designed for a class-room where little space is available. Such benches, however, can be placed back to back in a laboratory. Still, where a school board places science benches in a classroom, intending shortly to have a room properly fitted for science teaching, it would be better to put in the regular combined physical and chemical benches described in Chapter III, and place them close together and in smaller number. They will, of course, produce a more cramped condition, and should only serve as a temporary provision.

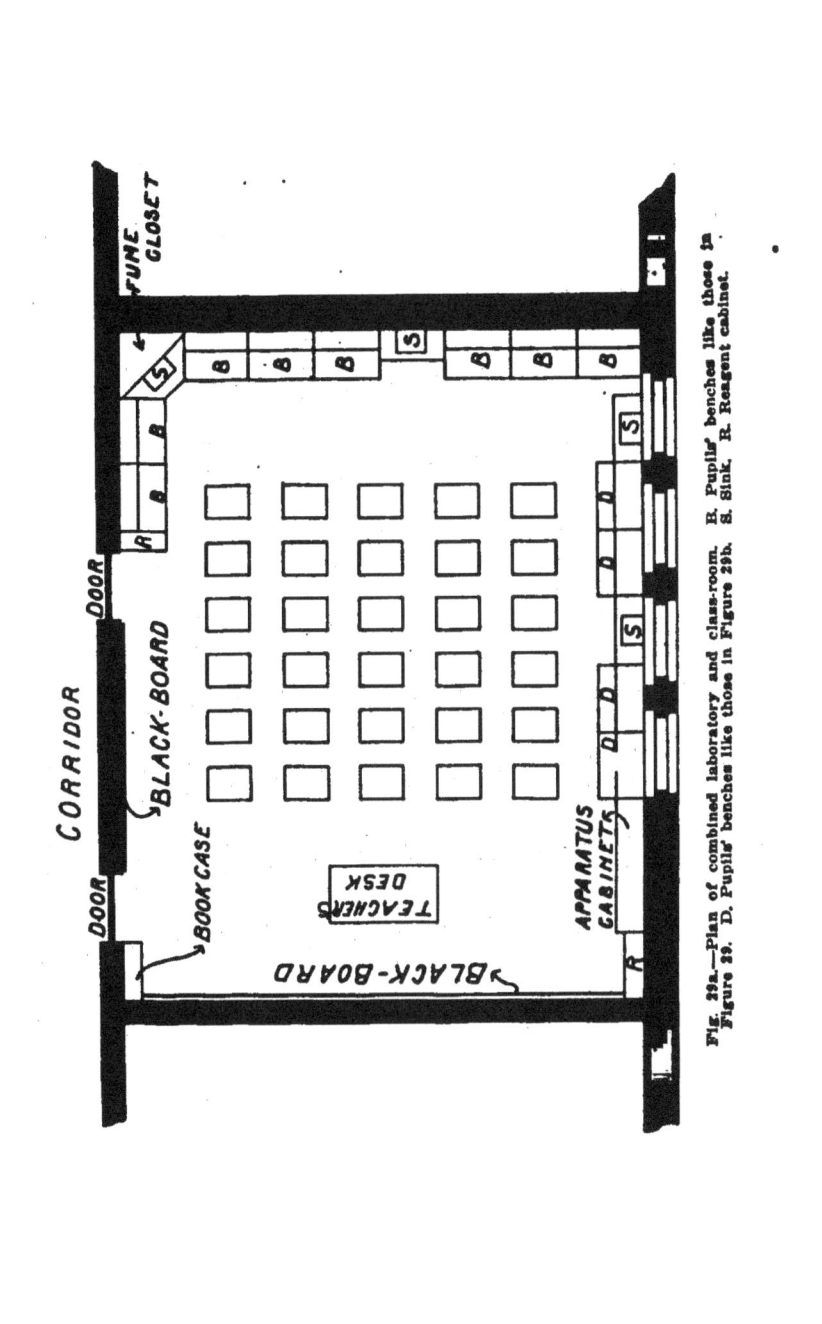

Fig. 29a.—Plan of combined laboratory and class-room. B. Pupils' benches like those in Figure 29. D. Pupils' benches like those in Figure 29b. S. Sink. R. Reagent cabinet.

50b   LABORATORY ACCOMMODATION.

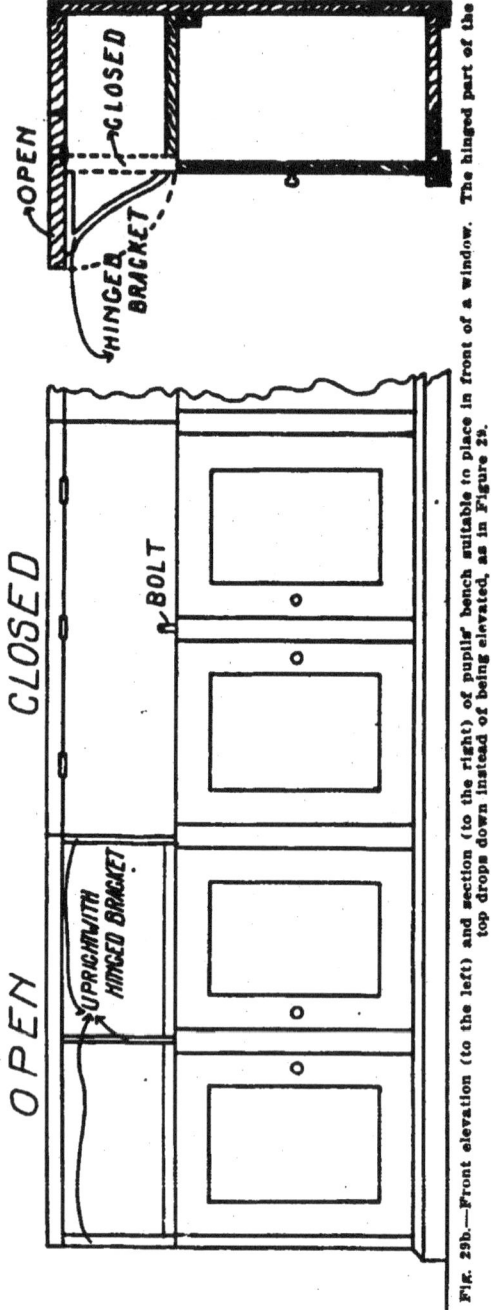

Fig. 29b.—Front elevation (to the left) and section (to the right) of pupils' bench suitable to place in front of a window. The hinged part of the top drops down instead of being elevated, as in Figure 29.

CHAPTER III

COMBINED PHYSICAL

AND

CHEMICAL LABORATORY

THE laboratory furniture of a school in which all the experimental work in science is performed in the class-room has been described in the preceding Chapter, and such an arrangement should obtain only under exceptional circumstances. The more usual condition is that in which one room is set aside exclusively to be used as a laboratory, with one or two smaller rooms that may be used for the storage of apparatus, specimens, etc. The better grades of continuation schools and the smaller high schools should all have at least this accommodation. Larger high schools and collegiate institutes should have at least two rooms, one for a physical and the other for a chemical laboratory, and, of course, the larger schools will have still more elaborate equipment. It is the combined physical and chemical laboratory that will be described in this chapter

ADVANTAGES AND DISADVANTAGES

Such a laboratory possesses advantages, in some respects, over separate physical and chemical laboratories, and, of course, still greater advantages over the class-room that is also used for a laboratory. The disturbance due to the combination of class-room and laboratory disappears. There can be economy in the amount of apparatus required in such a room, as certain apparatus is used in both physics and chemistry, such as Bunsen burners, alcohol-lamps, retort-stands, beakers, etc.; while in the school with separate laboratories, either duplicate sets have to be provided, or a great deal of time is wasted in carrying apparatus from room to room, and much irritating confusion arises from the fact that the pieces are not always put back in the right drawer or cupboard. Such a laboratory takes up less room than the separate science rooms and is certainly less expensive to equip and maintain. These are considerations of importance.

On the other hand, such an arrangement has serious disadvantages that more than counterbalance the good points already mentioned. Unless the school is small, or the matter of expense is serious, the combined laboratory is not to be recommended. The pupils' benches which are suitable for physics are not convenient for chemistry. In a chemistry bench every pupil must have ready access to a sink, while in the physics bench the opening of the sink is inconvenient, as a plain, level surface of large area is required. Individual benches of small size are best for chemical work, while in physical experiments longer benches, on which long pieces of apparatus may be placed, are a necessity; a stone top, also, is most resistent to the reagents of the chemical laboratory, though quite unsuited to the physics bench, where objects have to be clamped to the top; the chemical benches require the space underneath to be taken up with pupil's lockers, while the physics benches are better if they have open spaces below. In a school of moderate size it is frequently necessary to have more than one science class at the same time, and in the one-laboratory school some of these classes must be held in ordinary class-rooms; in this way experimental work is liable to be neglected. In the one-laboratory school, facilities for carrying off the corrosive gases are not likely to be very efficient; these gases are bound to be very injurious to the delicate physical apparatus, and cause considerable depreciation in the value of the equipment.

THE PUPIL'S BENCH

The arrangement and structure of benches, as illustrated and described, reduce these disadvantages to a minimum. Drawings of the combined bench used for physics and chemistry are shown in Figures 30 and 31. Figures 32, 33, 34, and 35 show working drawings of the bench which, if studied carefully, will make its structure clear. Such a bench is only beginning to be used in this country but is very largely used in Great Britain. It is probably the most efficient bench for a combined laboratory yet devised. W. & J. George, of Hatton Hall, London, England, were, it is believed, the first to place it on the market. The bench about to be described is modelled after theirs, though with some modifications which make it more suitable for Ontario schools.

Each bench is 7 ft. long and 4 ft. wide, and will accommodate four pupils. This gives each pupil a working surface of 3½ ft. long and 2 ft. wide, or where two work together, as is necessary in some experiments, the two have a bench top 7 ft. long, which is ample for any experiments in physics. The bench should be of such a height that the pupil, when standing, should be able to work with the forearm approximately horizontal: from 33 in. to 36 in. will be the most suitable height for high school pupils.

The top should be made preferably of teak, as no other wood can compare with this for such a purpose. It is tough, does not warp and, being filled with resin, is quite impermeable. If its expense is prohibitive, maple strips one inch wide, thoroughly glued together with a waterproof glue (see page 11) will answer well; but such a top may be expected to warp a little and also to separate more or less where glued together. Georgia, or pitch pine, is also suitable for this purpose, as it is much harder than white pine and its resinous character makes it impervious. The most novel feature of this bench from a Canadian standpoint is the style of the reagent shelves. These are arranged in sets of two, one above the other, and are 17 in. long, 8 in. wide, and 18 in. high. Each has a strip running lengthwise along the middle to divide it into two sides—one for a pupil on each side of the bench. In order to prevent the bottles falling out, a low strip, forming a low apron, runs along the front of the shelf. This strip does not run quite to one end, thus facilitating the cleaning of the shelf. Each shelf is 8 in. high, which will allow for ordinary 8 oz. reagent bottles. Five or six bottles may be placed on each shelf. These latter have the end pieces projecting almost as far below the bench top as they rise above it, (Fig. 33). In order to give strength, a cross-piece is put between the lower ends. This shelf can be lowered and raised like a window sash. A cord with a lead weight at one end, after passing over a pulley, has the other end attached to the base of the end piece of the shelf. The lead weight is more than heavy enough to raise the shelves. The cord is so adjusted in length that, when the shelves are raised so that the bottom one is level with the top of the bench, the weight rests on a support not shown in the Figure. The shelves can be depressed until the top of the upper shelf is continuous with the top of the bench, and a snap holds them in this position, which, when drawn back, allows them to rise owing to the force of the weight. A chain somewhat similar to a

COMBINED SCIENCE BENCH

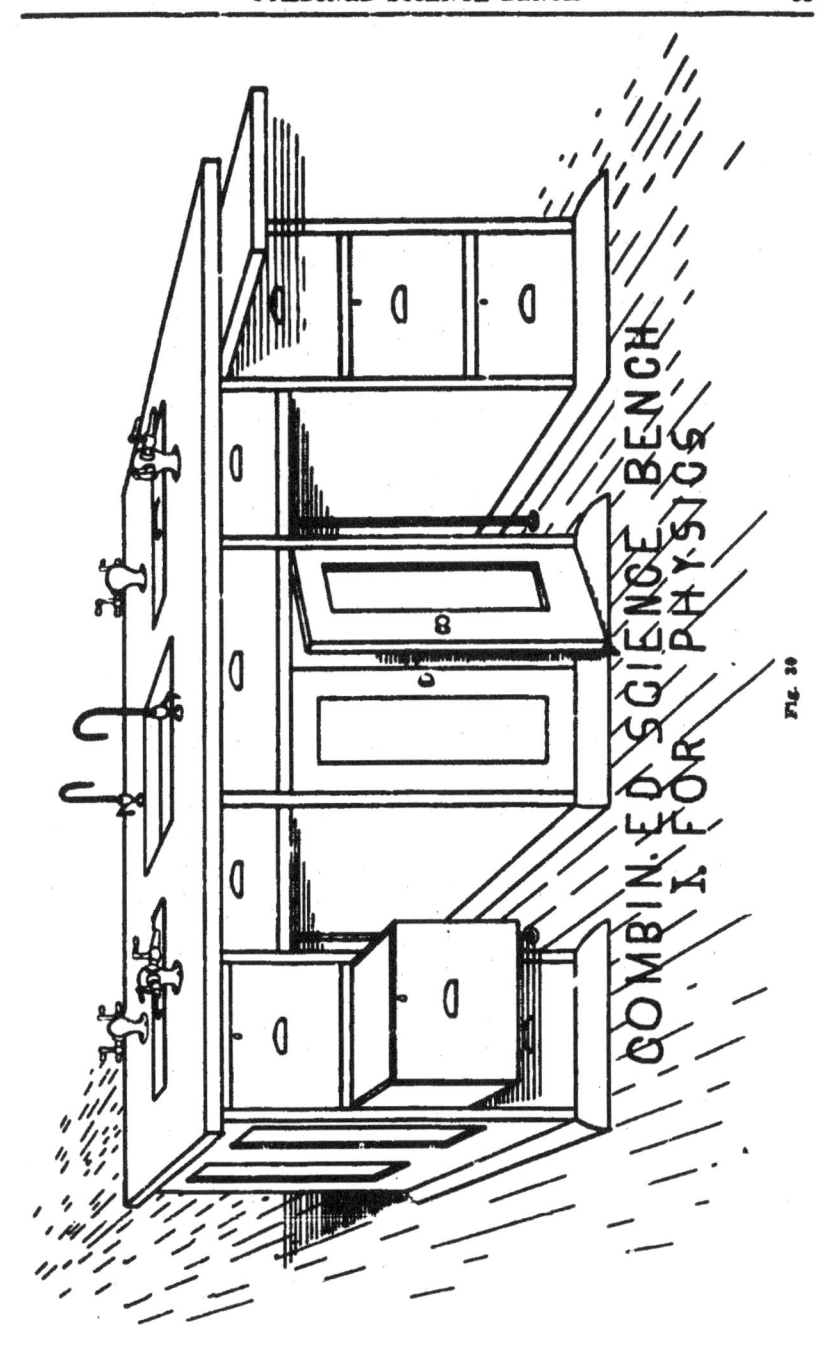

FIG. 20 — COMBINED SCIENCE BENCH FOR PHYSICS

54 LABORATORY ACCOMMODATION

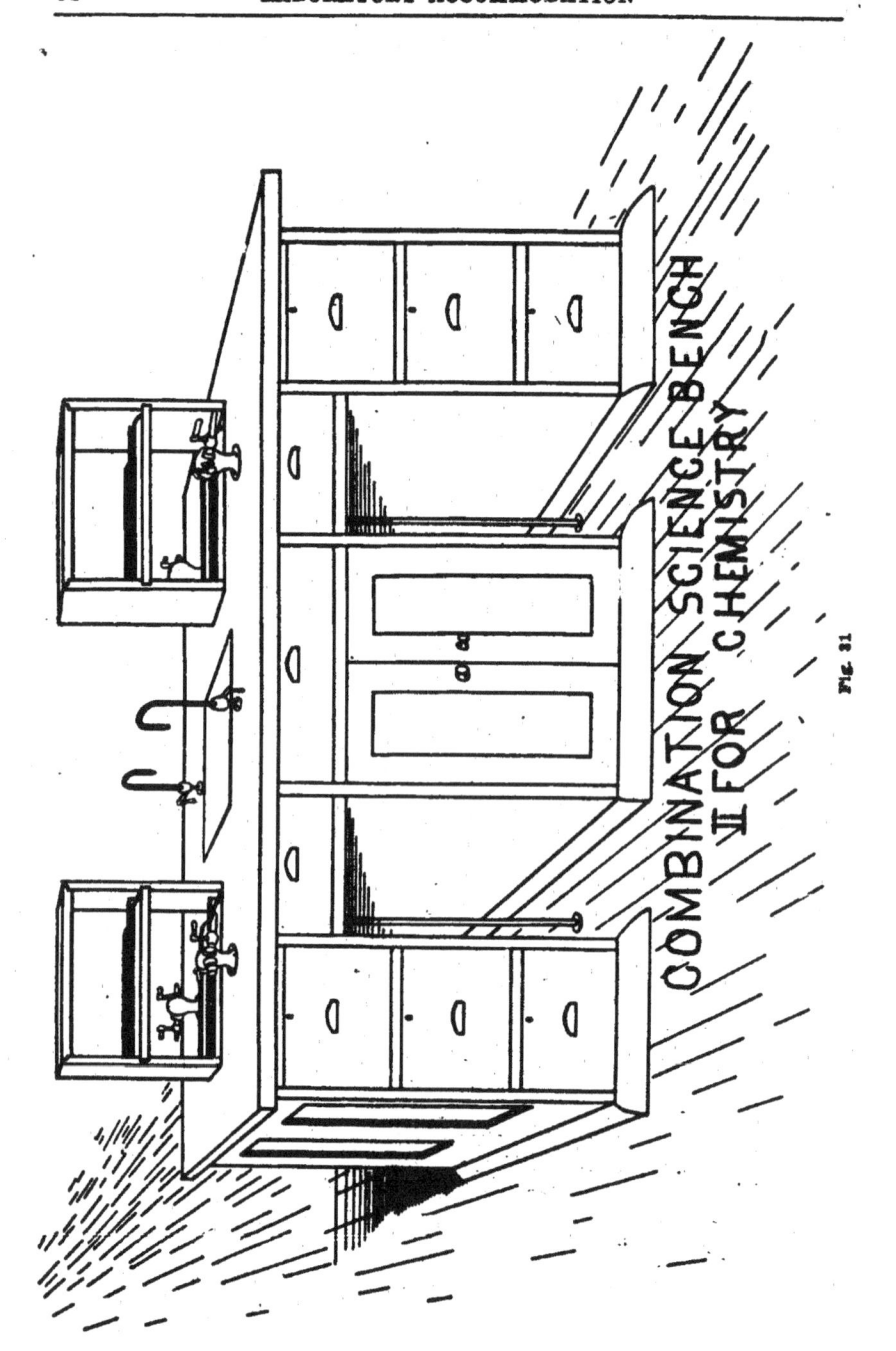

FIG. 21.—COMBINATION SCIENCE BENCH FOR CHEMISTRY

FIG. 22.—Combined science bench

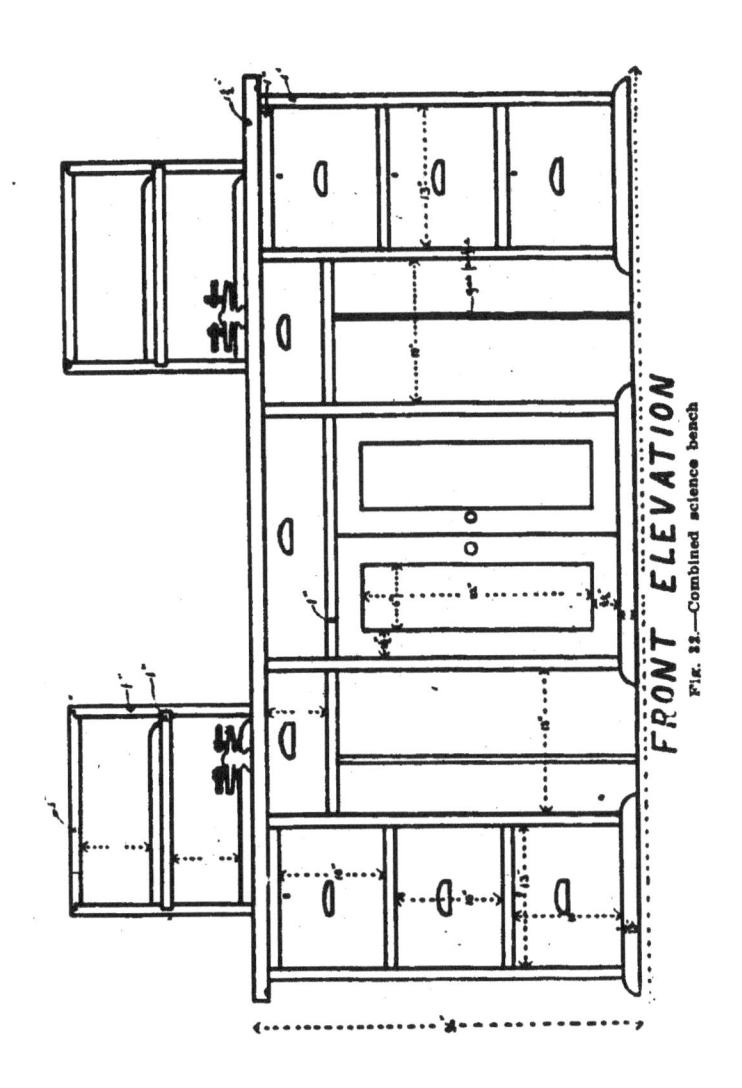

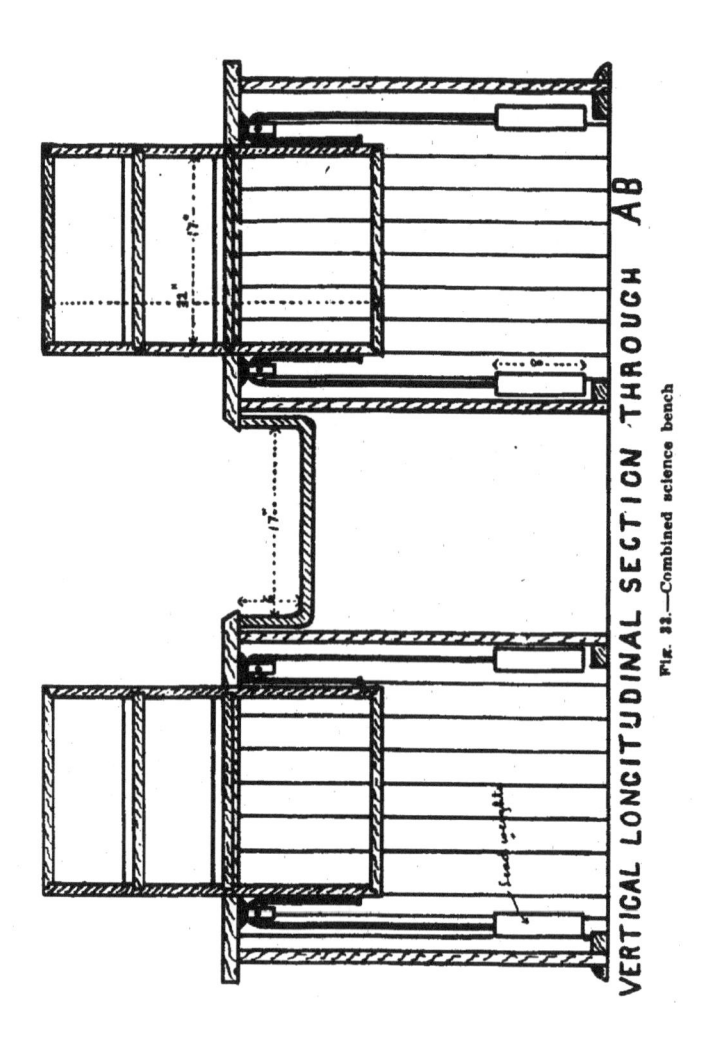

FIG. 32.—Combined science bench. Vertical longitudinal section through AB.

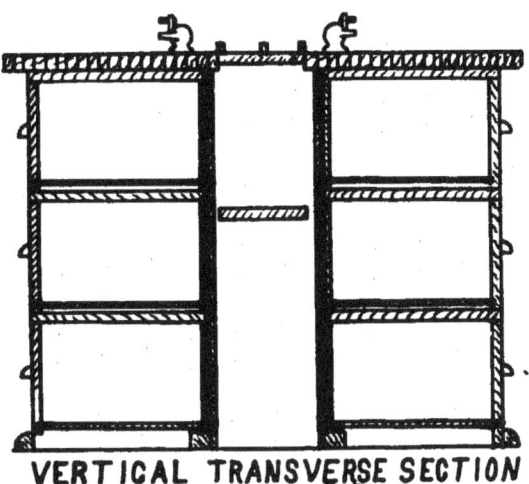

VERTICAL TRANSVERSE SECTION THROUGH CD

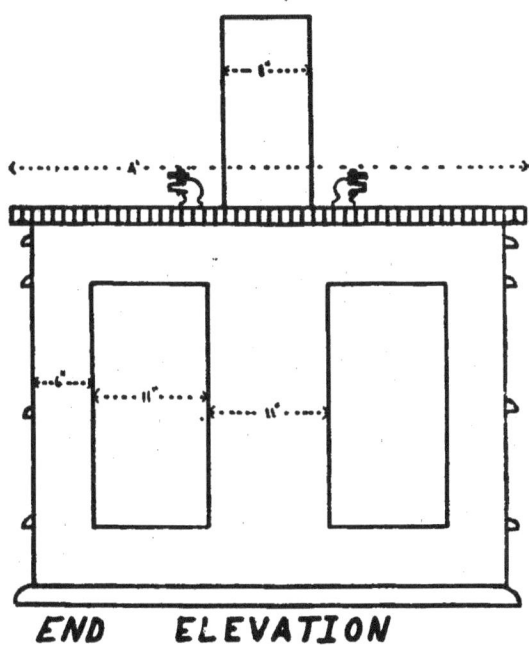

END ELEVATION

Fig. 54.—Combined science bench

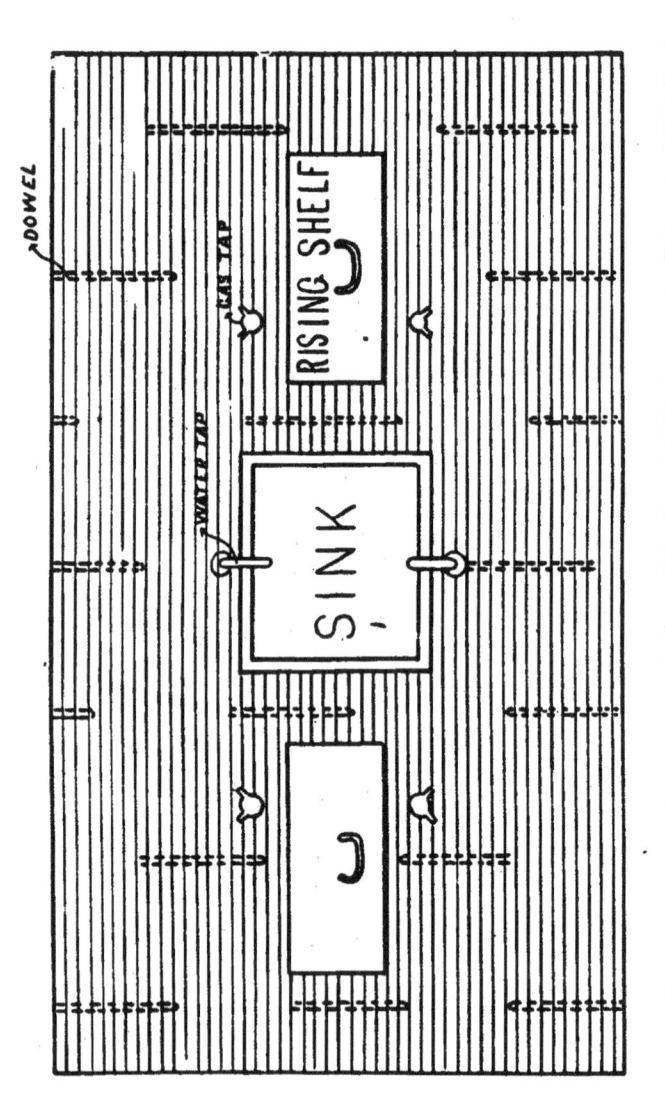

Fig. 35. COMBINED PHYSICS AND CHEMISTRY BENCH PLAN.

bicycle chain may be used instead of the sash cord and is better. Partitions of matched boards run from the top to the bottom of the bench on each side of the shelf, thus separating it entirely from the drawers below the bench top. This arrangement overcomes several of the objections to a combined physical and chemical bench. The best science teachers now consider any shelves rising above the top of the bench as a disadvantage; for they do not allow the teacher to have an unobstructed view of the whole class. This is particularly objectionable where the laboratory is also used as a demonstration and lecture-room, because the shelves prevent the pupils from seeing the experiments performed on the demonstration bench, and they also give mischievous pupils opportunities to get out of the master's sight. The adjustable shelves overcome this difficulty. When physical experiments are being performed, and when demonstrations are being given, the shelves are lowered, and they are raised only during chemical experiments. The reagent bottles are also protected from the dust of the room. Six drawers are in each side, three being toward each end, and besides these there is a cupboard and three common drawers on each side. The three drawers one above the other are to serve as lockers for the pupils. Each drawer is about 16 in. deep, 10 in. high, and 13 in. wide. It holds flasks, beakers, test-tubes, racks, etc. A slat about 4 in. high placed across the bottom of the drawer on the inside about 4 in. from the front, in which flasks, beakers, etc., are placed, will prove valuable, when the drawer is quickly opened or closed, in preventing apparatus from sliding along the bottom of the drawers and being broken. The three drawers furnish sufficient accommodation for three classes in chemistry, which will probably be the maximum number in schools having the combined laboratory. Each of these drawers should have a Yale cylinder lock, all the locks to have different keys and all to be opened by one master-key. Duplicate keys should go with each lock. The other three drawers and the cupboard on each side have no locks. They are occupied by the apparatus which is not likely to be broken, such as Bunsens, retort stands, crucible tongs, etc. These are used in common by all the classes in physics and chemistry. A shelf that pulls out is placed above each tier of drawers. This gives a clean surface on which the student's note-book may be placed A complete partition should be put over the bottom and middle lockers in each tier, so that they cannot be pulled out and the contents of the one below taken. All the drawers should have a button on the back, in order to prevent them from being pulled entirely out inadvertently and the contents upset or broken. This button, however, when turned to a horizontal position, should allow them to be completely withdrawn, as this is necessary from time to time in order to clean them. One or two gas-taps rise above the top of the bench at the back of each pupil's place. The drawings (Figures 33 and 35), show a single large sink 17 in. long by 14 in. wide at the centre of each bench top. Each sink should have a cover, which may be placed on it so that the top will be flush with the bench top. This sink has a tap at each side, which will be used by the two pupils working on that side of the bench. Jointed water-taps may be supplied, which can be folded over into the sink, and thus give a clear sweep for the whole top (with the exception of the gas-taps) for experimental work in physics. If the electrical supply is distributed to each bench, suitable terminals may be placed at the end of the bench top, one set for each pupil. The drawings do not show uprights with a cross-beam such as is used on physical benches (see Fig. 55). Such uprights may easily be added, as they do not offer much obstruction to the view and will prove very useful in physical work.

Many variations may be made in this desk to suit individual needs. The benches may be made long enough to accommodate six pupils or even more, and

LABORATORY ACCOMMODATION

COMBINED PHYSICAL AND CHEMICAL LABORATORY

Fig. 36

A - BALANCE TABLE
B - STUDENTS BENCH
C - TEACHERS BENCH
D - SHELVES FOR REAGENTS
E - LANTERN SCREEN
F - FUME CLOSET
G - BLACKBOARD
H - REAGENT CUPBOARD
J - BLOCK OF ALBERENE STONE
K - FUME VENT
L - TEACHERS WORK TABLE
M - APPARATUS CABINET
N - LANTERN STAND
O - SHELVES FOR APPARATUS
P - TABLE

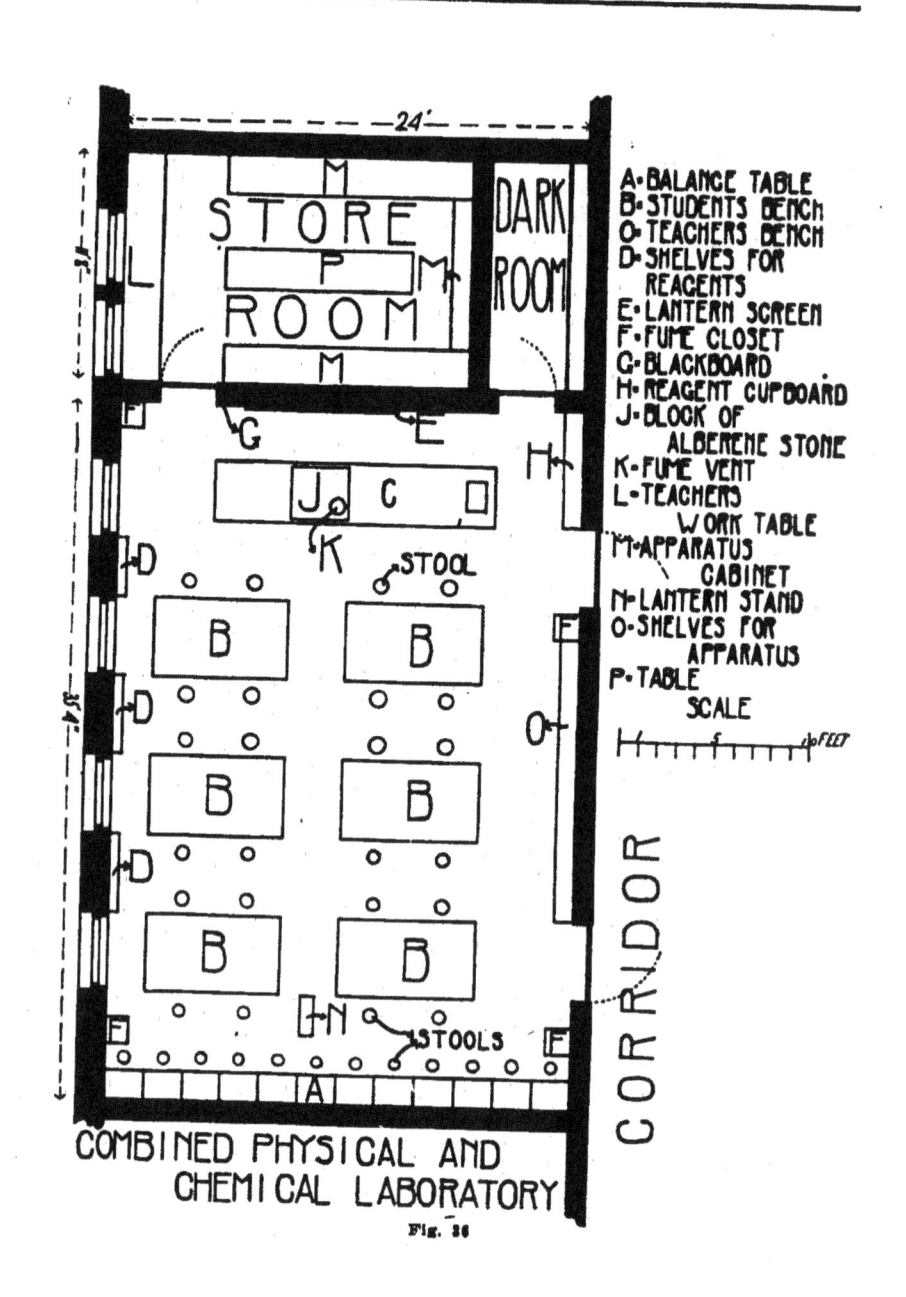

then fewer benches would be required. This may be necessary in order to make them fit into a room that is very long and narrow, or into one that is almost square. The adjustable shelves may be omitted, if each pupil is not supplied with a set of reagents, or the reagents may be kept on small shelves on the walls; but reagent shelves permanently fixed above the top are not to be recommended. Two smaller sinks might be used instead of the one large one and there might be a less number of drawers, but this will be at the expense of efficiency. The qualities of material and finish will also vary to suit the finances of the board and to harmonize with the other furnishings of the building.

The material of the top has already been discussed. The exposed parts of the body may be made of pine, ash, maple, or birch, according to taste. The drawers may be made of basswood with birch slides. If uprights are used, they should be made of birch or teak. The top and all exposed parts should be finished as described on pages 10 and 11. The taps, both water and gas, should be gun-metal, as brass and nickel will tarnish and not look well. The drawer pulls are best made of wood, as metal will not withstand the acid fumes. They should project as little as possible.

ARRANGEMENT OF FURNITURE

The laboratory should be of such a size that the benches can be placed in the most convenient positions and yet give adequate space for the pupils and sufficient room for the teacher to move among them when assisting in the work. It should also have accommodation for a lantern stand, draught closets, and some shelves for reagents, also shelves for storing the sets of pupils' apparatus. There must be at least one additional apartment to serve as a store-room, and a small dark-room will be found valuable, but is not absolutely necessary.

The benches should be placed with their ends directly in front of the windows, as shown in Figure 36. This secures good side light for all the working places. The teacher's demonstration bench (C) is also placed opposite a window, so that a porte lumière placed in the window will throw light directly across the bench. Of course it is possible to have a hole drilled in the wall and a porte lumière placed in this opening.

Every science room should be equipped with a projection lantern and a stand (N); it can be placed at the back of the room in the aisle between the rows of benches. An opaque screen (E) on a spring roller is placed above the blackboard.

Even in a school with a single laboratory, provision should be made for balance tables, as these require a firm horizontal base to rest upon, are usually injured by being carried to the pupils' benches, and are certainly injured by the corroding gases discharged into the room during experimental work in chemistry. These tables are best placed against the wall, and as they must be free from all jarring they should be fixed to it by brackets having no attachment to the floor. Full particulars are given on page 81.

While a few of the more generally used chemicals will be kept on the reagent shelves in the pupils' benches, it is convenient to have other shelves at accessible places around the room on which other commonly used chemicals are kept, as well as a stock supply of the reagents in the bottles on the shelves of the benches from which the pupil's supply is replenished. These may be placed on the walls between the windows (D) in tiers of two or three shelves. The bottoms of these shelves should be made of plate glass or slate; or if of wood they should be well protected

COMBINED SCIENCE AND LECTURE ROOM

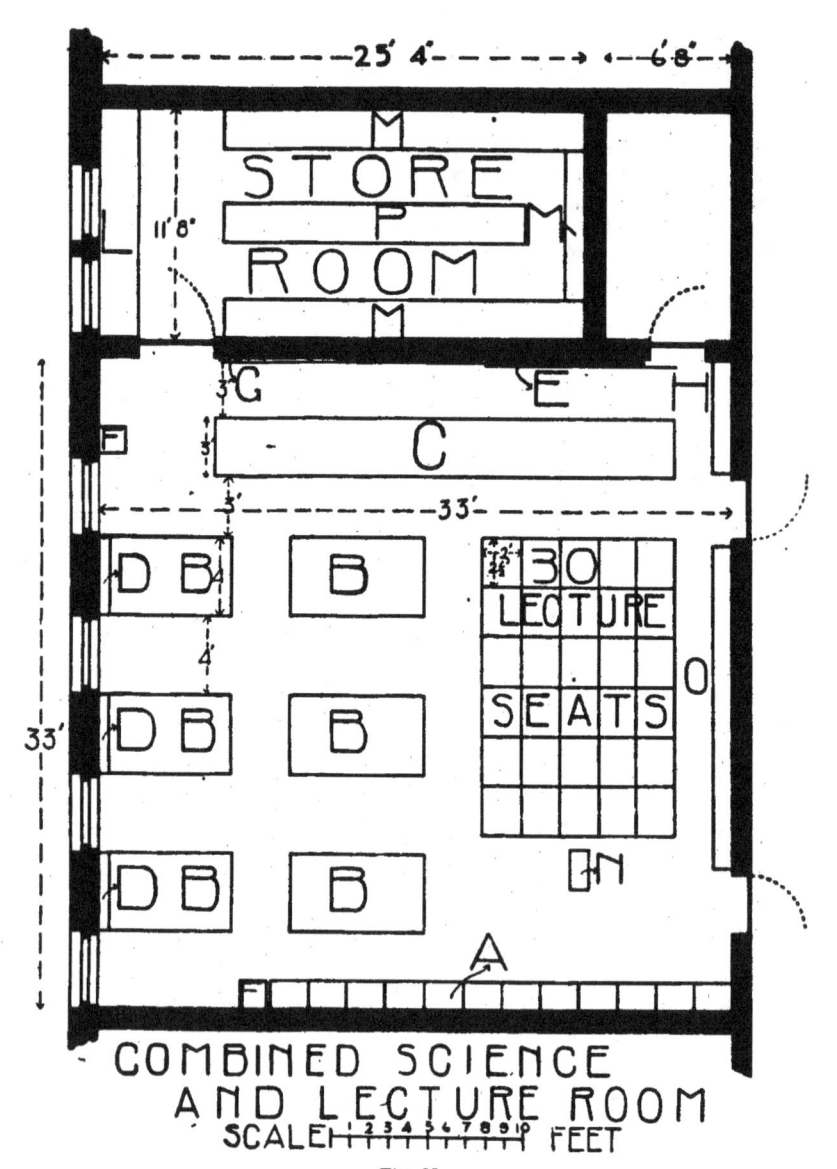

Fig. 37
(Letters have same significance as in Fig. 36.)

by an acid-proof finish. One large reagent cabinet (H) should be placed near the demonstrator's bench, in which all the reagents, both solid and in solution, should be kept. The structure of this is described fully on page 76.

Draught closets (F) are placed at the four corners of the laboratory, one being convenient for the teacher, the others close to the pupils' benches. These need not be of large size, but must have a strong artificial draught, preferably by means of a motor fan. They are fully described on page 83.

The store-room is a necessity in such a laboratory, as physical apparatus would soon be ruined if kept in a laboratory where chemical experiments are being performed. The store-room has apparatus cabinets (M) around the interior walls. For description of these see page 101.

A table (P) in the middle of the store-room is very convenient for the purpose of setting up apparatus and laying pieces preparatory to putting them in the cabinets. A work bench (L) may be placed along the outer wall just below the windows; this should have a sink, and should be fitted also for working in wood, iron, and glass.

Figures 37 and 38 show plans of two science rooms of larger size than the one illustrated in Figure 36. These combine the laboratory with the lecture-room. This arrangement is one that should be aimed at, even in small schools, for the additional space and equipment required are insignificant, while the conveniences for doing effective work are greatly increased. It is difficult to teach a lesson or demonstrate an experiment to a class distributed over a large room and seated uncomfortably at science benches, half of them facing the back of the room. A set of seats compactly placed near the demonstration bench gives a much more favourable condition. All the pupils can observe clearly any experiment or explanation on the black-board and, as the teacher has his class under closer observation, discipline becomes much easier.

The letters in Figure 37 have the same significance as those in Figure 36; Figure 37 shows the arrangement in a square room and Figure 38 in a long, narrow room. The general arrangement in both is similar to that of Figure 36 and calls for no additional comment. The position of the lecture seats in Figure 38 is superior to that in Figure 37, as the light is much better. In both cases there is no aisle next the windows, as it is necessary to place the benches against the wall between the windows in order to economize space. Altogether, there is much to be said in favour of the long, narrow room for laboratory purposes.

Very great variations can be introduced into this arrangement. In many continuation schools, the room at the disposal of the teacher of science is much smaller than any of these illustrated. Such a room as pictured here is the ideal to be aimed at. If the room set apart for science is small, the benches may be decreased in size, the spaces between them diminished, and at one side of the room they may be placed against the wall. In schools with a small science room, the number in a laboratory class will usually be small, and probably four tables instead of six will give sufficient equipment. It must always be remembered, however, that, while all these changes reduce the cost of equipment, they also diminish the efficiency of the laboratory and consequently prove to be an unwise economy.

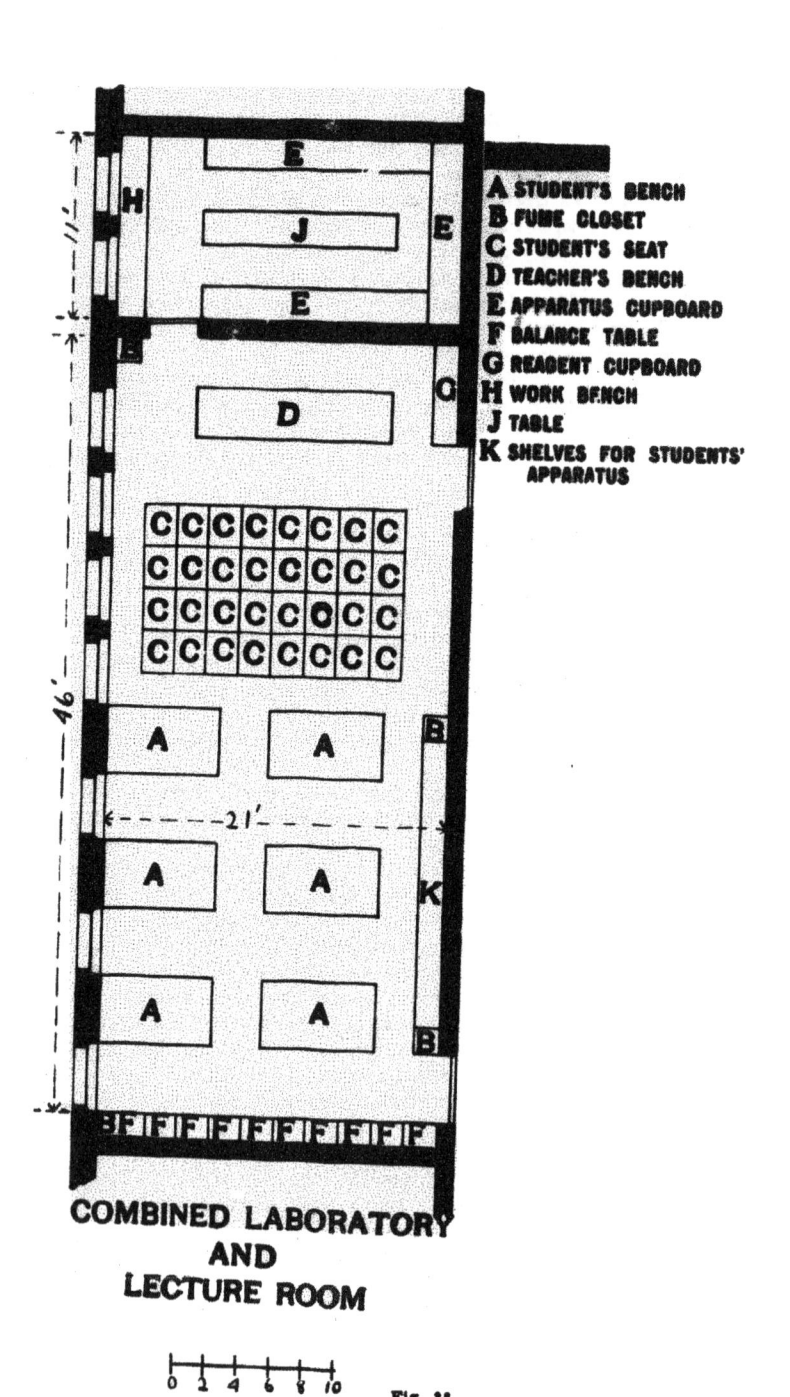

A STUDENT'S BENCH
B FUME CLOSET
C STUDENT'S SEAT
D TEACHER'S BENCH
E APPARATUS CUPBOARD
F BALANCE TABLE
G REAGENT CUPBOARD
H WORK BENCH
J TABLE
K SHELVES FOR STUDENTS' APPARATUS

COMBINED LABORATORY
AND
LECTURE ROOM

Fig. 38

CHAPTER IV

CHEMICAL LABORATORY

THE situation of the chemical laboratory has already been discussed (see page 3). The room should be large and airy, with numerous windows that can be readily opened from both top and bottom, so that it can be emptied of irritating gases with the greatest rapidity. For the same reason the ventilation of this room should be particularly perfect. It it is on the same ventilating circuit as the rest of the building, the flues leading into it and out from it should be proportionately larger. The essentials in construction and arrangement are simplicity, ample space, promotion of easy discipline, and minimum amount of movement on the part of the pupils. The benches and other furniture should not be constructed to fit the room, but the latter should be made of such size and proportion as to accommodate the furniture.

LIGHTING

The illumination should be as adequate as possible. The windows are usually confined to one side and, if so, they should be large and close together, the whole side being as nearly as possible composed of windows. These should extend as close to the ceiling as circumstances will permit. If the room is situated on the upper storey a large skylight is a valuable addition, as it gives the best light for looking down into evaporating dishes, beakers, or bottles.

FURNITURE

The most important pieces of furniture are the pupils' work benches, preferably single ones, which should supply twenty-four working places. Besides these, a teacher's demonstration bench, as long as possible, should be placed at the front of the room. One or more reagent cabinets should be conveniently placed for the use of the teacher. Draught closets are a necessity. These are placed, preferably, on the pupils' benches, but in case that is not feasible, then several should be placed along the walls where they will be accessible to the pupils. Apparatus cabinets are placed in a small room off the main laboratory. Rigid shelves, on which are kept the balances inclosed in dust-proof glass cases, are necessary and, if at all possible, they should be in a separate room adjoining the laboratory, and separated from it by a transparent glass partition.

All the above furniture is absolutely necessary in any modern chemical laboratory. Other pieces of furniture will add greatly to the efficiency of the work but are not so essential. One or more side shelves on the walls are convenient to contain supplies of reagents from which the pupils may stock the reagent bottles on their benches; they will also contain other reagents that are frequently used. A table covered with an asbestos or stone top is useful for glass blowing and other work with the blast lamp; and another containing a large sand-bath, on which the pupils' evaporating dishes may be heated, will prove a great time-saver. A key board and a bulletin-board are also useful.

The different pieces of furniture will first be described individually, and then the best arrangement of them in the laboratory will be discussed.

THE PUPIL'S BENCH

The most important fitting is the pupil's bench, and it may well be described first. Undoubtedly, the individual bench is to be preferred. Every reason that can be given for the single desk in the class-room can be still more strongly advanced for the individual bench in the chemical laboratory. There are only two possible objections to such a bench—it is more expensive and it occupies more floor space. Compared with the advantages, these objections are "penny wise, pound foolish". When a bench is occupied by several pupils, their apparatus is spread out on a common top and cannot well be kept separate; there is much talk and discussion; and discipline becomes a much more difficult matter. If each has his own bench, there is no excuse for argument or talking and no temptation to appropriate a neighbour's apparatus.

A bench top 3½ ft. long is sufficient for each pupil. The width should be such that a pupil, when standing at the bench, can reach across the top of it without bending. For the average high school pupil this will be about 2 ft. or a little more. As the pupil will usually be standing when working at the bench, it should be of such a height that the forearm will rest comfortably on the top. For pupils up to sixteen years of age, 2 ft. 9 in. or 2 ft. 10 in. is about the right height, and for all above that age, 3 ft. All work fairly comfortably at benches three feet high. So a bench 3½ ft. by 2 ft. by 3 ft. will be of proper dimensions. Figures 39, 40, 41 show details of a suitable bench which will now be fully described.

The bench is made with a flat top, and it is advantageous to have a raised edge around the ends and back. This prevents objects from rolling or being pushed off the bench and also prevents water from running over the edges. The top should project 1 in. beyond the body on the side at which the pupil works, and on the under side of this a gutter should be cut to act as a drip. This prevents water which runs over the edge from running in on the under surface of the top. The sink should be placed as close as possible to the left-hand side and to the back, but never at the centre of the top. The length of the sink should be across the top. The tap should be placed behind the sink where it will be out of the way. The gas-tap rises above the top near the middle of the bench close to the back. On each side of the gas-tap metal sockets are sunk in the top, into which rods which act as retort stands may be screwed. This does away with the ordinary retort stand, which is always a nuisance, particularly to put away.

If a hood is present, it should be placed behind the sink, as in the illustration. It will there be so situated that a flask on a ring attached to the rod will be close to the mouth of the hood. Such an arrangement gives a clear amount of free table top of maximum extent, and all the fixtures in the most convenient positions. Taps at the front of the bench are always in the way if projecting above the bench top and, if placed below, they limit the amount of available space for drawers and cupboards. The water-tap should not be at the end of the sink, as it is liable to be struck by the arms when a person passes along the aisle.

Below the top are drawers on each side and a recess in the middle to receive the knees and feet when the pupil is sitting down. On the right side of the bench it is best to have three drawers all of the same size; these should be as deep as possible, so that they may hold test-tube racks and other tall apparatus. The greatest depth available is about 10 in. They should be 1 ft. wide and run right to the back of the bench. Each drawer should have a partition across it

Fig. 39.—Pupils' chemical bench

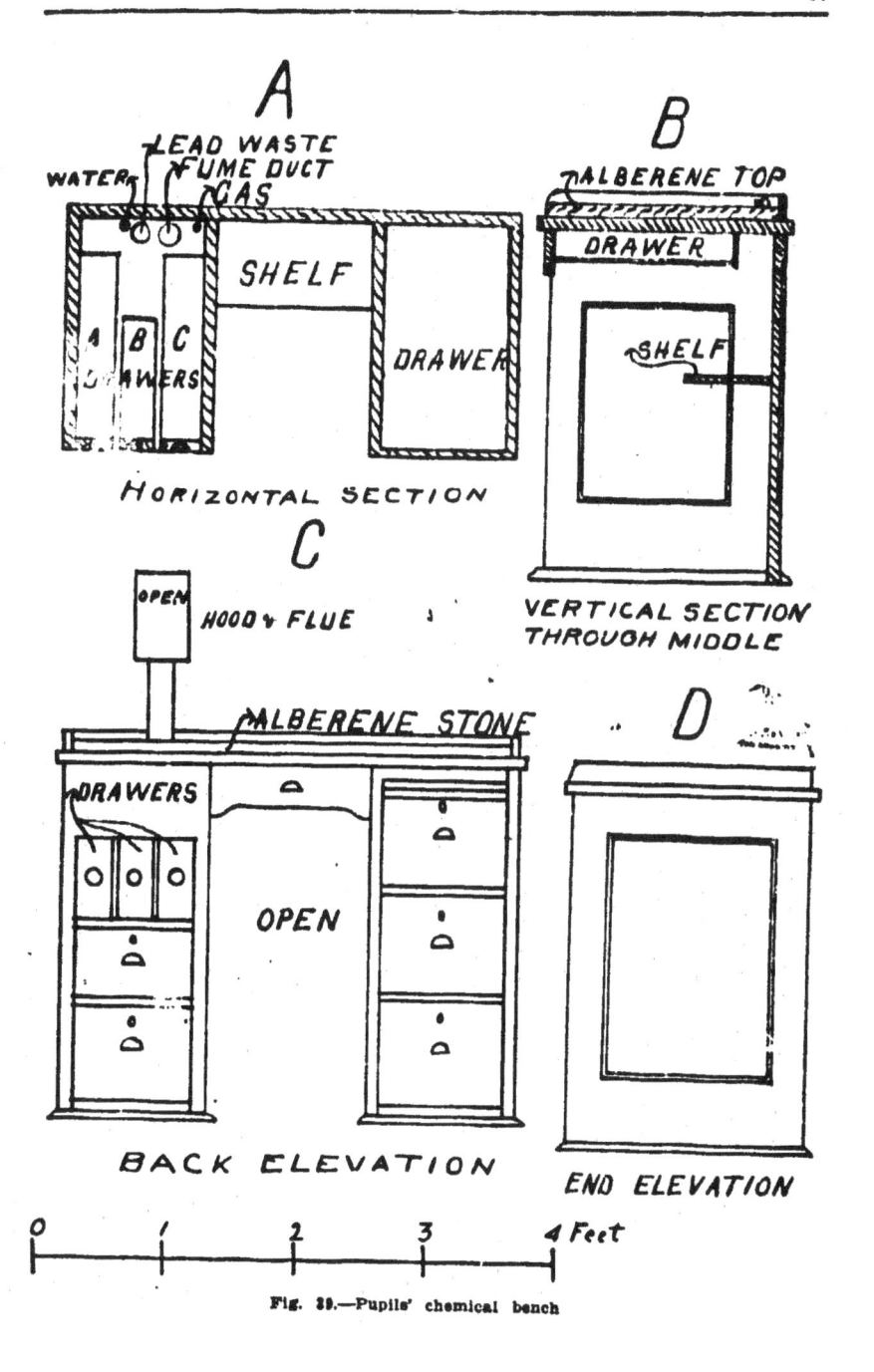

near the front and, in the narrow compartment thus produced, beakers, flasks, and other glass-ware should be placed, for if they are left loose in the drawer they are liable to be broken by the jar of opening and closing the drawer. The drawers should each have a button at the back, which will prevent them from being pulled completely out, as this is liable to be done accidentally, with a consequent destruction of glass-ware. This button, when turned in a horizontal position, allows the drawer to be entirely removed, which is occasionally necessary

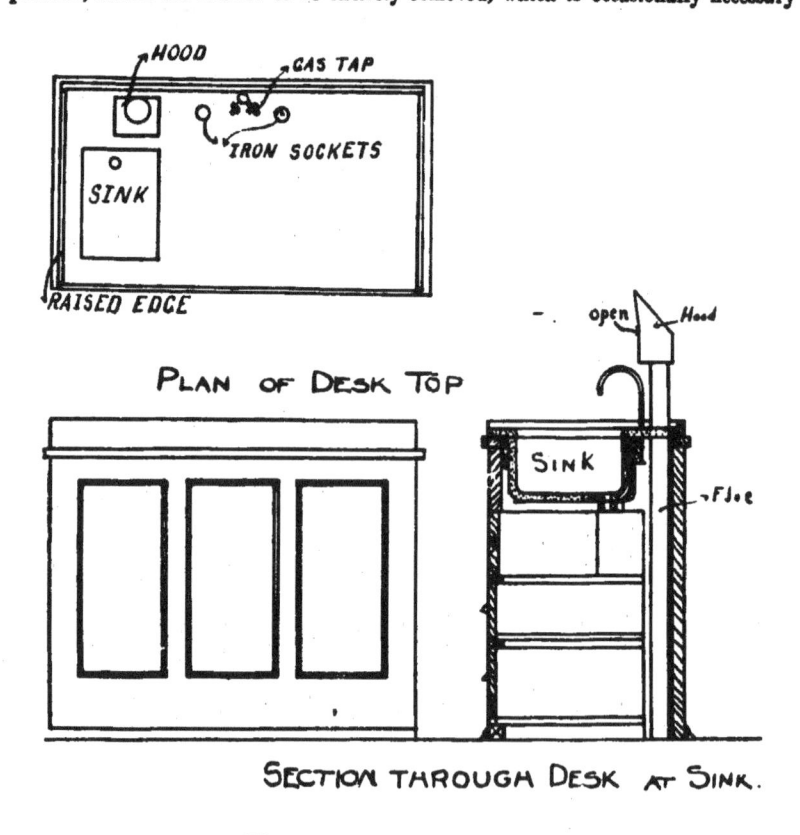

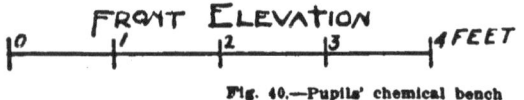

Fig. 40.—Pupils' chemical bench

in order that it may be cleaned. Above this tier of drawers is placed a sliding shelf, which, when pulled out, may be used as a support for a note-book. This is a convenience but not a necessity.

On the left side, the two bottom drawers are exactly similar to those on the right. But above these are three drawers, A, B, C, (Fig. 41), which are used for containing reagent bottles. These drawers are 3 in. wide, 7 in. deep, and as

PUPIL'S BENCH

long as possible. The front and back are of wood, while the sides and bottom are of sheet-iron covered with acid-proof paint. The right side is not more than 2 in. high, so that the labels of the reagent bottles may be seen. These drawers can be placed on the bench when the bottles are to be used. A shallow drawer is placed above the recess under the middle of the bench. The five large drawers are to be used for lockers in which pupils store their individual apparatus. Between each two drawers placed one above the other a complete partition must be built; otherwise it is an easy matter to pull out a drawer and appropriate the apparatus in the one just beneath it. These lockers are all furnished with Yale cylinder locks, each unlocked by a different key, and all the drawers in the laboratory are controlled by one master-key. Each bench is thus equipped to accommodate five classes. In the recess is a shallow shelf on which may be placed pneumatic troughs or other large pieces of apparatus that will not fit into the drawers. It is necessary to have some of the apparatus common to all the pupils,

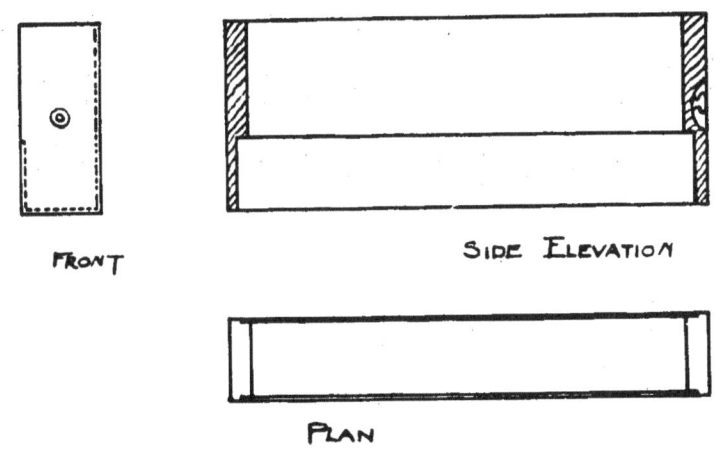

FRONT   SIDE ELEVATION

PLAN

Fig. 41.—Reagent drawer marked A, B, C in Fig 39, A

as it is impossible usually to purchase complete outfits for each locker. This common apparatus, consisting of mortars, burners, metal gauze, and other pieces not likely to be broken, is placed in the shallow drawer above the recess.

A sink 12 in. long, 10 in. wide, and 5 in. deep is a good size. It should be of the very best earthenware, white glazed inside and cane-glazed outside. It requires no rim either on the outside or inside, as it is fixed beneath the top by means of iron brackets. The top of the bench should project slightly over the edge of the sink to prevent the water splashing out. The plug and socket at the outlet of the sink should not be of brass, as the chemicals will soon corrode this metal. A very suitable arrangement is one in which the socket in the base is made of lead or porcelain and in which the aperture in the socket is filled by a grating of the same material. A porcelain plug is attached to the sink which can be inserted into the socket above the grating (see Fig. 6 and description). A large overflow is necessary in order to prevent flooding. The most suitable overflow is one that consists of a tunnel in the body of the earthenware of the sink itself that runs down through the side and along in the bottom to empty through the side of the opening at the bottom. (Section through desk at sink in Figure 40 illustrates this point.) A standing waste is not to be recommended, as it serves no particular purpose where a plug and overflow are provided, and it occupies a considerable part of the sink. The tap should have a swan-neck (Fig. 5) and should be of such a height that the opening is about 1 ft. from the bottom of the sink. The valve should open by means of a wheel screw. The gas-taps should just project about 1 in. above the bench top and should be horizontal, the terminal part being about $3/8$ in. in diameter, so that a gas-tube will slide over it easily but tightly. The valve in it works by a lever handle. Neither the gas- nor the water-taps should be made of brass nor should they be nickel-plated, as the surface will rapidly become unsightly. Gun-metal is by far the best material from which to make them. (See pages 19, 20, and Fig. 5 for fuller descriptions of these taps.)

As has been already stated, alberene stone is the most suitable material for the top, as it is chemical proof and not so hard as to injure glassware. Maple or birch strips glued together properly and treated with an acid-proof finish make the next best top. Glass and slate are not to be recommended, as the former is too hard and the latter too porous. It should hardly be necessary to add that a marble top is entirely unsuitable, as every drop of acid will corrode it. (See pages 10, 11 for complete description of bench tops.)

The hoods need some description. They are of the shape indicated in the drawing and are open in front. The best material to use is copper, but galvanized iron gives good results. The floor of the hood is made of metal which is per- forated over the vent-tube. The hood has a collar on the base which slips over the vent-pipe and allows it to be rotated to bring the open side into any suitable position. It may also be lifted off entirely, flush with the desk, but in practice it will seldom be found necessary to do this. The whole hood is covered with aluminium paint.

The materials composing the body of the bench are determined partly by taste and partly by the cost. There are certain woods that are more suitable than others. White pine, ash, maple, or birch will all give good results, but oak is too porous and too liable to shrink unevenly, while elm warps too much and is liable to splinter. The unexposed parts are preferably of white pine, though basswood is frequently used. The sliding sides of the drawers are made of birch, which is smooth and satiny.

The finish of the bench will be in keeping with the rest of the room trimmings. A description of a suitable finish has been already given (page 10). The pulls on the drawers are preferably of wood, as metal is sure to tarnish rapidly, and the less these pulls project the better. Any panelling should be quite shallow and have no projecting mouldings to catch the dust.

The above is the most suitable bench, but it can be subjected to many modifica- tions to suit the conditions of different schools. Where cheapness or lack of room space is a consideration, it is advisable to construct a bench twice as long as the one described, with a single sink and hood at the middle, so that it can accommodate two pupils. This sink will serve to divide the top into two working places for the pupils. The alberene top may be replaced by one made of wood, and the number of drawers may be diminished in smaller schools where there are only two or three classes in chemistry. The hoods on each bench may be replaced by several fume cupboards along the wall. While any of these changes may be introduced to diminish the cost, in every case the change diminishes the usefulness of the bench.

THE DEMONSTRATION BENCH

The size and structure of the demonstration bench will depend largely on whether the teacher's experiments are to be performed in a separate lecture-room or in the chemical laboratory. If the former condition obtains, the teacher's bench in the chemical laboratory will require little elaboration and may be fitted underneath with a series of drawers in which to keep supplies that are being continually required by the pupils. Generally, demonstrations will take place in the laboratory itself, and a bench suitable for such demonstrations will be described. (Figs. 42 and 43).

The size of such a bench will depend much on the size of the room. It is doubtful if it can be made too long. Where experiments for different classes have to be set up, a top at least 12 ft. long is required, and one of twice that length could be utilized to advantage. There is not much advantage in having it more than 3 ft. wide, and even a width of $2\frac{1}{2}$ ft. will be found sufficient and convenient. Three feet is the proper height. It should never be placed upon a raised platform, as this brings the pupil's eye below the level of the top of the bench, when really the eye should be in such a position that it can look down upon the apparatus from above.

The structure of the top is of great importance. It should be made of strips 2 in. thick, well fastened together with waterproof glue and dowelled as described on page 10. Several iron bolts passing across all the strips, which can be tightened up from time to time by means of a nut, will also be valuable in preventing the strips from becoming separated. The head of the bolt and the nut should not project, but be well sunk in the sides of the top. The latter should project over the body of the bench fully 5 in. at the back, 4 in. at the ends, and about 1 in. at the front. A gutter should be cut out of the under side all around to prevent the water that drips down the sides from running in on the under side of the top. A slab of alberene stone, (B) $2\frac{1}{2}$ ft. long by 2 ft. wide and 1 in. thick should be sunk into the top, so as to be flush with its surface. This is placed near the centre of the bench, as this will be the part upon which the most of the demonstrations will actually take place. Where there is any probability of chemicals being spilled, this slab must be used.

In the bench represented by drawings in Figures 42 and 43 another recess is cut out from the top to make a mercury tray. This is only $\frac{1}{2}$ in. deep at one end and increases regularly in depth to 1 in. at the other end. Along this end is placed a gutter (H) increasing in depth toward the tubular outlet (J). The tubular outlet (O) is made of glass or iron and leads into a bottle placed on a shelf (R) below. This recess is filled ordinarily by a close-fitting wooden cover which has its top flush with the main surface. This cover has two flush handles, Fig. 43 (E), by means of which it can be lifted in or out of place. As this cover is only $\frac{1}{2}$ in. thick at one end, it should be made of three or four ply, well-fastened together with waterproof glue. If the cover is made of one thickness of wood, it will soon warp and crack until it becomes useless. The purpose of this shallow depression in the top is to prevent the loss of mercury by spilling. All experiments, such as the one to prove Boyle's law, in which this expensive liquid is used, are to be performed over this recess, and any mercury that is dropped will be directed by the slanting surfaces to the bottle beneath. This mercury tray may be omitted from a demonstration bench used for chemistry alone, but it is a useful though not a necessary addition in a bench that is also used for demonstration

72   LABORATORY ACCOMMODATION

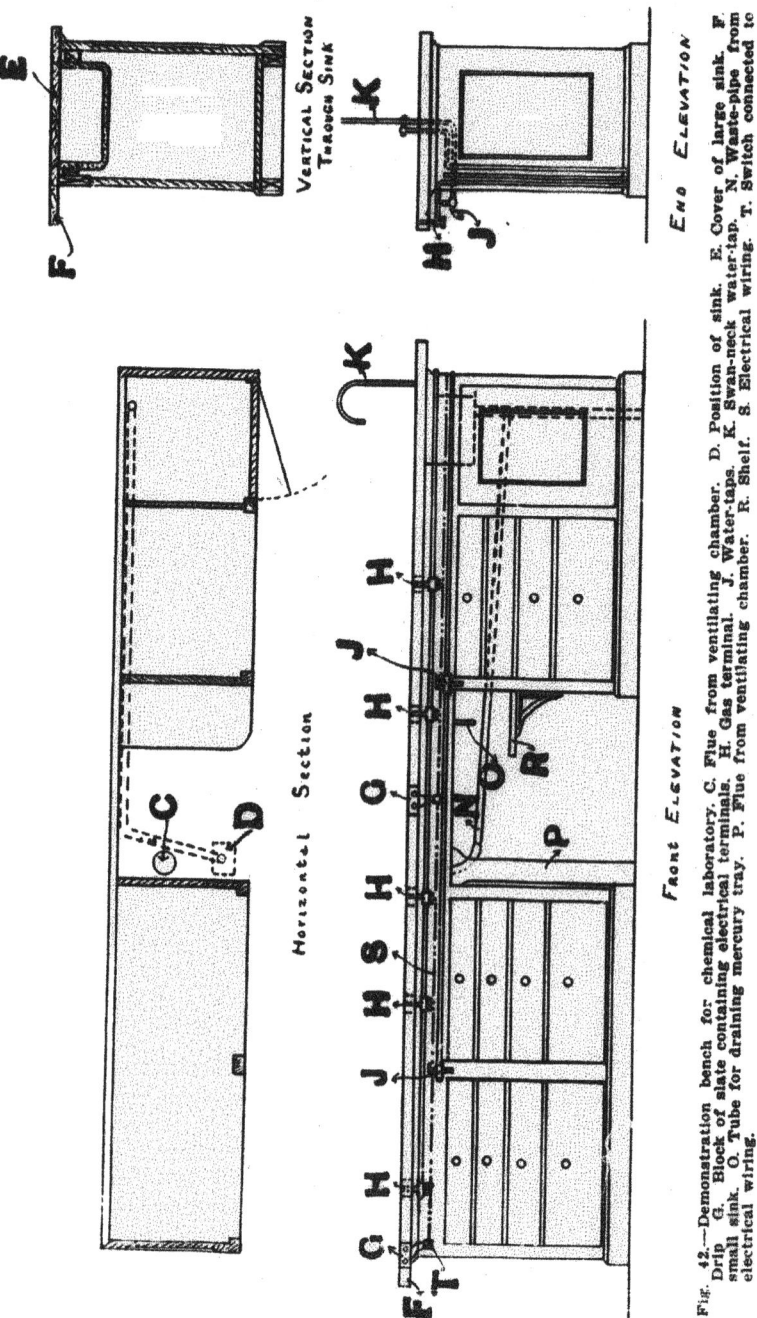

Fig. 42.—Demonstration bench for chemical laboratory. C. Flue from ventilating chamber. D. Position of sink. E. Cover of large sink. F. Drip. G. Block of slate containing electrical terminals. H. Gas terminal. J. Water-taps. K. Swan-neck water-tap. N. Waste-pipe from small sink. O. Tube for draining mercury tray. P. Flue from ventilating chamber. R. Shelf. S. Electrical wiring. T. Switch connected to electrical wiring.

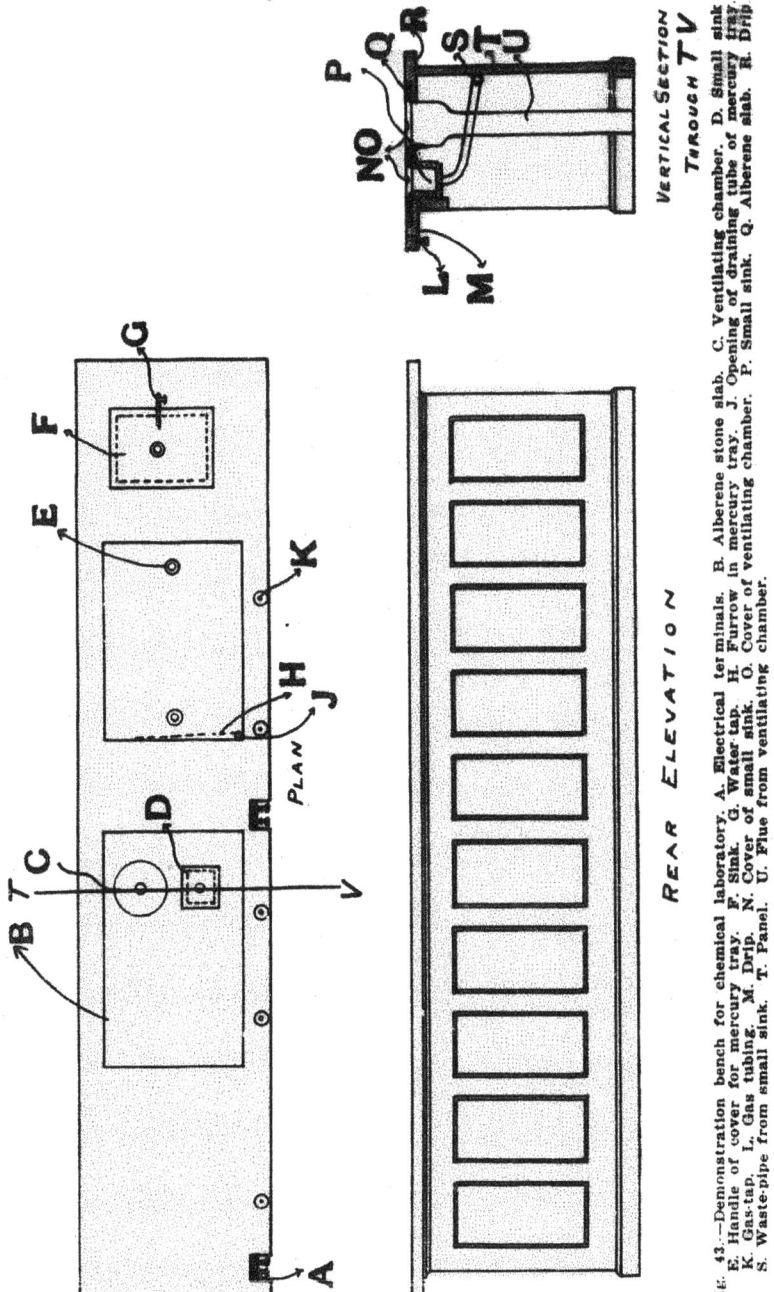

DEMONSTRATION BENCH

Fig. 43.—Demonstration bench for chemical laboratory. A. Electrical terminals. B. Alberene stone slab. C. Ventilating chamber. D. Small sink. E. Handle of cover for mercury tray. F. Sink. G. Water-tap. H. Furrow in mercury tray. J. Opening of draining tube of mercury tray. K. Gas-tap. L. Gas tubing. M. Drip. N. Cover of small sink. O. Cover of ventilating chamber. P. Small sink. Q. Alberene slab. R. Drip slab. S. Waste-pipe from small sink. T. Panel. U. Flue from ventilating chamber.

work in physics. Its only disadvantages are that dirt and water are liable to accumulate in the cracks around the cover unless it fits very tight, in which case it may at times be difficult to remove.

There should be no projections above the top except the water-tap, which is close to one end. Gas-taps and handles will all be flush. Even the water-tap need not project above, for there is now on the market a tap with a hinged joint of such a character that it can be folded down into the sink, and when the cover is placed on the latter there is a complete sweep of horizontal surface on the whole bench top.

The main sink (F) (Fig. 43) should be placed at one end, preferably toward the demonstrator's right hand when facing his class. The tap (K) will be to the right of the sink. This sink should be of large size and of the same character as those in the pupils' benches. (See pages 19 and 20.) It should be at least 16 in. long, 12 in. wide, and 6 in. deep. A sink of even greater size would be none too large. The tap should have connections with both hot and cold water, and the neck should be so high that the tallest bottle may be placed under it.

It is an advantage to have a tap with a secondary nozzle on a level with the top of the sink, as in Figure 44, each nozzle working by its own valve. The lower nozzle is used except when water is required to fill some tall vessel. When there is a swan-neck nozzle alone for filling the sink, much water is splashed out over the top of the bench. Besides the main sink, it is advantageous, but not necessary, to have a very small sink (D) toward the middle of the bench in the alberene stone. This sink would have no tap, and is largely used for carrying off running water which it may be necessary to use in experiments for cooling liquids or condensing vapours that may be given off. A water-pipe runs along parallel with the gas-pipe under the back of the bench and has two taps (J) along it. These should project as little as possible. They are used for supplying running water for condensers, aspirators, etc. All the taps will have small corrugated nozzles over which rubber tubing may be placed.

The gas supply runs along under the edge of the bench projecting toward the demonstrator and has taps attached to it every two feet. These taps pass up through round openings in the bench top and almost flush with the surface of the latter. The handle for opening and closing the valve of the gas-tap is situated below and must be convenient to reach. The nozzles must be tapering and corrugated, so that a rubber attachment can be slipped over them with ease. If the circular hole cut in the bench top is too small, much inconvenience will be experienced in slipping rubber tubing over the gas-tap, so the hole should be at least 2 in in diameter, and the upper edge should

Fig. 44.—Water-tap with secondary nozzles for demonstration bench

be bevelled off. An absolutely essential attachment is a hood for taking off irritating and bad-smelling gases. This can be placed directly on the bench, or it may be built as a closet against or within the wall behind the bench, and a sliding blackboard may be placed in front of it. Ordinarily the black-board is down in front. When the draught closet is to be used, the black-board is raised out of the way, and the experiment is performed in the closet. Such a demonstration draught closet should be painted within with a white silica paint and should be lighted by electric light from above. Such a closet has been found quite unnecessary if the opening of a shaft connected with a powerful draught is placed on the bench top itself. The following arrangement has been found most convenient: In the alberene stone is cut a circular opening (C, Fig. 43) about 8 or 10 in. in diameter; this is the upper end of a galvanized iron shaft (U), as shown in the illustration. This shaft is connected with a fan, as will be described later. (See page 86.) Over the top of the opening is placed a metal grating, which is on a level with the bottom of the alberene stone. On this grating is placed the apparatus from which the fumes are to be withdrawn. When not in use the opening is closed by a tight-fitting cover (O) flush with the surface of the stone. Objection may be made to such an arrangement that it will only take away heavy gases, such as chlorine, which naturally sink through the air, but that the lighter ones will rise and mix with the atmosphere of the room. In practice it has been found that with a powerful draught not only the heavy gases but also the light ones are sucked through the opening, and the air in the room is kept free from all irritating and offensive odours. It is quite possible to have rising up above the bench top to a height of about 15 in. a tube 3 in. in diameter. This tube turns till the opening faces downward, and the open end terminates in a wide funnel which is placed directly above the galvanized iron shaft in the bench top just described. This funnel can be connected below the bench top with the same exit tube as the opening in the top. Such a funnel should work on a telescopic joint, so that it can be placed at various heights to make it suitable for different experiments, and it should be removable entirely from the bench when not in use. The opening of the funnel must be at least as wide as the down-draught opening in the bench top.

There will be terminals for using the electric current. These terminals should be suitable not only for experimental demonstrations, but also for connecting up the lantern, as the latter is used continually in the demonstration work. There should be at least two terminals on the bench; three will be still better. These terminals should be blocks of slate (Fig. 42, G, and Fig. 43, A) sunk in the edge of the bench top toward the demonstrator. These blocks contain the terminals, which are of the ordinary English type and project out flush with the edge of the top. Each of these has its own switch beneath. A very convenient terminal to have in addition to these is a plug and socket; the latter being attached just underneath the top of the bench, and the former having attached to it two wires ending freely. The free ends of the wires are attached to the apparatus through which a current is required, and the plug is pushed into the socket when a connection is necessary. The best form of plug and socket to use for this purpose is one in which the two slit-like openings in the end of the socket are at right angles to each other, and the metal terminals on the plug are arranged similarly, so that the plug can only be inserted in one way. By always having the insulation on the two wires coloured differently, and by always keeping one colour of insulation for the positive wire and one for the negative, the sign of the terminals can always be distinguished.

The arrangement of the parts underneath the top of the bench is a matter of choice on the part of the teacher. Each will have to determine his requirements and distribute the space between drawers and cupboards accordingly. A large number of small drawers will prove most convenient, but will add greatly to the cost. A smaller number of large drawers, some of which have dividing partitions, will be almost as useful and much less expensive. Three sets of drawers and a cupboard at one end have been selected in the illustration, Figure 42. Under the middle is a recess. The drawers are of various depths, the ones toward the bottom being the deepest. The drawers can be constructed with partitions of various kinds. Some are pigeon-holed, the spaces being suitable for containing small objects, such as corks, binding posts, etc. Others have longitudinal partitions, making narrow compartments to contain tubing, deflagrating spoons, etc. One set of cupboards is very essential. In it can be placed all tall stands and other bulky pieces of apparatus which are frequently used.

The material and finish is largely determined by that of the pupils' benches and other furniture. All that was said regarding them on page 9 applies equally to this bench. The severe montony of a plain front and ends may be overcome by a series of vertical panels, as in Figures 42 and 43, but these should be not more than $3/8$ in. deep and with no mouldings to catch the dust. The front should be constructed in one piece and fastened to the body with screws, so that it can easily be removed in order to expose the plumbing. The kind of finish has been already described. (See page 10.) The top is always finished in black with one of the acid-proof preparations described on page 11. The pulls for the drawers and cupboards are made preferably of wood of the same kind as that from which the body is made. While not absolutely necessary, it is advantageous to have the drawers and cupboard fitted with locks, as it may be advisable to have some of the drawers continually under lock and key. If locks are added, they should all be of the same kind, so that one key will control all, and this key should be the same one that served as a master-key for all the pupils' lockers. In fact, the teacher should aim to have all the locks on drawers, cupboards, etc., of one or at most two kinds, so that all can be unlocked with the minimum number of keys, as it is exceedingly troublesome for the science teacher to be compelled to carry a large bunch of keys and to have to hunt out the proper one for every drawer or door he wishes to open.

The Reagent Cabinets

In constructing this cabinet the chief aim is to produce a piece of furniture in which as many bottles as possible can be so placed that the labels of all may be read, that each can be removed with ease, and that each occupies the minimum amount of space. The least suitable of all is a deep cupboard with a series of plain shelves one above the other. All the depth except a few inches is lost, for bottles, to be at all convenient, can be arranged in only a single row, and any space lying behind them is largely wasted.

The reagent cabinet illustrated in Figures 45 and 46 is both convenient and compact. The dimensions are determined by the number of bottles it is necessary to store. Before having one constructed, the teacher should make an estimate of the number of bottles required to store the reagents, also the different sizes of the bottles, and the number of each size. It is well to have only a few sizes, and those containing 250c.c., 500c.c., and 2,000c.c. will be found convenient. The amount of space required for each kind should be calculated, and then cabinets should be constructed in which the shelves will give this estimated accommodation and also allow space for the addition of new reagents.

Four main shelves (B) run across the cabinet. On each of these is placed a series of raised shelves increasing in height toward the back. Each shelf is just wide enough to accommodate the bottles that are to be placed upon it, so that their width will vary considerably. In practice, it has been found that two or three widths are sufficient. The height of each shelf will be determined by the height of the bottle that is to be placed in the row in front of it. It should be of such a height that the bottles on the shelf in front do not cover the labels on the bottles that are on the shelf behind. It should also be of such a height that the bottles can

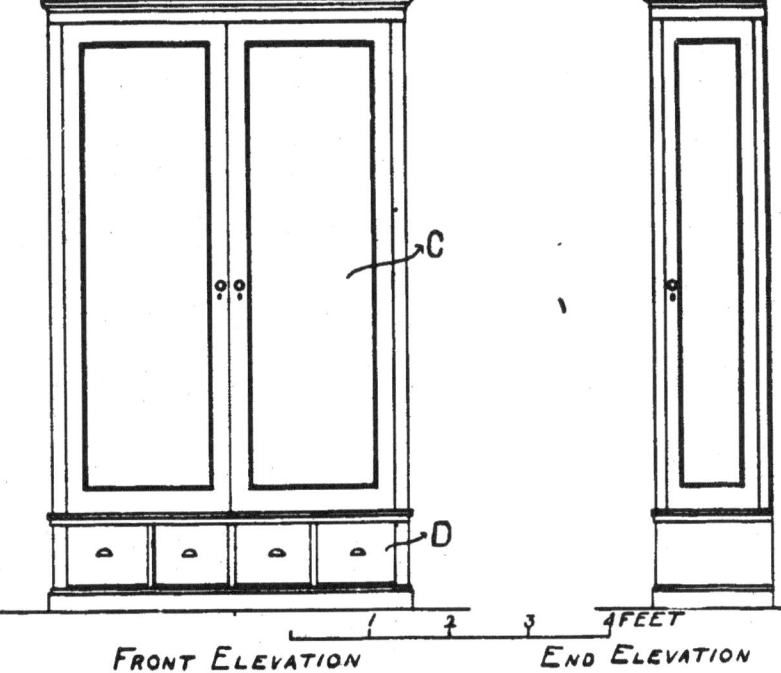

FRONT ELEVATION   END ELEVATION
Fig. 45.—Reagent cabinet. C. Glass in door. D. Drawer.

be taken out without danger of knocking over those of the row in front during the operation. The top shelves should never be so high that they cannot be reached by the teacher while standing on the floor, for it is very vexatious to have to get a stool to stand upon in order to take down or replace a reagent bottle. The shelves are so constructed that a series of long, narrow inclosed spaces (A) lie below them. A door is placed on the end of the cabinet so as to make these accessible. They are very convenient for holding glass tubing, burettes, and other long, narrow pieces of apparatus that usually are difficult to store.

Beneath the shelves a row of drawers (D) is placed. These can be used for a variety of purposes. There will always be quantities of reagents left over in packages after filling the regular bottles, and these can be kept in these drawers. A pair of doors are placed along the front. Usually these have glass running from the top to the bottom. Such a glass front is convenient because the labels can be viewed without opening the door, and a person can see if the particular reagent required is in that cabinet. There are objections, however, to a glass front. Light always acts on some chemicals, and they will remain unchanged better if the case excludes the light. Besides, the glass will continually become covered with a white deposit that is formed as a result of the gradual leakage of vapours from the reagents. It will be noticed that the cabinet in which hydrochloric acid is stored always produces this white deposit, and, undoubtedly, it is largely due to ammonium chloride formed from this acid uniting with ammonia gas. The bottles and glass

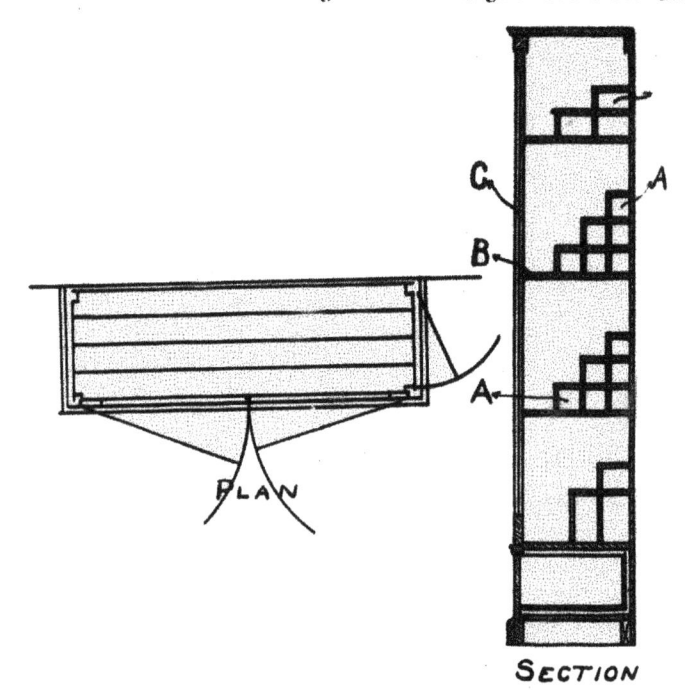

Fig. 46.—Reagent cabinet. A. Openings underneath the shelves accessible from the door on the end. B. Shelf. C. Glass in door.

front will be kept much cleaner if the hydrochloric acid and ammonium hydroxide are excluded from the regular cabinet. The general construction in respect to material and finish is similar to that of the other furniture. All pulls and knobs should be of wood or porcelain. The shelves, if constructed of wood, should be finished with a good paraffin finish, according to instructions given on page 12. The black acid-proof finish is not suitable here, as it is not absolutely acid-proof. While it is quite satisfactory on a bench top, where the corrosive material is soon wiped off, it is not so effective on a reagent shelf, where the liquid may drip down and be in contact with the wood for days before it is noticed. The best material for reagent shelves is plate glass, where its cost does not make it prohibitive.

REAGENT SHELVES

Besides a reagent cabinet, one or more sets of shelves on the wall are convenient. These will contain the reagents from which the pupils replenish the reagent bottles in their own benches, and also those that are being continually used by the pupils. Three shelves extend as high as a pupil can reach when the bottles are large. The shelves may be of wood but are preferably of plate glass. The bottom one is wide enough to serve as a narrow table. This serves as a receptacle for the pupils to place their small bottles upon while they are filling them from the stock supply on the shelf. This bottom shelf should be of wood or alberene stone and should have a narrow ledge in front of it, so that no spilled

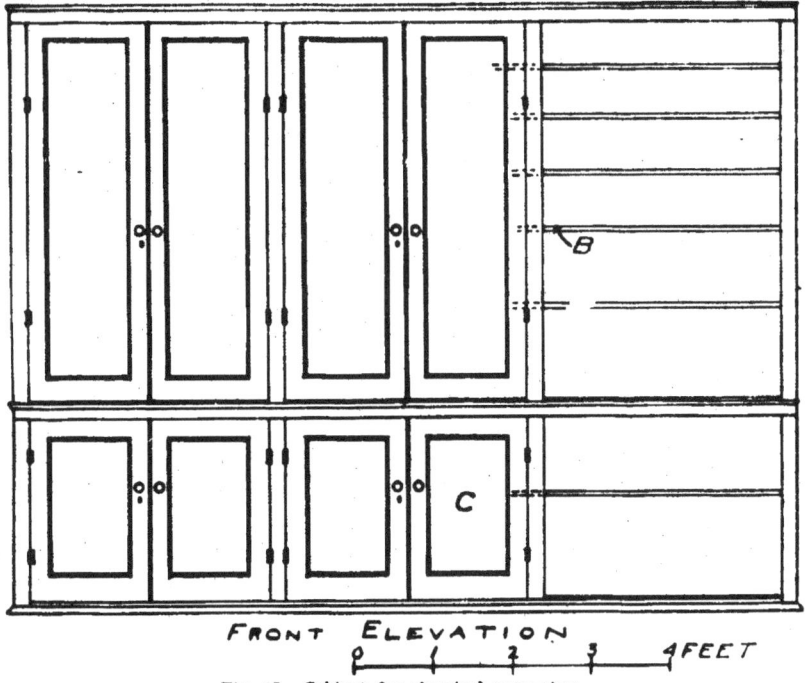

Fig. 47.—Cabinet for chemical apparatus

material will fall on the floor. If this shelf is built of wood, it must be thoroughly paraffined, because a good deal of spilling of both solids and liquids will take place where pupils are pouring chemicals from one bottle into another. As this wide shelf at the bottom is used, instead of the demonstration bench, for placing all materials upon to which pupils are to help themselves, the demonstrator's bench can thus be kept cleaner and more tidy.

APPARATUS CABINET

A good deal of bulky material used in the chemical laboratory has to be given storage room. A year's supply of beakers, flasks, gas jars, and bottles, are purchased at one time, and they must be placed under lock and key. Some prefer

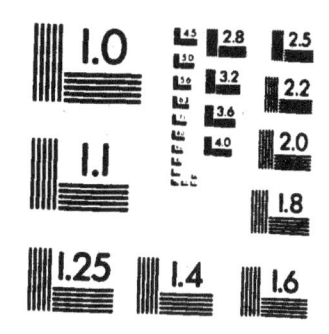

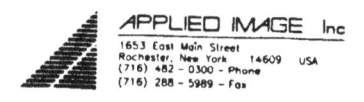

bins and shelves, but a cabinet is usually found most serviceable. A cabinet suitable for this purpose (Figs. 47 and 48) consists of an upper part with glazed doors and a lower, deeper part with wooden doors. In the upper part will be kept all special apparatus used for demonstration experiments, together with other small stuff. Below will be stored the supplies of bulkier apparatus, such as bottles, gas jars, test-tube racks, etc. It will be found convenient to have the shelves in the

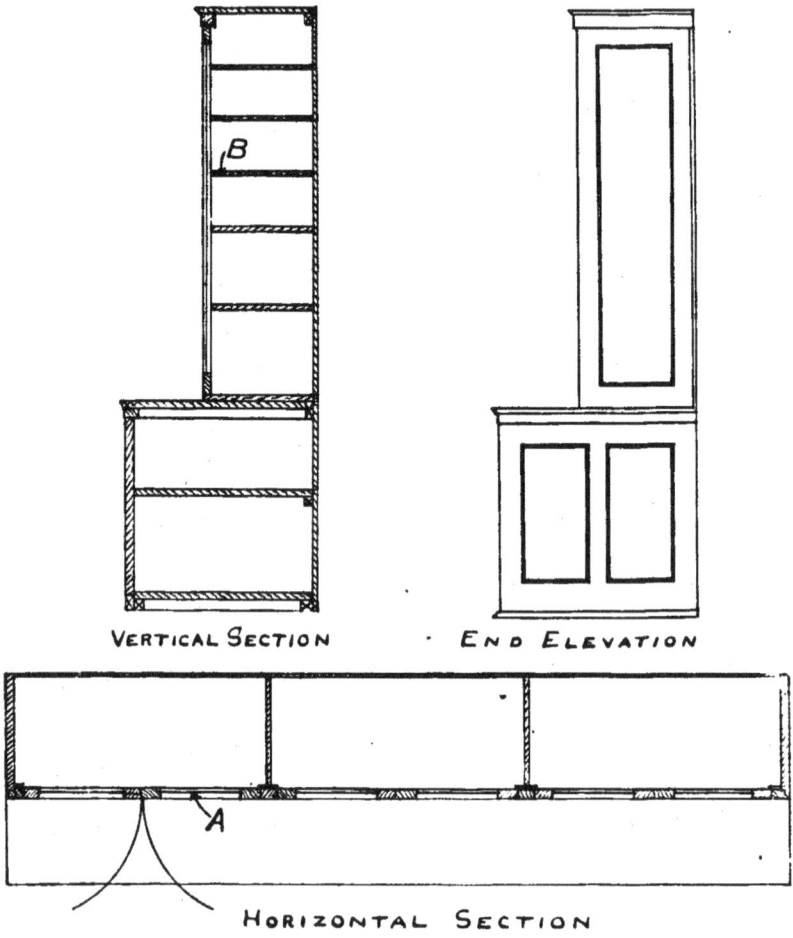

VERTICAL SECTION · END ELEVATION

HORIZONTAL SECTION

Fig. 48.—Cabinet for chemical apparatus. A. Glass in door. B. Shelves.

upper part adjustable. Adjustments can be made by small holes bored into the sides into which metal studs fit, or by means of a perforated metal strip along each corner into which the metal studs, or brackets, fit. The latter arrangement will give better permanent results. Whether it is preferable to have hinged or sliding doors will be determined by the place in which the cabinet is to stand, and to a certain extent by its size. If it is placed in a narrow storage room where there is not much space in front of it for doors to swing, and particularly if the doors are long and heavy, then the sliding door is to be preferred. But where the store-room is wide, or the cabinet is placed in the laboratory where there is sufficient space in front, the doors can be made light and allowed to swing on hinges.

The depth of the upper part of the cabinet is 1½ ft., while that of the lower part is 2½ ft. This leaves a ledge 1 ft. wide at the top of the lower part. The total height is 7½ ft. Then the upper shelf can scarcely be reached from the floor, and only material seldom required will be placed there. The wide part is 2½ ft. high and the narrower part is 5 ft. high.

Nothing additional need be said about the material and finish, as both will be similar to the other furniture of the laboratory already described. (See page 9, where the matter is fully discussed.) The shelves are 1 in. thick, and must be supported every 3 ft.; in order that there may be no sagging. If the doors are on hinges they will be 1½ ft. wide, of light weight, and with a pane of glass as large as possible to throw a good light to the back of the cabinet. One fixed shelf

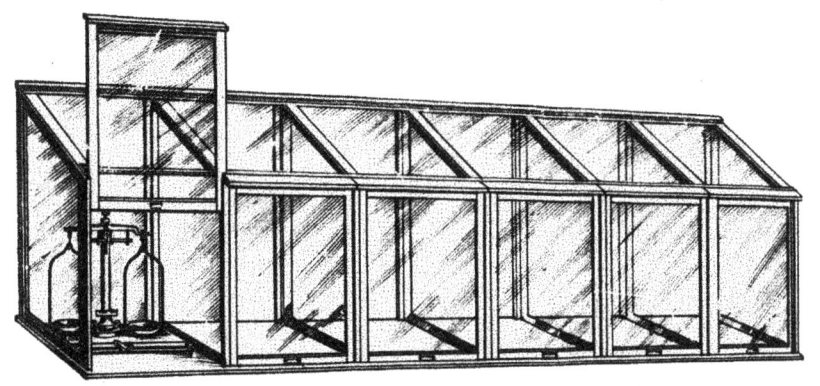

Fig. 49.—Balance shelf, with glazed cases for protecting the balances

will be sufficient in the lower wide part and five adjustable ones in the upper part. It will be found that by fixing special pieces of apparatus on hooks and brackets fastened into the back and ends of the cabinet, much shelf space can be economized and these pieces of apparatus will be more easily found when required. All the doors will have locks controlled by one key, and this key should be capable of opening all the cabinet doors in the laboratories.

BALANCE SHELF

Balances are undoubtedly the most important pieces of apparatus used in the chemical laboratory, and great care should be bestowed upon the selection of suitable ones. They are delicate mechanisms and require great care, so it is not satisfactory to have them carried from place to place. Fixed shelves should be provided, on which they are kept permanently, and when pupils wish to make a weighing, they should go to the balance situated in its fixed position. Such a shelf should be, (1) absolutely firm, (2) perfectly level, and (3) serve as a protection for the balances against corrosive gases, draughts, and changes of tempera-

82　LABORATORY ACCOMMODATION

Fig. 50.—Balance shelf, with glazed cases for protecting the balances. A. Wall to which shelf is attached. B. Counterbalance for raising front. D. Pulley. E. Plate glass or slate slab on which balance feet rest. F. Iron bracket. H. Drawer.

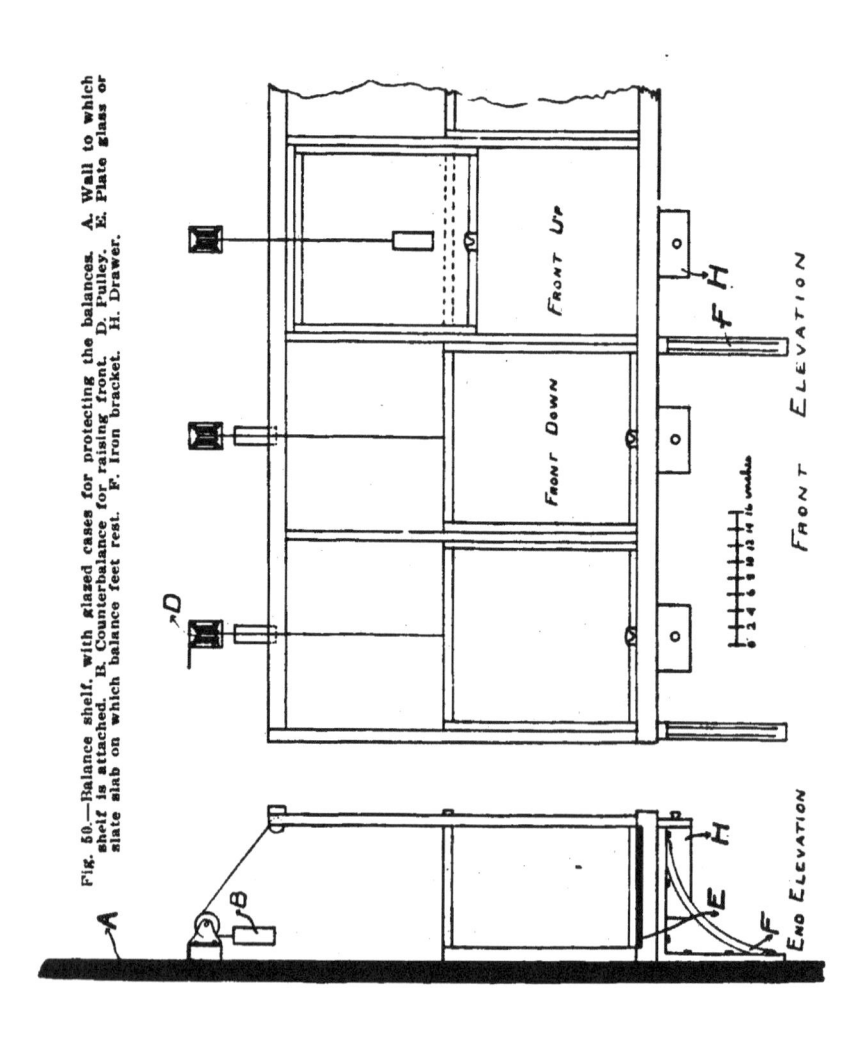

ture. To produce the first two qualities, the shelf (Figs. 49 and 50) is attached to a solid wall, preferably one of solid brick which goes right to the foundation. The shelf should have no connection whatever with the floor, as the walking and other disturbances in the laboratory are sure to cause vibrations. To avoid corrosive fumes, draughts, and changes of temperature, the balances must be kept in glass covers with fronts that will rise like a window sash. Some balances of the Dutch pattern have the case and balance immovably attached. Usually it will be found more satisfactory to have the balance quite separate and to have the inclosing case attached to the shelf.

The shelf is attached to the wall by heavy iron brackets which give it the necessary rigidity. These should extend at least 15 in. down the wall and the same distance under the shelf. The shelf is 18 in. wide and long enough to allow 2 ft. for each balance. If there are 12 balances—which will be the usual number—the shelf or shelves will be 24 ft. in total length. It should be of such a height that the pupil when sitting on a stool will have his eye a little below the beam of the balance; 22 in. from the floor to the top of the shelf is about correct. The shelf may be made of slate, alberene stone, or wood covered with plate glass. If of slate or alberene stone the material should be thick enough to allow the edges to be raised $\frac{1}{2}$ in. This raised edge prevents weights from being lost by rolling off the shelf. If wood is used it should be built up of strips in the same way as the laboratory benches already described. (See page 11.) As a wooden top is to be covered with glass, the chief characteristic of the wood selected should be freedom from warping; white-wood, pitch-pine, or maple are satisfactory in this respect. As the feet of the balances are made of brass and terminate in sharp points, it is quite essential that they do not rest on wood, as these points will sink into it and it will be impossible to keep the balances level. So the wooden top should be covered with a piece of English polished plate glass $\frac{1}{2}$ in. thick. A shallow wooden apron rises $\frac{1}{2}$ in. above the glass around the margin of the shelf. (Omitted in the drawing.) Below the shelf, opposite each balance, is placed a small drawer deep enough to take the box of weights.

On these shelves are placed the glass cases for the protection of the balances. Each balance may have a case quite separate, or they may all be united into one continuous case along the whole shelf. If the former condition obtains, the cases should have no bottom, so that the balance will rest directly on the glass. The case has a wooden framework with the front, back, ends, and top made of glass. The front glass is in a sash that rises up. It may have a weight fastened to it by a cord over a pulley, as shown in Figure 50, or it may be fastened by a spring clip when it is pushed up.

Draught Closets

Adequate means of getting rid of the evil-smelling gases produced in the chemical laboratory are much too frequently omitted from even the more recently constructed buildings. It is most important that such a condition of affairs should not continue. Experiments involving the production of such gases cannot be avoided if the courses in chemistry are to be adequately taught, and there is no good reason why the science pupils, as well as the teacher, should have to bear the irritations to the eyes and throat, the headaches, the sickness of stomach, as well as the permanent weakening of some of the vital organs from these gases, when they can be avoided by proper draught closets emptied by suitable ventilating flues. Not only do the pupils in the chemical laboratory suffer, but a small escape of sulphuretted hydrogen will soon penetrate every class-room in the building and the work of the whole school will be seriously disturbed. There is at least one collegiate institute in the Province where an epidemic of pneumonia broke out among the students of chemistry, and the physician blamed it directly to the escape of chlorine gas into the room, which irritated and weakened the delicate lung tissues.

In the description of the pupils' benches already given, full particulars will be found regarding the hoods placed on these benches. These are recommended as most serviceable for getting rid of the gases. Then, too, the pupil can reach one of the hoods without leaving his bench, so that there will be no temptation for him to avoid taking the time or trouble to go to a common draught closet, where it may be necessary to wait his turn. Even where these individual hoods are present, there should be at least one other large draught closet with a sink in it, into which may be emptied the contents of flasks and test-tubes that contain the refuse from which chlorine, sulphur dioxide, hydrogen sulphide, and other offensive gases have been generated. The sink in this closet is also useful for washing out gas generators and other apparatus from which noxious gases might escape. For schools where the installation of individual hoods is too expensive, and also for those already constructed where the adding of these conveniences is impossible, wall draught closets may be substituted. These are most convenient if distributed around the room so that they are easily accessible to all the benches. This distribution requires so great a length of exit flues that in some laboratories the different draught closets are placed side by side.

Fig. 51.—Draught closet. In this the front consists of two sashes like a window.

It will be sufficient to give details, Fig. 52, and illustration (Fig. 51) of a single one. The closet should be no larger than is absolutely necessary for the convenience of the pupils who work at it, for the less the cubical capacity, the more frequently the air in it is changed. It will be constructed against a wall and may be placed on a pair of brackets, so that its floor stands

DRAUGHT CLOSET

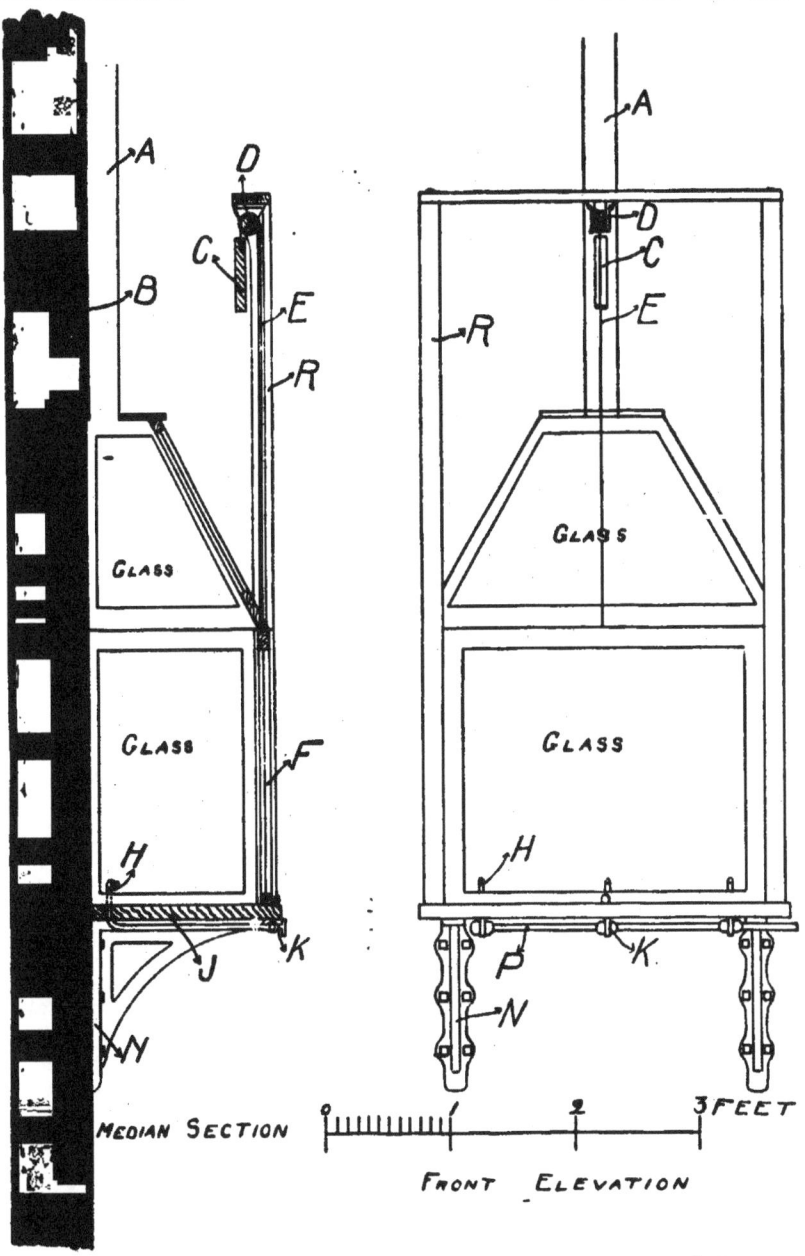

85

Fig. 52.—Draught closet. A. Flue. B. Wall to which the closet is attached. C. Counterbalancing weight. D. Pulley. E. Wire attaching front to weight. F. Glass in front. H. Gas-tap. J. Slate- or alberene-stone base. K. Valve of gas-tap. N. Iron bracket. P. Gas-pipe. R. Upright supports.

at the same height as the working top of the pupil's bench, namely, 3 ft. A small one will be 2 ft. long, 1½ ft. deep, and a little over 2 ft. high. The sides, front, and top are of glass in order to give as much light as possible. If the cupboard is constructed within the thickness of the wall, then, of course, only the front can be composed of glass, and the whole interior should be made white with silica paint. The whole of the front should be constructed of a movable sash properly weighted with counterbalancing weights, Figure 52 (C). This front sash should be capable of rising 2 ft., so that an iron stand can be easily placed within. The two outer corners should project upward 2½ to 3 ft. above the top to form guides (R) for the sash to run in when it is elevated; these guides are sometimes hollow in order that they may contain the counterbalancing weights, but it is much more satisfactory to have the weights suspended, as in the illustration. Ordinary sash-cord is unsuitable for draught closets, as the gases soon weaken it by their chemical action. A wire cord or a chain is more satisfactory. A strong piece of catgut is used with satisfaction in some laboratories. Indeed the weights may be entirely abandoned, provided a suitable catch is used. This catch should be made of some hard wood and should be well soaked in paraffin; it should also work in a hardwood rack. When a counterweight is used, it may be arranged in a similar manner to those described and illustrated already under balance cases. (Figs. 49 and 50.) The top of the cupboard should not be flat, but should slope upward from front to back and also from each side, so that all gases will be directed toward the fume flue situated at the top toward the back. The panes of glass are placed as close as possible to the inner side of the framework, and the angles of the frame are bevelled off. This is particularly important in the sliding front sash. When it is raised, a narrow slit will be left between the inner side of the glass and the roof, and this provides a means of exit for the gases into the laboratory. If the glass is put in the frame close to the inner side, this slit will be narrowed. A rubber flap should be placed along the front of the roof, pressing against this front frame, so that when the sash is raised this flap will touch the glass and close this space; otherwise, there is likely to be much leakage into the room when the sash is raised at the bottom, as it usually is during an experiment. If the closet is built in the wall this difficulty will be overcome. No metal pulls should be attached to the sliding front, but knobs of wood or porcelain must be used. The floor of this closet should be constructed to resist all chemicals, for not merely the corroding fumes must be withstood, but also the chemicals spilled, and there will be more spilling here than on the benches, as pupils are working in cramped quarters. Alberene stone is undoubtedly the best base, but slate is satisfactory also. If wood is used, it should be thoroughly seasoned and finished with paraffin or acid-proof paint. (Page 11). No gas or water-pipes should enter the closet; these should all terminate at the front or it on a level with the floor of the closet (Fig. 52), and, when required, rubber tubing should connect them with the closet. If the gas-taps project into the closet, as in the illustration, Figure 52, then the lever valve should be located at the front and on a level with its floors, so that the gas can be regulated with ease from the outside. For a large closet several gas-taps are required, the number depending on the number of pupils who require to use the closet at one time. Special Bunsen burners made of porcelain may be used, as they are particularly suitable for draught closets, withstanding the corroding gases well. As has been stated, the flue is attached at the top and back of the closet. The size of the flue will depend on the size of the closet, but it is better to have it too large than too small. In the course of the flue there should be no sharp turns. Some recommend a second exit near the bottom to carry off the heavy gases that settle downward. There is some slight advantage in such an arrangement, but if there is a good draught a second outlet is not required; and such an outlet near the bottom will always be troublesome where it is necessary to use burners, as the flames of them will be deflected toward the outlet. Moisture may tend to collect on the sloping roof of the chamber, and it will run down the sloping sides unless a small trough around the base of the roof drains it into a vessel provided for the purpose. Figure 51 shows a draught closet somewhat different from the one described. Only the lower part of the front is movable, the water and gas-taps are all placed outside the closet at the front, and there is a sink within. This has two exit flues, a square one at the top and a round one at the bottom.

The flues may be made of various materials, but a good deal of care should be taken in their selection, as the fumes passing through will be in continuous contact with their surface. Glazed earthenware pipes are used in the very best laboratories, but these will always be confined to a very few schools on account of their expense. Galvanized iron or copper pipes serve the purpose very well, but the inside of these should be covered with some resistant material, such as pitch or a chemical-proof paint. The flues should be connected to a main flue, and the cross-section of the main one increases as it passes along, so that its cross-section is always equal to that of all the ducts emptying into it up to that point. These flues should not run under the floor but along the ceiling of the room below the chemical laboratory, so that all parts will be exposed and accessible.

A draught closet without a special forced draught for exhausting it is a very poor affair indeed. If the flue runs merely into a chimney, the probability is that it will seldom or never work efficiently. The exhaust, even in winter when the furnaces are lighted, will not be rapid enough to keep the laboratory from becoming polluted, and in summer, when there is no draught due to fires, the current of air is as likely to move down as up. Such a tapping of the chimney is also sure to interfere with the proper draught of the furnace below. A draught caused by a gas-jet at the entrance to the flue is better, but it is not at all satisfactory unless the gas-flame is so powerful as to make it expensive. The only suitable exhaust is that produced by a powerful fan run by a water or electric motor. This should be quite independent of the general ventilating system of the school. Such a fan must be of adequate size. The cubical contents of all the hoods and draught closets should be calculated, and a fan and motor should be selected that will exhaust this volume of air at least three times every minute. The noise of the fan and motor may be transmitted along the metal flues to the laboratory and be an unpleasant disturbance. This may be largely eliminated by breaking the continuity of the metal piping by cutting out a few inches of the latter and replacing it by a canvas sleeve. The motor itself should be placed on a felt pad, and this will also assist in diminishing the transmission of the noise.

Some makeshift substitutes for a draught closet have been described in books. One such makeshift is a sort of box that can be placed in an open window so that the sash fits down on it, but it is difficult to see what advantage it has over simply placing the apparatus outside of the window on a flat sill; and let it be again stated, that a wide, horizontal window-sill is an excellent arrangement for the chemical laboratory.

7 LA

In using the draught closets it must always be remembered that a gas can only pass freely out of a chamber through a flue when there is an opening by which air can freely pass in to take its place. Whenever the draught closet is being used it will probably be of advantage to leave the front sash up so that there will be a narrow slit below along which air may enter the chamber.

Even with the best of draught closets the success with which the chemical laboratory is kept free from evil-smelling gases will depend on the disciplinary powers of the teacher. From the first day that pupils enter the laboratory they must be trained to work close to the hoods on all occasions when gases are being generated, or to perform their work in the draught closets, as the case may be. If permitted, a careless pupil will let the room become filled with fumes, even if he has a hood at his elbow.

The Blast Lamp Table

Most of our secondary schools are without a gas supply. While in this *Educational Pamphlet* we have always recommended private gas plants where acetylene or gasolene is used, it is probable that a good many schools will still adhere conservatively to the antiquated, inefficient alcohol lamps. The laboratories that have no gas supply, and all laboratories, to some extent, require several powerful lamps for producing intense heat for glass-blowing as well as for many chemical experiments. These lamps may be used on the pupil's or teacher's benches, but it is advantageous to have a special bench for them, where the pupils may come when they desire to use the blast lamp. If the lamps used burn alcohol, kerosene, or gasolene, no continuous forced draught will be required, but where gas of any kind is used, some method of producing a steady blast of air will be necessary. The most common method of producing this is by means of a foot bellows. The main objection to the foot bellows is that the pumping takes so much effort that it distracts the attention from the manipulation that is necessary to blow the glass, or whatever the process may be. A cheap and satisfactory substitute for the foot bellows is a water blast, which runs by means of the water pressure in the water-works pipes. All that is necessary is to turn on the tap and let the water run, and a blast of air strong enough to run any lamp is produced. Water blasts are now produced powerful enough to run three lamps at once. This piece of apparatus will be described more fully in discussing the lecture-room (page 140).

The blast lamp table may be constructed in a very simple manner. Its size and shape will depend on the number who will require to use it at one time, and it will be partly determined by the amount of space that can be given up to it. The main consideration is the composition of the top. If possible this should be made of stone. Either alberene stone or slate will give very satisfactory results. Plate glass and wood are entirely unsuitable, for the intense heat is almost sure to crack the former, and the heated glass and metal coming in contact with the latter will soon deface it. If a wooden top is used it should be covered with sheet lead. The lead should be dressed over a fillet which stands up slightly all around the edge of the bench top. This prevents objects from falling on the floor. Zinc may replace lead on the bench top. But both these tops are much inferior to the ones made of stone. The metal covering, under the different changes of heat, is sure to rise up in places on the bench top. Asbestos-covered tops are occasionally used, but they are far from satisfactory, for any material spilled soaks in and cannot be got rid of, and the asbestos becomes rough and soon wears through. As pupils

FRONT ELEVATION

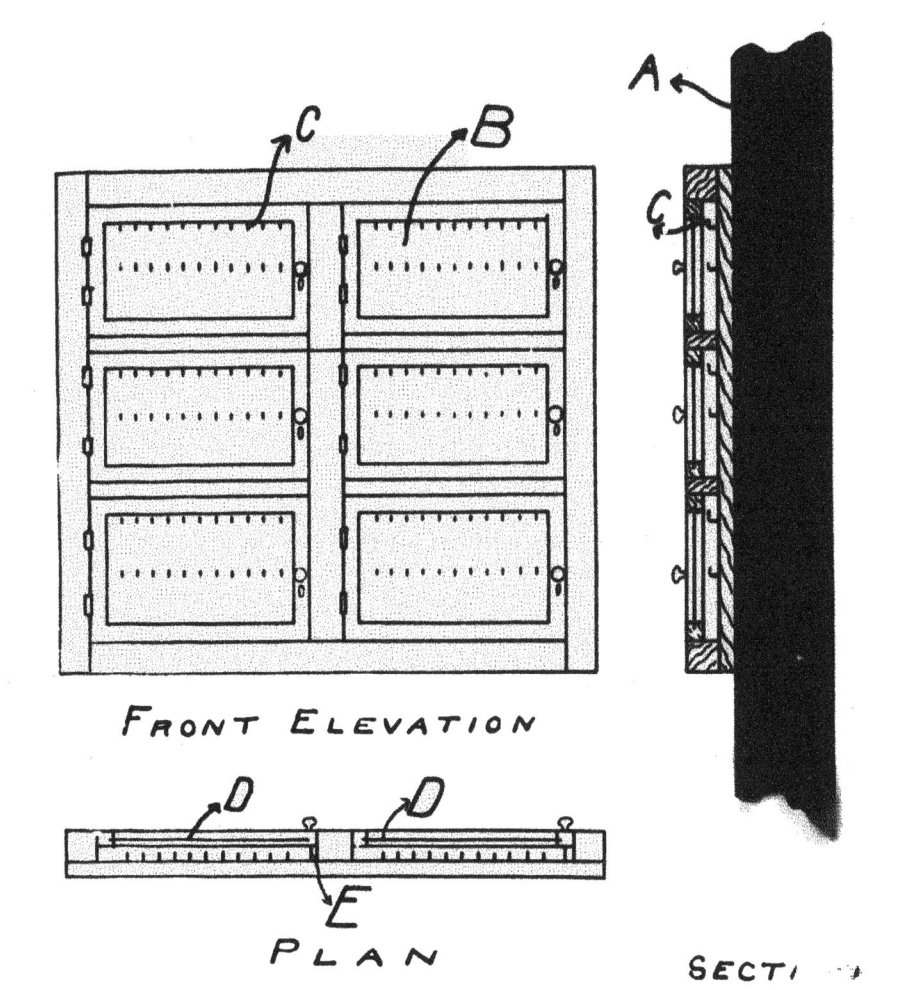

PLAN

SECTION

generally stand while working at such a table, the height should be 3 ft. A convenient width is 2 ft., if all work on one side, or 4 ft. if they work on both sides. As much gas may be used, a large main should lead directly to the bench.

THE KEYBOARD

In the chemical laboratory it is absolutely essential that each pupil should have his own locker, and this must be furnished with a lock that can be opened only by his key and by the master-key carried by the teacher. These keys must always be bought in duplicate, so that if the pupil's is lost, a duplicate can be made. It is never safe to let him have the duplicate, as, if it is lost, it may prove a matter of great difficulty to get it replaced. There are various ways of managing the pupils' keys. Each pupil may be given the key and allowed to carry it with him; if it is lost, he must replace it. To such an arrangement as this there are some objections. Many keys are lost, it may be a week or more before substitutes can be made, and during this time the teacher has to lock and unlock the drawers with his master-key. Then there is the bother of continually getting new keys made and collecting the money for them. The greatest objection to this method is the fact that pupils will continually forget their keys, especially the girls, who have no pockets; the imposition of fines will not prevent this. Moreover, the pupils often leave the school and town, carrying the keys away with them. The more satisfactory method is to have an inclosed keyboard with compartments for each class, as illustrated in Figure 53. Each compartment has a separate glass front (B) that can be closed and locked. Every locker in the room will have a number placed on it, and there will be a peg (C) with a corresponding number on the keyboard. The keyboard will be placed near the door, and as a class enters, their compartment will be opened and each pupil takes off his key as he passes to his bench. At the end of the class period, the keys are returned and the teacher locks the board, seeing at a glance that all the keys have been returned. The illustrations will show the details of its structure. It should be very shallow, the whole thickness not being more than 3 in. The key pegs (C) are ordinary right-angled brass screw hooks. The knobs of each door are of porcelain, and all the compartments are opened by the same key. The illustration shows one composed of six compartments, which would be used for a school where there are six different classes in chemistry.

ARRANGEMENT OF FURNITURE IN THE LABORATORY

The position of each piece of furniture in the room is a matter of vital importance. Every pupil should be placed where he will have the best light possible and where he will have the maximum amount of free space and not be interfered with by adjoining pupils. The cabinets, draught closets, etc., should be put in those positions in the room where they will be most accessible to the pupils and the teacher. If the room is to be used also for demonstration and teaching, the arrangement of the benches should be such as to make the room convenient to both teacher and pupils for that purpose. No one definite arrangement can be given as best for all laboratories, as so much depends on the size and position of the room, the character of the furniture, and the number and position of auxiliary rooms.

Some laboratories have the pupils' benches on different levels, the platforms increasing in height as they recede from the teacher's bench. This is not to be recommended even where all the demonstration is carried on in the room. Such an arrangement makes it too awkward for both pupils and teacher to move about the room, and interferes seriously with the utilization of the walls for storage. It is better to have the whole floor on one level, there being no platform for the benches of either pupils or teacher.

Figure 54 gives a floor plan of a well-arranged and commodious chemical laboratory. The main room is 39 ft. by 28 ft., and two auxiliary rooms are respectively 14 ft. by 9 ft., and 8½ ft. by 9 ft. in size. The room will be considered to run north and south with the windows on the west. It will be noticed that the whole west wall is as completely occupied by windows as the structural requirements will admit. Each window is about 4 ft. wide and goes right to the ceiling. Such an arrangement gives adequate lighting; one seldom sees a laboratory in which the lighting is as good as it might be if the windows were built properly. The window-sill is horizontal and fully a foot wide, so as to give a shelf on which apparatus may be placed to cool or on which a generating flask is placed to exhaust itself because it is obnoxious or dangerous in the room. The partition between the balance-room and the main laboratory is composed largely of transparent glass, so that the teacher has a full view of the pupils in this room. The partitions on each side of the hall between the balance-room and the store-room are of glass also, the one on the balance-room side being transparent, the one on the store-room side being translucent. The glass of these latter two partitions should extend quite to the top, in order that the store-room may get as much light as possible.

The pupils' benches are so arranged as to have them face the front and to have the light come from the left. This should always be the arrangement. The aisles are usually 2 ft. wide, the one next the windows, however, being 1 ft. wider, while the one on the side next the hall is 5 ft. in width; this is quite wide, because the side shelves, which are placed along here, extend out 1 ft. or more. Between each 2 benches from front to rear is a space of 3 ft.; this gives sufficient room for the teacher to move freely about the room.

The teacher's demonstration bench runs right across the front of the room, and one end of it might readily be utilized for blow-pipe work. The back of it is 3 ft. out from the wall. This wall has a black-board that can be raised or lowered, which extends along behind the bench. It should be at least 6 or 8 ft. wide, and the bottom of it should, in its lowest position, extend nearly to the floor, so that the top is just at the right height for writing on. At its highest position the bottom should be at least 6 ft. above the floor. Such a black-board may be constructed of slate or of ground glass backed with some black material; the former will probably be found the more satisfactory material. In the partition behind the demonstration bench is a draught closet in which demonstration experiments may be performed. The main reagent cabinets are placed in the two corners next the demonstration bench; the side shelves are located along the inner wall. The keyboard is just inside the entrance door. A lantern screen is placed on a roller above the blackboard and a lantern shelf is placed in line with it at the back of the room. This shelf can be folded up against the wall when not in use. The lantern should be left on it only when actually in use, as it would be injurious to it to leave it in the chemical laboratory for any length of time. Along the outer wall between the windows are placed the three shelves for jars of distilled water. The balance-room is well lighted and is not entered directly from the laboratory but through a hall passing from the chemical to the physical laboratory. Situated in this position, it

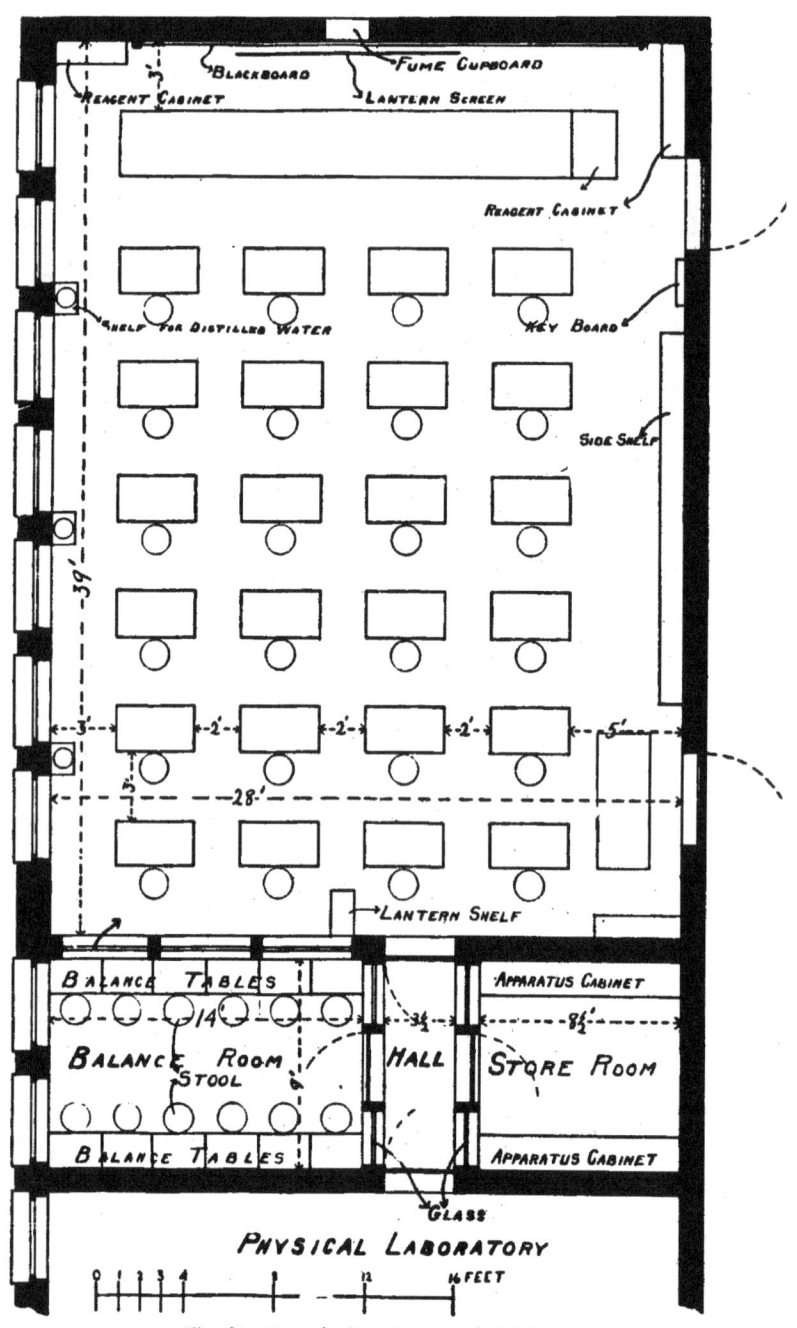

Fig. 54.—Ground plan of a chemical laboratory

can be utilized by classes in both physics and chemistry. The balance shelves are arranged along each side so as to give each pupil a little more than two feet of space. The store-room is placed just across the hall from it and is convenient for both the physical and the chemical laboratories. It has its cabinets, shelves, and bins arranged along the walls.

The walls of the laboratory should be finished in a light grayish-green colour and the ceiling in white. No lead paints should be used in any part of this laboratory. All the gas, water, drainage, and other conduits should pass through the floor and just below the ceiling of the room below. The practice of placing pipes under the floor is not to be recommended in connection with laboratories, as they are too difficult to get at for repairs.

There may be a good deal of elasticity about the above arrangement without disturbing the essentials; by diminishing the size of the aisles the 24 benches can be placed in a smaller room; some of the furniture may be entirely omitted.

No draught closets have been placed about the room. It has been assumed that each pupil's bench has a hood, and, of course, then they are not necessary. If no hoods are on the pupil's benches, then several of these draught closets must be placed in the room. Figure 36 will suggest good positions for them.

The balance-room has been placed between the physical and the chemical laboratory, for in this position the same balances can be used in both. A hall passes from one laboratory to the other and, the balance-room being entered from this hall, pupils can work in it from either laboratory without disturbing classes in the other. The partition between it and the chemical laboratory is made of transparent glass, and this should come down quite low, so that the teacher in the laboratory has an unobstructed view of the pupils while they are using the balances. The lighting in the balance-room should be particularly bright and, therefore, two large windows are placed in the end. If it is located on the top flat, a large skylight would greatly supplement the side light. It will be noticed that the balance-room is not entered directly from the chemical laboratory but from the hall. This is a rather important arrangement, for fumes are liable to be carried into the balance-room through the door when the opening is direct.

The store-room is situated between the physical and chemical laboratories also. This is an obvious advantage, as many of the pieces of glassware are used in both. As it has no windows, the whole end partitions of both it and the balance room are of translucent glass. This glass should extend right to the ceiling, and the doors should be made largely of glass also. This produces a fair amount of light for this room. The storage cabinets already described (page 79, Fig. 47 and 48) are arranged along the sides. A table down the middle, on which apparatus may be placed temporarily, will complete the equipment. If there is no preparation room, a sink with a draining-board will be useful in this room if a place can be found for it.

CHAPTER V

PHYSICAL LABORATORY

SITUATION

A LABORATORY suitable for both physics and chemistry has already been described in Chapter III. Here it is intended to describe the furniture and its arrangement in a laboratory used exclusively for the teaching of physics, it being assumed that the school is also equipped with a chemical and, perhaps, with a biological laboratory.

The room itself will be situated adjoining the other science rooms. Where the school has a chemical laboratory also, it is well to place the physical laboratory on one side of the store-room and balance-room, and the chemical laboratory on the other side, so that the balances and apparatus will be convenient for use in both laboratories.

The room should be quite lofty—not less than fourteen feet high—and should be situated in a part as free from vibration as possible, also in a position free from magnetic influences. It should never be situated near a boiler nor near a dynamo or motor, and must be kept well away from the ventilating fans. Under no circumstances should it be placed in the basement. The lighting is certain to be defective, and more objectionable still, the dampness of the spring and summer is certain to be ruinous to the apparatus and furniture.

LIGHTING

The lighting should be as perfect as possible. Large windows reaching nearly to the top of the room and as close together as possible should occupy one wall. Overhead lighting by means of skylights will be an advantage and, when this is obtained, the side windows do not require to be so large or numerous, though there is no danger of admitting too much light. The windows must all be adapted for closing with dark blinds, as for many experiments in physics a darkened room is necessary. These dark blinds will be fully described later (page 132).

The character and finish of the walls and floor will be similar to those of the other laboratories which are discussed on page 5.

FURNITURE

The furniture necessary for equipping the physical laboratory is quite simple. The most essential pieces are the working benches for the pupils. A demonstration bench for the use of the teacher will be necessary where a lecture-room is not attached, and even where there is such a room some kind of bench is necessary on which apparatus and reagents may be placed for the use of pupils in performing their experiments. Storage cabinets will be placed either in the laboratory itself or in a store-room. A number of shelves with boxes in which sets of apparatus are placed is a great convenience, for the boxes are the means of saving much time in the distributing and collecting of apparatus used for pupils' experiments. Sinks are not necessary on each working bench, but a number should be provided for washing glassware and for other purposes. Boards attached along one wall at different heights are invaluable for the insertion of hooks and pegs and for the suspension of apparatus.

Where sets of balances are used for physics alone, some balance shelves will be necessary and may well be placed in the room itself. These pieces of furniture will be described individually, and then their arrangement in the laboratory will be more fully discussed.

The Pupil's Bench

This is the most important piece of furniture, and great care should be exercised in selecting one that will be as suitable as possible for all the varied uses to which it is put. The chemistry bench already described, would not be suitable for the work in physics. The raised edge passing around three sides of the margin of the top would be continually in the way, as would the upright rods for retort rings. The sink holes would also be in the way. The amount of bench top required for the performance of an experiment in physics varies much more widely than it does for practical work in chemistry and biology. In working with lenses and mirrors a continuous stretch of 6 or 8 ft. is required, while in many other experiments a very small amount of space is all that is necessary. Some recommend individual benches that are not fastened to the floor. These may be placed two or three together, when a long, continuous bench top is required. Such an arrangement has points to recommend it; it gives all the advantages of the individual bench and supplies a variety of sizes of working places to suit all experiments. But the objections to such a bench are so serious that, however desirable individual working places in the physical laboratory may be, it cannot be recommended. Loose benches will always be out of alignment and will give the room a very untidy appearance. Such benches are very noisy, as they are being continually moved, and there will be numerous disputes as a result of one pupil encroaching on the place of another. The physics bench, as we shall presently see, requires to be very heavy, to give solidity, and such a bench is unsuitable for transferring from place to place. Some form of cross-bar from which pulleys, levers, etc., may be suspended is necessary, and if this is situated on a single bench it makes the latter topheavy. Besides, a physics bench should have gas and electrical connections for each pupil, and these must be capable of disconnection at the floor if the benches are movable; this condition will continually produce trouble.

The bench that will prove most satisfactory is one long enough to accommodate two working places at a side; these can be made double, so that two work at each side, or single, with only two working at the bench; in the latter case twelve such benches will be required; in the former, six. An advantage of the double benches is that one pair of uprights will suffice for the workers on both sides of the bench. While six sets of uprights will not interfere seriously with the teacher's observation of the pupils, twice that number produce a bewildering effect. On the other hand, the disadvantages of pupils facing the two opposite directions are obvious. Altogether the advantages are decidedly in favour of a bench that accommodates four working places, two on each side. Such a bench will now be fully described and illustrated (Figs. 55 and 56).

A bench with a top 7 ft. long and $3\frac{1}{2}$ ft. wide will be of a good size. This gives each pupil a bench space $3\frac{1}{2}$ ft. long and $1\frac{3}{4}$ ft. wide, which is ample. Where longer free spaces are required, two pupils can work together and then a space 7 ft. long is provided. The height should be such that the top is convenient for work when the pupils are standing, as much of the work will be done under these

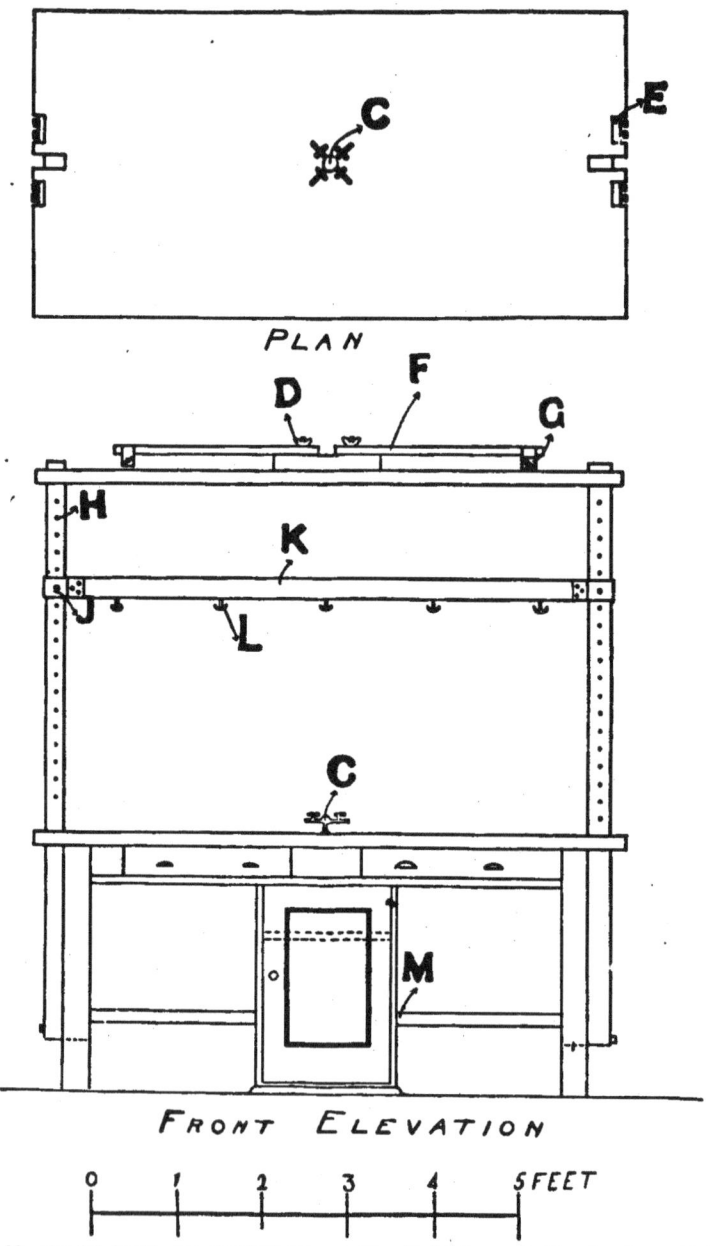

Fig. 55.—Pupils' bench for physical laboratory C. Gas-tap. D. Thumb-screw. E. Electrical terminals. F. Horizontal swinging arm. G. Clamp. H. Holes in upright. J. Brass collar. K. Movable horizontal beam. L. Brass hook. M. Shelf underneath table.

conditions. When standing, the forearm should rest on the top of the bench, while the upper arm hangs freely. For pupils up to sixteen years of age, the height of the bench top should be about 2 ft. 9 in., for those older than that the height should be nearly 3 ft., no mistake will be made if they are constructed anywhere between these two heights. The cross-bar above the bench top has a swinging arm (F), which, when swung at right angles to the cross-bar, extends out far enough to allow a suspension beyond the edge of the top; this arm should be high enough to allow a suspension of at least two metres without touching the floor.

The whole top should be perfectly flat without any projections above except, perhaps, the gas-taps. The top should project out beyond the body at least 4 in. all around, in order that clamps or vises may be attached to it. A drip (O) in the form of a small gutter should run around the under surface of the top about 1 in. from the edge; this prevents water running in on the under surface and staining the body. It is neither necessary nor advisable to have sinks on each bench; a few placed at convenient positions around the walls will supply all the accommodation necessary in this respect. The electrical terminals will be placed in the ends of the bench, as shown in Figure 56. A gas tube which rises through the middle of the bench terminates in four gas-taps, one for each pupil. The two uprights rise from the ends. This arrangement leaves the whole top of the bench free from projections, except the gas-taps. The material for the top should always be wood. Stone or glass of any kind are both unsuitable and unnecessary. As chemicals are not used to any extent in physical experiments, the danger of mutilating the top with corrosive materials is slight. The stone and glass are cold and unpleasant to the touch, and pieces of apparatus cannot easily be clamped to them. The ideal wood is teak, but maple or birch give satisfactory results. If the latter woods are used, the top should be built up of narrow strips about one inch in width glued together with a waterproof glue, recipes for which are given on page 11: the pieces should be further bound together by dowels, after the method described on page 11 and illustrated in Figure 35. Two inches in thickness is none too great for the top, as the more solidly built the bench is the better. The top should be finished in black with an acid-proof finish, as described already on page 12. The legs and framework should be very heavy and strong to produce a bench not easily jarred and as free from vibration as possible.

The top is supported by four strong legs at least 4 in. square. Two shallow drawers and a cupboard are placed on each side. The cupboard is central, opening by a single door. It should have a shelf dividing it into two compartments, a shallow one above and a deep one below. This latter compartment should be high enough to take retort stands. The two drawers are toward the ends, and beneath them is an open space in which the feet and knees of the pupil may be placed while sitting at the bench. These drawers and cupboards are not to serve as lockers, for each pupil is not supplied with a set of apparatus in physics; they contain tubing, burners, and other pieces of apparatus that are being continually used. Cross-pieces pass across the ends near the bottom of the legs to strengthen the framework. Beneath the top, with one end resting on this cross-piece, runs a longitudinal shelf (M) 8 in. wide. All of these pieces should be massive.

Some arrangement must be made for having a cross-beam for suspending apparatus. The arrangement shown in the illustration is a very useful one. From the ends rise uprights which are bolted firmly to the top and the cross-pieces between the legs. A fixed beam joins the two upper ends of these uprights. Below this fixed beam is the sliding beam (K). This is a wooden scantling 2 in. by 4 in., just long enough to slide between the ends. On each end it has a heavy brass socket (J) just large enough to slide freely around the uprights. The sliding beam is fixed in any position by a pin which passes through an opening in the brass socket and in the upright. The openings (H) in the uprights may be placed 2 in. apart or even closer. The pin is attached by a chain to the end of the movable cross-beam. If the pin is not attached, it will never be found when wanted.

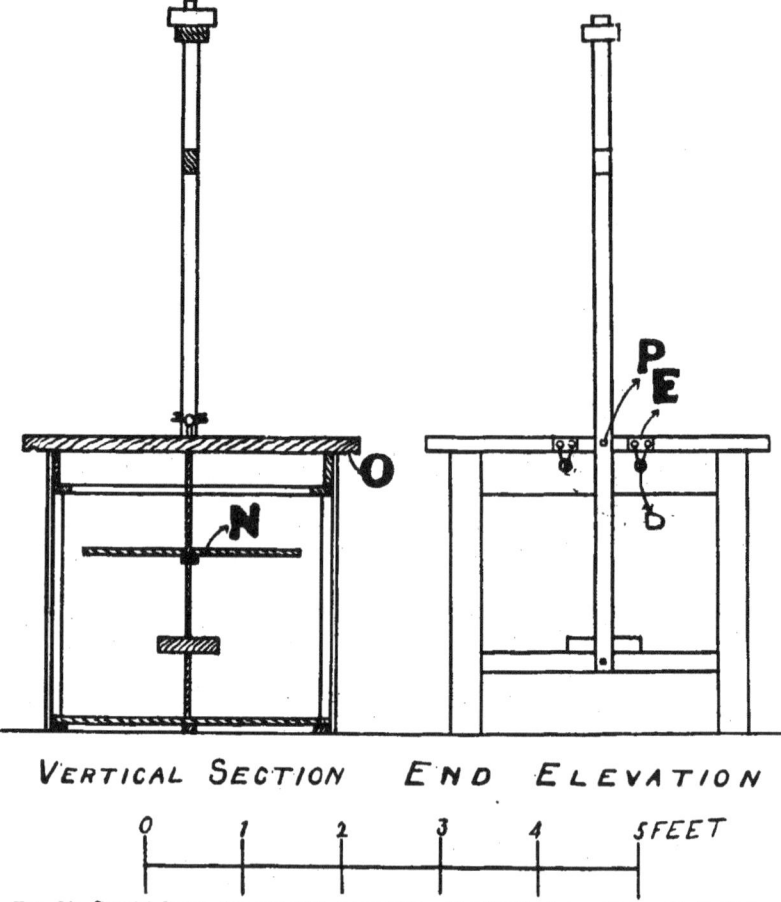

Fig. 56.—Pupils' bench for physical laboratory. E. Electrical terminals. N. Shelf in cupboard. O. Drip. P. Bolt.

Hooks of brass are attached on the under side of the beam for suspensions. One inconvenience of such an arrangement is that the suspended apparatus is along the middle of the bench and is a little difficult to reach by the pupil standing at the bench. This can be overcome by having flush sockets in the sides of the beam into which brass rods are screwed; the suspensions are made from these brass rods, which extend out as far or farther than the margin of the bench. These are not shown in the drawing. Two horizontal arms (F) are placed on the top of the fixed, horizontal beam. These have a bolt passing through them at the end toward the centre, while the other end is free. They are fastened to the bolt by a thumbscrew (D) in such a way that, by loosening the screw, the free end may be swung out, and by tightening the screw it may be fixed in any position. When swung out at right angles to the beam the end reaches beyond the edge of the bench top. Over this free end slides a heavy brass collar (G) prolonged below into a hanger with a tightening screw (Fig. 57). This is for the attachment of a thread or wire, which is placed between the two jaws and held firmly by tightening the thumbscrew (T). This arm, as has already been stated, is for making pendulum suspensions of considerable length.

The gas-pipe rises from the floor and terminates in the centre of the bench top; four taps run diagonally from this. The taps are of gun-metal or brass and have lever handles to the valves. The tap should terminate in a corrugated nozzle over which rubber tubing may be pushed. (See page 19.)

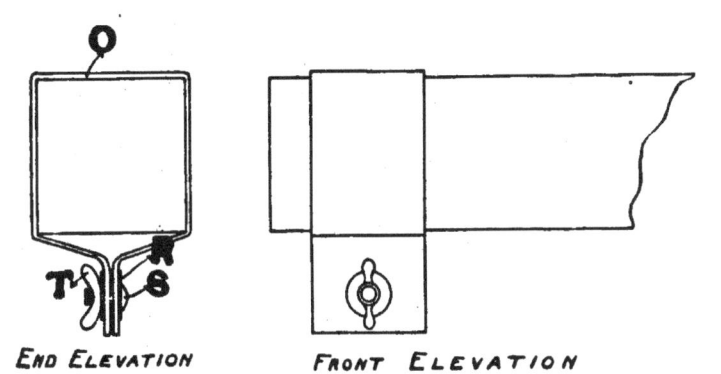

Fig. 57.—End of horizontal swing arm on the top of cross-beam of physical bench. O. Brass collar. S. Tightening screw. T. Thumb-screw. R. Washer.

A word should be said about the electrical terminals. If the current utilized is taken from the mains of the town or is produced by a generator in the building, the underwriters will demand that all the wiring and terminals shall be inclosed within pipes. The wires cannot terminate in binding posts fastened directly to the woodwork of the bench, so the terminals should be fixed in blocks of slate which are screwed to the bench. Figure 58 will give a good idea of the best method of having the wiring and terminals attached to the bench. It represents a part of the end of a pupil's bench. The wires are represented by heavy lines and are drawn diagrammatically, as the wires really pass through iron pipes which are not represented in the drawing. The wires come up alongside the vertical support (D), passing up the end. Before they send off branches to the terminals, fuses (J) are put in the circuit, one on each wire. The only fuse admitted should be one that screws into a socket and that may be replaced by an incandescent lamp. Branch wires connected in multiple with the mains go to each set of terminals, and each wire has a switch (G) on its course. This switch may be of any of the types used in house wiring, but the small button switch with "on" and "off" marked on it has been found the most satisfactory, as the pupils can always tell whether the circuit is closed or open. The nature of the terminals (C) is important. In Figure 58 the section through A B will give a good idea of the most suitable form. A piece is cut from the end of the bench top about 3 in. long and 2 in. wide. The cut is not made through the whole thickness of the top, except in the outer inch. In the inner part of the cut half an inch is left on the lower side to serve as a shelf for the slate block (K) to rest upon. The figure of the section through A B will make this clear. The binding posts (L) are fixed in the piece of slate or marble (K) that occupies this recess. The stone block is fastened to the shelf below by the bolts (M) Figure 58. It fills the inner part of the cut and extends ¼ in. into the outer part, leaving ¾ of an inch for the projection of the

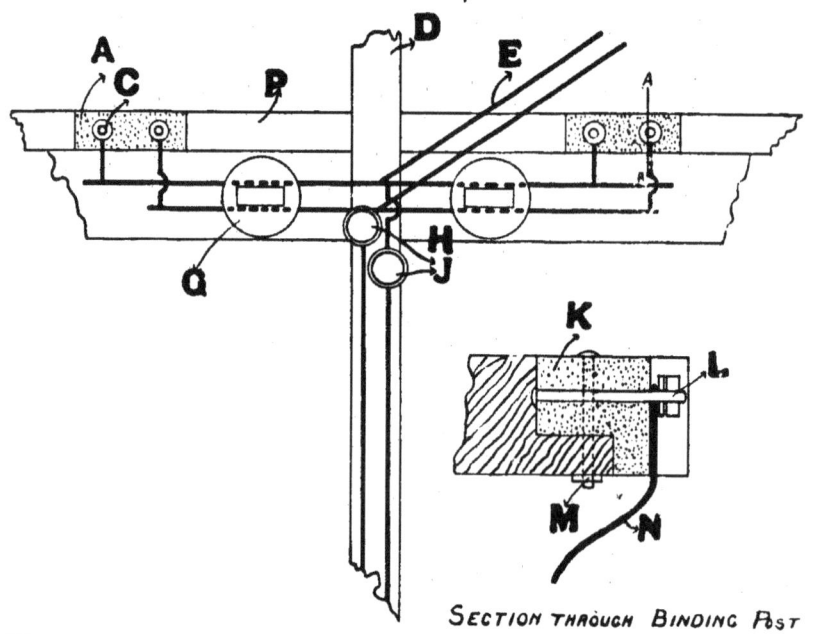

Fig. 58.—The upper diagrammatic drawing shows a part of the end of the physical bench to show the electrical wiring and terminals. The small figure below and to the right is a section through A B of the upper figure. The pipes through which the wires pass are omitted. A. Slate-block. C. Binding-post. D. Upright. E. Wires passing to terminals at the other end of the bench. G. Switch. H, J. Fuse. K. Section of slate slab. L. Binding post in section. M. **Fastening** bolt. N. Wire to terminal. P. End of top of table.

metal terminals. These consist of binding posts which are horizontal, and must not project beyond the end of the bench top, for if they do the pupils will be continually tearing their clothes on them. The binding posts may be either of the bolt and nut variety as in the illustration (L), or they may have an eyelet to receive the wire; the former will prove the more suitable, as, in the use of the latter a fine wire will not hold tight, and a stranded wire can only be passed through the eyelet with difficulty. The washer and thumbscrew between which the wire is held should be large, and the contact surfaces quite flat. When in use, if a small source of electricity is required, as a few storage cells, two 15-ampere fuses may be left in the circuit. If, on the other hand, the lighting circuit is being used for experimental work, or for any purpose requiring a strong current, then the pupils would be likely to blow out these fuses by carelessly or wilfully making a short circuit. There must be protection, therefore, against this contingency. If one fuse is removed and an incandescent bulb is screwed into its place, then complete protection against the blowing out of fuses is obtained, and sufficient current is allowed to pass for all ordinary experiments. Different candle-power lamps allow different currents to pass; if the voltage is 110, a 16-C.P. carbon-film lamp gives ½ ampere, a 32-C.P. lamp gives 1 ampere, etc. By having several sets of lamps, a considerable variety of currents can be distributed to the desks from a 110 volt main. If there is no main source of electrical supply and no wiring to the bench, the longitudinal shelf underneath will serve to hold a battery from which the current may be taken; the most suitable cells for such a battery have been already discussed on pages 30-32.

Teachers' Demonstration Bench

The structure of this bench will depend largely on the use to be made of it. If the science department contains a lecture-room for demonstrations, then the table in the physical laboratory need not be so elaborate as when a lecture-room is absent, for it will serve largely as a supply table for apparatus to be distributed to the pupils. If it is used also for demonstration purposes, the structure and equipment will be similar to that of the demonstration bench already described on pages 71-76, and illustrated in Figures 42 and 43. However, in the bench for the physical laboratory, the fume duct may be omitted without much loss. Figures 59 and 60 are illustrations of a simplified form of bench in which the fume vent, the second sink, and the mercury tray have been omitted. The details as to the top, drawers, finish, material, etc., are the same as those of the chemical demonstration bench described fully on pages 71-76, and need not be described again. One feature which it is necessary to add to the demonstration bench already described to make it suitable for physical demonstrations is an adjustable cross-bar. From this bar suspensions may be made. The heavy, permanent bars of the pupil's bench would be quite unsuitable on the teacher's bench, as they would seriously obstruct the pupils' view of the black-board and of the lantern screen. The most suitable arrangement is that illustrated in the drawings. The brass flush-threaded sockets are sunk into the bench top. Into these sockets are screwed two cylindrical uprights (Fig. 59, (L)), (Fig. 60, (B)), 1 in. in diameter and 5 ft. high. The cross-bar (B), Figure 59, is made of 1 in. tubing of sufficient strength. Figure 61 shows how it slides on the vertical pieces. It has a collar (B) screwed into each end, which slides over the uprights and can be fixed securely at any point by means of a set-screw with a large, milled head (A). This cross-bar has hooks (N) on its lower side. The whole arrangement can be taken down when not required for use.

Apparatus Cabinet

Much greater care is necessary in the planning of storage cabinets for the physical apparatus than in planning them for the chemical apparatus. The former is much more easily injured than the latter, as it is not so largely made of glass as of wood and metal. The physical apparatus is also of all shapes and sizes and very difficult to store. A cabinet of large dimensions is most convenient, so that pieces of apparatus of great length, height, or width can find a place in it. Figure 62 gives illustrations of a very convenient cabinet. It is 7½ ft. high and 2 ft. in

102   LABORATORY ACCOMMODATION

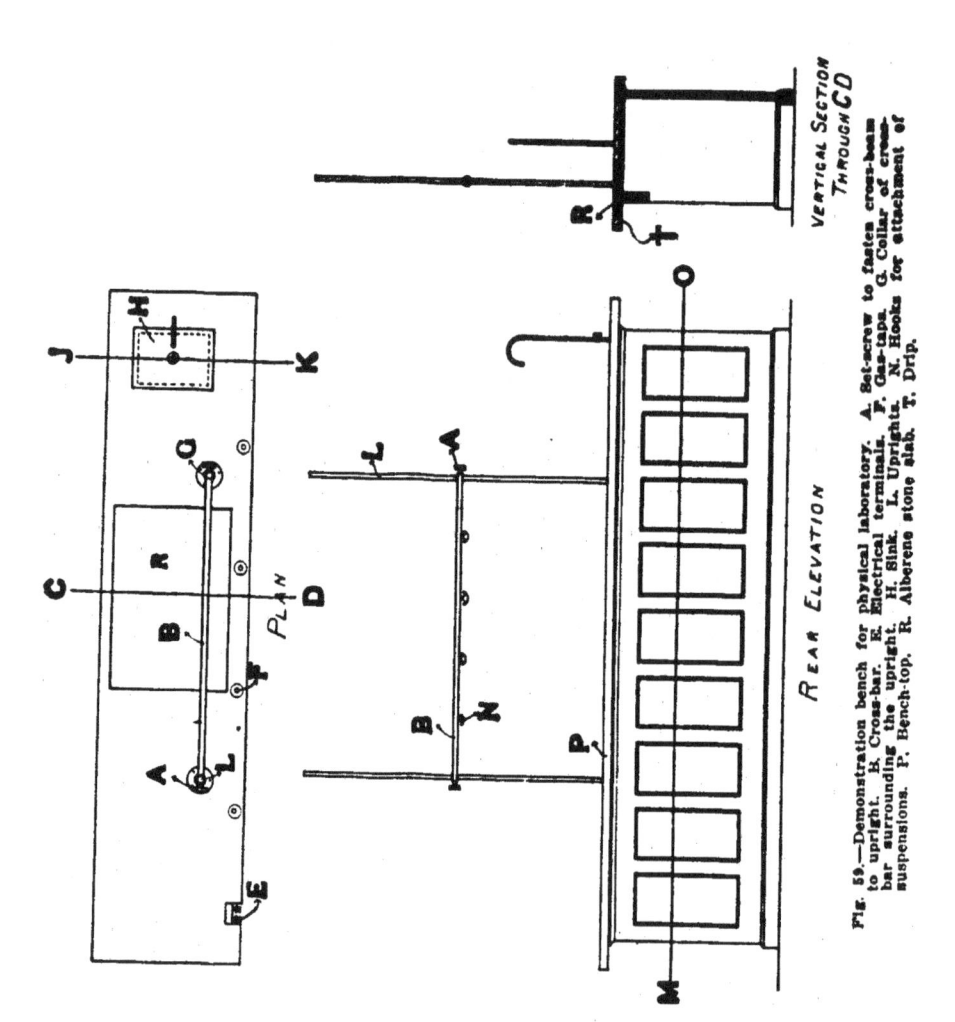

Fig. 59.—Demonstration bench for physical laboratory. A. Set-screw to fasten cross-beam to upright. B. Cross-bar. E. Electrical terminals. F. Gas-taps. G. Collar of cross-bar surrounding the upright. H. Sink. L. Uprights. N. Hooks for attachment of suspensions. P. Bench-top. R. Alberene stone slab. T. Drip.

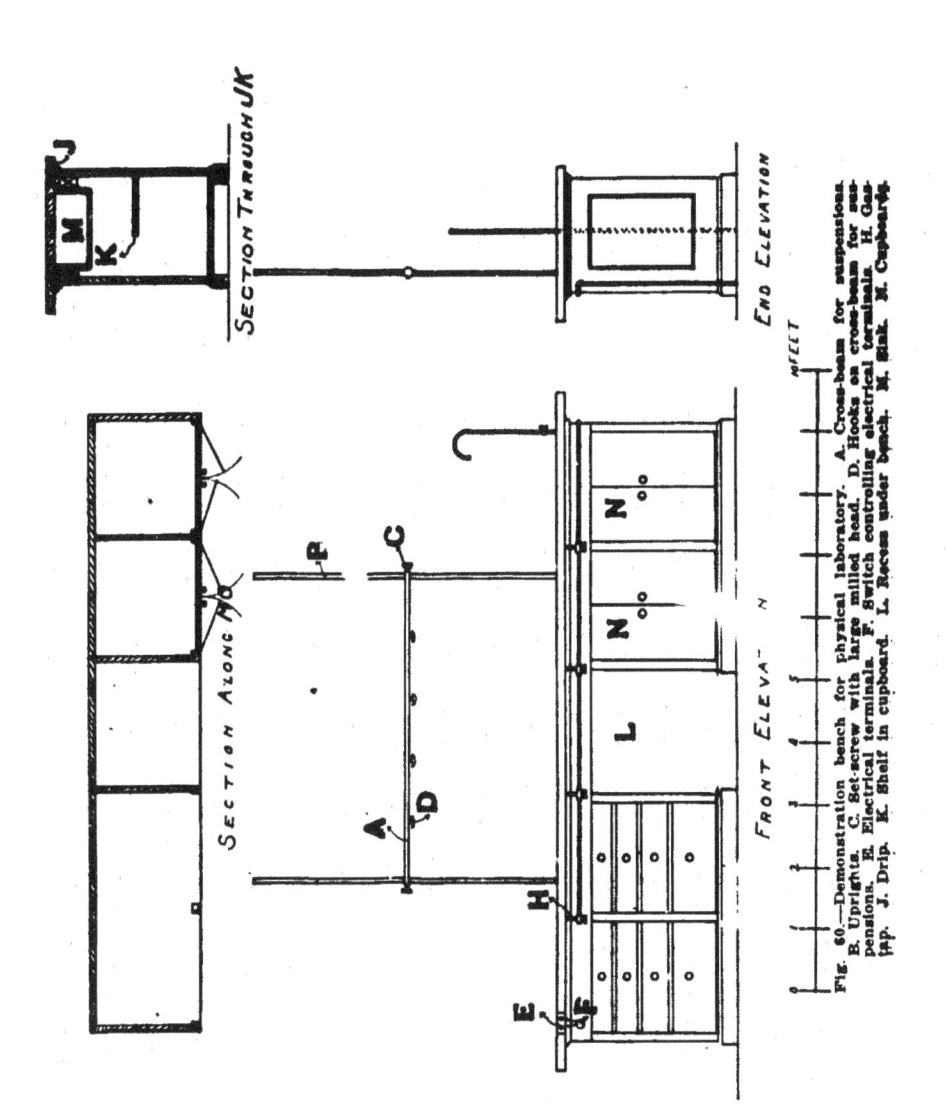

Fig. 60.—Demonstration bench for physical laboratory. A. Cross-beam for suspensions. B. Uprights. C. Set-screw with large milled head. D. Hooks on cross-beam for suspensions. E. Electrical terminals. F. Switch controlling electrical terminals. H. Gas tap. J. Drip. K. Shelf in cupboard. L. Recess under bench. M. Sink. N. Cupboards.

available depth. The length will depend on the size of the space in which it is placed. Along the bottom is a row of drawers of about 1 ft. in depth. These will prove invaluable for storing unsightly material and odds and ends. The whole upper part is one continuous space with no vertical partitions. The ends and front are of glass. The whole front is occupied by doors. Swinging and sliding doors both have their advantages and disadvantages, and these have been discussed already (page 81). Here, where the doors are large and heavy, the sliding ones are preferable. These should have, on the under side, ball-bearing slides which run on a steel track. This arrangement is cheap, and the doors run with the greatest ease. Two shelves go right along the cabinet from end to end. It is not advisable to have these adjustable, as they are so large and heavy that such an arrangement would be of doubtful advantage. By means of hooks, nails, and brackets, much material can be stored against the walls. Shallow shelves across the ends and along the back between the main shelves will also increase its

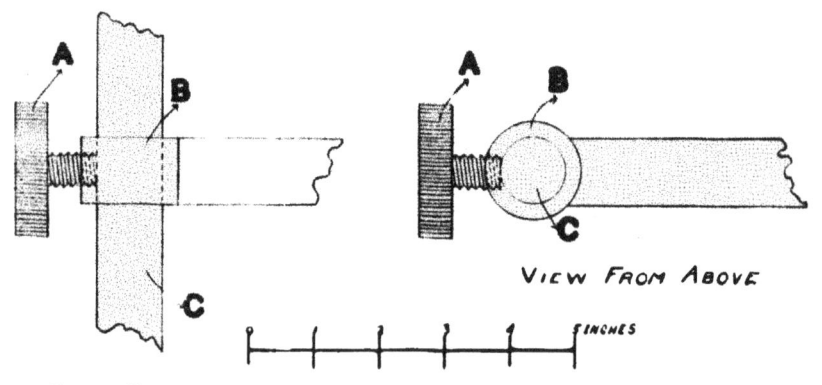

Fig. 61.—Enlarged view of a part of the uprights and cross-beam of demonstration bench for physical laboratory. A. Milled head of screw, which presses against the upright and fixes the cross-beam. B. The collar on end of cross-beam that slides on upright. C. The uprights.

storage capacity. The details of the material and finish are similar to those already described for the chemical cabinet on page 9. All the doors are locked by the same key, and a spring lock will be most suitable on this cabinet. The top is made perfectly flat with no space at the back between it and the wall, so that it can be used, if found necessary, for storing some of the bulkier pieces.

· SHELVES

A set of shelves should be constructed on the wall. These should hold a set of uniform boxes. In these are stored the apparatus used for individual experiments. For this work sets of twelve or twenty-four pieces are frequently on hand, such as calorimeters, magnets, prisms, burners, etc. These are stored in the boxes, which have labels on the ends showing their contents. In distributing apparatus to the class, a pupil passes among the class with one of these boxes and leaves one piece with each pupil; they are collected in the same way. Another way of

CABINET

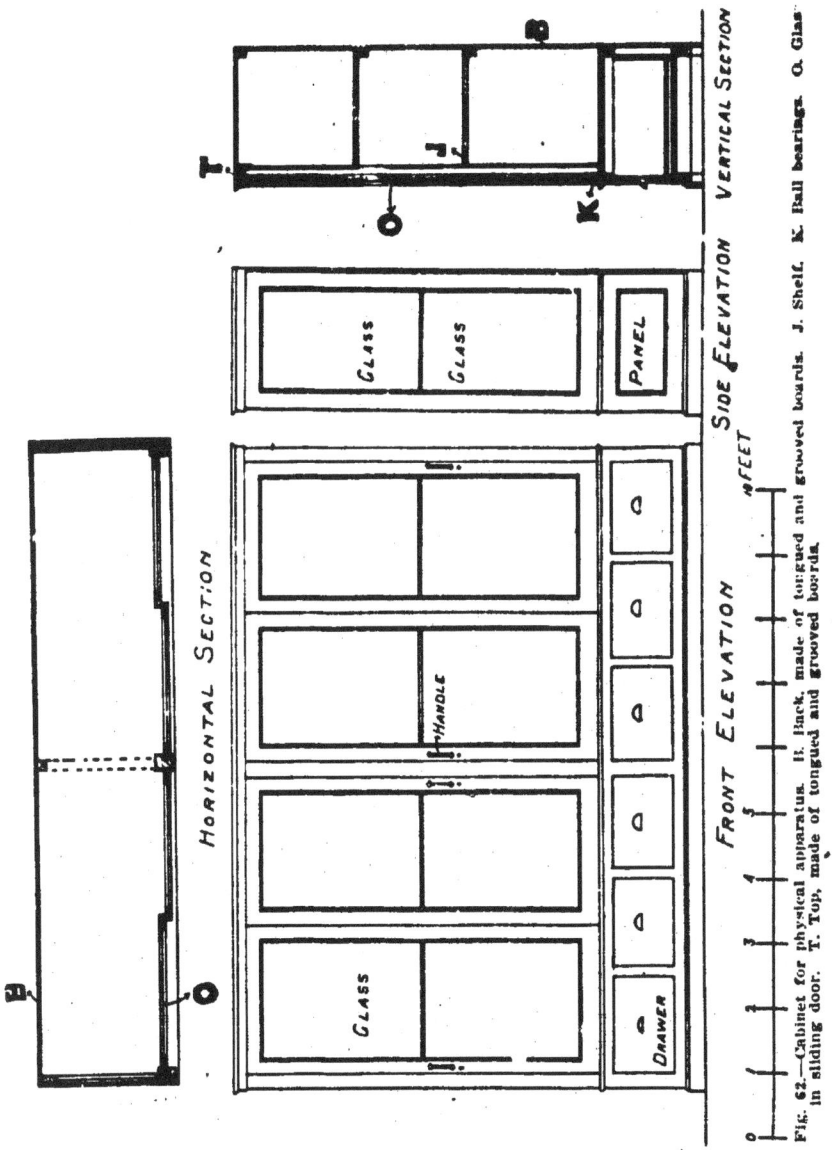

Fig. 62.—Cabinet for physical apparatus. B. Back, made of tongued and grooved boards. J. Shelf. K. Ball bearings. O. Glass in sliding door. T. Top, made of tongued and grooved boards.

using these boxes is to have one for each pupil's place in the physical laboratory. Before the class begins work these may be set out in a row and the apparatus placed in each, so that when the class enters the laboratory each pupil comes forward to the shelf and takes his box to his place and is at once ready for work, with all his apparatus convenient.

The shelves are 10 in. in depth and are placed 1 ft. apart. The length will depend on the amount of available wall space—the longer the better. The boxes are of uniform size, 14 in. long, 10 in. wide, and 6 in. high. The twenty-four that are used for distributing the apparatus to the pupils' benches are painted dull black except the under side of the bottom, which is painted white so that they can be used by the pupils as screens in performing experiments in optics. Narrow strips are nailed along two sides of the bottom to prevent the white from being rubbed off.

Balance Shelves

These are quite similar in every respect to those of the chemical laboratory, and the reader is referred to pages 81-83, and Figures 49 and 50 for a complete description of them.

The Sinks

The laboratory sinks are best placed along the walls rather than on the pupils' benches. Figure 63 gives a good idea of a suitable sink. It is made of glazed stoneware of the kind already described on page 19. One about 14 in. by 10 in. is of a good size. The top and back are of slate. The top is about 3 ft. long and 1½ ft. wide, and is placed above the sink. It is counter-sunk with a slight depression all around the sink. Against the wall is a slate back about 1 ft. high. Around the top, at the front, and at the two ends, is an apron of slate projecting at least 2 in. above the top. This is to guard against the splashing of water on the floor. The junctures between the pieces of slate must all be water-tight. The slate comprising the top and the apron should be 1½ in. thick, and that of the back 1 in. The sink is supported on iron brackets. The slate may be replaced by wood but of course the results will not be so good. The best wood to use for such a purpose is teak, and if it is not available white-wood will stand the water fairly well.

Miscellaneous Furnishings

Some part of the wall of the laboratory should be constructed of unpainted wood. This can be used for holding nails and pegs on which apparatus may be hung. Many experiments in mechanics, such as the parallelogram of forces, may be performed here. If several vertical slats are attached to the wall and wooden boards are fastened to them horizontally, they will serve the purpose admirably.

A work bench is an essential part of the equipment of the science department of every high school. Such a bench, with a kit of mechanic's and carpenter's tools, together with a soldering outfit, will be a very valuable means of developing initiative on the part of both the pupils and teacher. It will pay for itself many times, as numerous pieces of apparatus will be repaired that otherwise would be thrown out, and much apparatus will be improvised that would otherwise have to be purchased. A regular manual-training bench will be fairly satisfactory, or any solidly built bench on which vises and an anvil can be placed will answer the purpose. This bench should be fastened rigidly to the floor.

SINK FOR PHYSICAL LABORATORY

A large sink with a draining-board in the store-room is handy. This will be similar to the other sinks in the physical laboratory, and should have the top and apron of slate or white-wood. The tap should have a long swan-neck, so that the tallest vessels may be placed under it. It should be connected with both hot and cold water. Behind it is placed vertically a teak draining-board with pegs slanting upward upon which glass vessels are placed to dry.

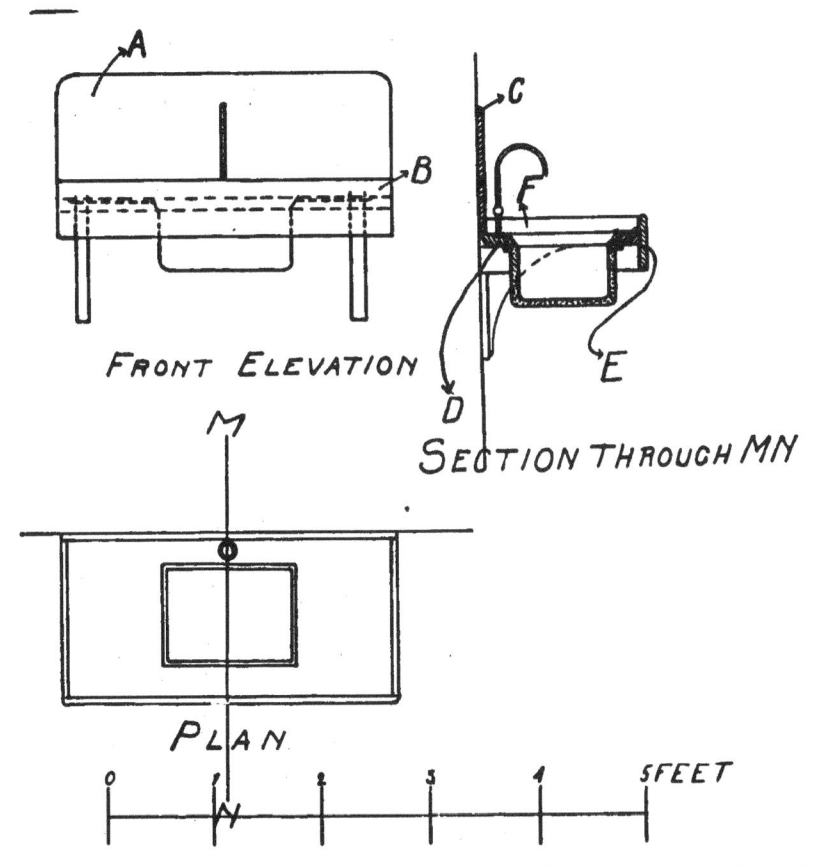

Fig. 63.—Sink for physical laboratory. A. Apron at back of sink. B. Apron at front of sink. D. Slate top surrounding sink. E. Apron at front of sink.

A long table in the store-room near the apparatus cabinet is a convenience. Pieces of apparatus are placed on it when the teacher is putting them in or taking them out of the cabinet. Apparatus may also be set up on this table preparatory to taking it into the demonstration room.

The stools have already been described and illustrated, page 13, Figure 2. If the bench tops are 36 in. high, the height of the stool should be 25 in.

ARRANGEMENT OF FURNITURE IN THE LABORATORY

Figure 64 will give a good idea of the relative sizes and arrangement of the furniture in a physical laboratory which is well equipped. The windows occupy the whole of one side except a few feet toward the front, near where the black-board is placed. When the black-board does not extend near to the side where the windows are, they might be brought, with advantage, even more closely to the front. The pupils' benches are in two rows of three each. Their ends must always be turned toward the windows, so that no pupil will have to work with the light behind him, for in that case he would be working in his own shadow. In this laboratory much greater freedom of movement is necessary than in the chemical laboratory. The pupils will sometimes be working at the ends of the bench and sometimes at the sides. It is therefore necessary not to crowd the benches. The aisles on the outsides are each 5 ft. wide, while the middle one is 4 ft wide. This space is not too great, and narrower aisles will cause inconvenience. The teacher's demonstration bench (N) is situated at the front end of the room in line with the window, so that the sunlight may be used for experimental work. Of course if a window is not in line with the bench a small opening can be bored in the wall, and in this a heliostat may be permanently placed. This bench should be made as long as possible. It is represented as extending as far out on each side as do the pupil's benches. A space of at least 4 ft. is left between the demonstration bench and the black-board. The lantern screen (P) is situated above the black-board (R). If all the demonstration work is performed on this bench, then two other pieces of furniture should be placed behind it on the wall. A small galvanometer, shelf, and screen (S) are placed above the black-board, where they can be plainly seen by the whole class. A water air-pump and water blast (O) will be placed at one end of the black-board. A full description of the structure and use of these two pieces of equipment will be given when discussing the equipment of the lecture and demonstration room. (Page 140, Figure 80.) The sinks (K) can be placed before the windows, as this is a space that usually cannot be well utilized for any other purpose. Three such sinks are sufficient. One will be placed in line with each pair of pupils' benches, so as to be as convenient for the pupils as possible. Assuming that there are separate physical balances, these can be placed most conveniently in the laboratory itself, as there is not the objection to placing them there that there is to having them in the chemical laboratory. The balance shelves are placed around the walls toward the back of the room. A set of shelves with boxes for pupils' apparatus occupies the space between the two doors by which the laboratory is entered from the hall. The wooden slats, fastened to the wall, may be placed on the only extensive piece of wall space remaining, which is toward the front of the room.

Besides the main laboratory, the drawing shows a separate store-room and a dark room. There is not the same objection to having apparatus cabinets in the physical laboratory that there is to having them in the chemical laboratory. A lack of sufficient wall space will usually prevent them from all being contained there, and a separate store-room will prove a great advantage. The two side walls of this store-room are occupied by the apparatus cabinets, and a table runs along between them. The front of the store-room next the window contains the work bench. Here there will be abundance of light for fine work. The sink for washing apparatus described on page 107 will be situated just opposite the door. If a lecture-room adjoins the laboratory, then this space will be occupied by a door, and other accommodation

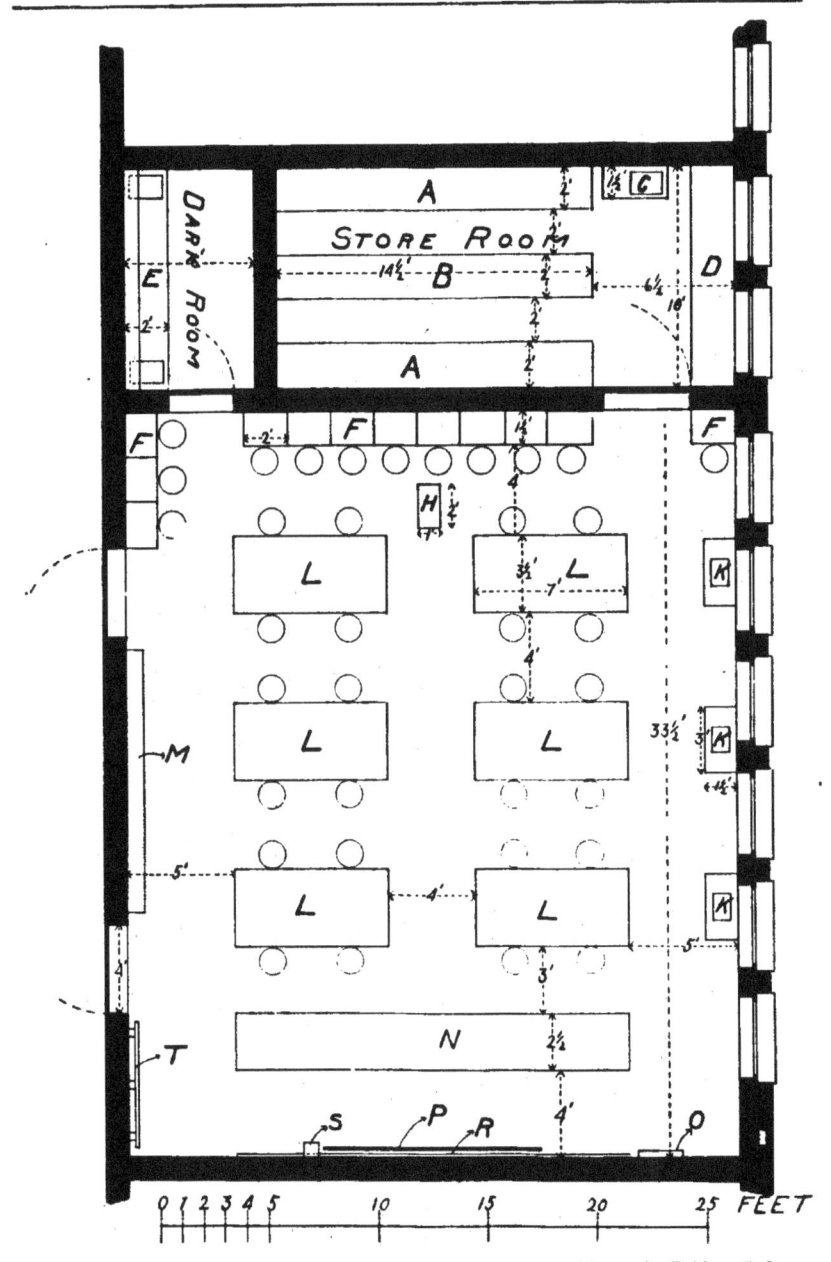

Fig. 64.—Ground plan of physical laboratory. A. Apparatus cabinet. B. Table. C. Large sink with draining board. D. Work bench. E. Table with two sinks in dark room. F. Balance tables. H. Lantern stand. K. laboratory sinks. L. Students' benches. M. Side shelf. N. Demonstration bench. O. Water air-pump and blast. P. Lantern screen. R. Black-board. S. Galvanometer shelf. T. Slats attached to Wall.

will have to be found for the sink by diminishing the size of one of the apparatus cabinets. The dark room has a door opening directly into the physical laboratory. The main equipment of the dark room will be for photographic work. Frequently, in optical experiments, it may be necessary to perform an experiment in an absolutely dark room, and the pupils working at it can pass directly into the dark room for the work.

ELECTRICAL WIRING OF PHYSICAL LABORATORY

Ordinary electricians know so little regarding the requirements of a science room that it is necessary to describe the details of the wiring of a physical laboratory when the current is supplied to each pupil's bench. The arrangement of the wires, switches, and fuses, on the end of each bench has already been described and illustrated. (See pages 99 and 100, Figure 58.) Figure 65 shows a plan of a room properly wired; horizontal wires are represented by lines parallel to the walls; vertical wires are represented by oblique lines. There are separate lines directly from the switchboard to the lantern stand (J) and to the demonstration bench (F), either of which can be turned on without sending any current to the pupils' benches. The advantage of this arrangement is quite obvious. From the switchboard (A) the mains to the pupils' benches pass down the middle aisle between the two rows of benches. Two wires are given off to each bench and a fuse box is put in the circuit of these two wires before they branch off to the pupils' terminals. From the two wires supplying the bench four circuits in parallel pass to the pupils' terminals, a switch being placed in the course of each. It is evident, as the circuits are in parallel, that one pupil's circuit getting out of order will not affect any of the others. When all are closed, if one happens to be turned off it will not seriously affect the strength of the current of the others. The mains must be made heavy enough to carry the whole current. It is evident that the current through the mains is the sum of all the currents through the pupils' circuits, and as each pupil should have at least 1 ampere available, these main wires must be capable of easily carrying 24 amperes. It is safest to put 30 ampere wires in the line and 30 ampere fuses in the main; 10 ampere fuses in the pupils' circuits are about right. The fuses for the lantern and for the teacher's bench should be 20 or 25 amperes. Of course a fuse and switch are placed in each circuit where it joins the switchboard. At the pupils' places, on the teacher's bench, and on the lantern stand, socket fuses are used; at the switchboard ordinary wire fuses will be most economical.

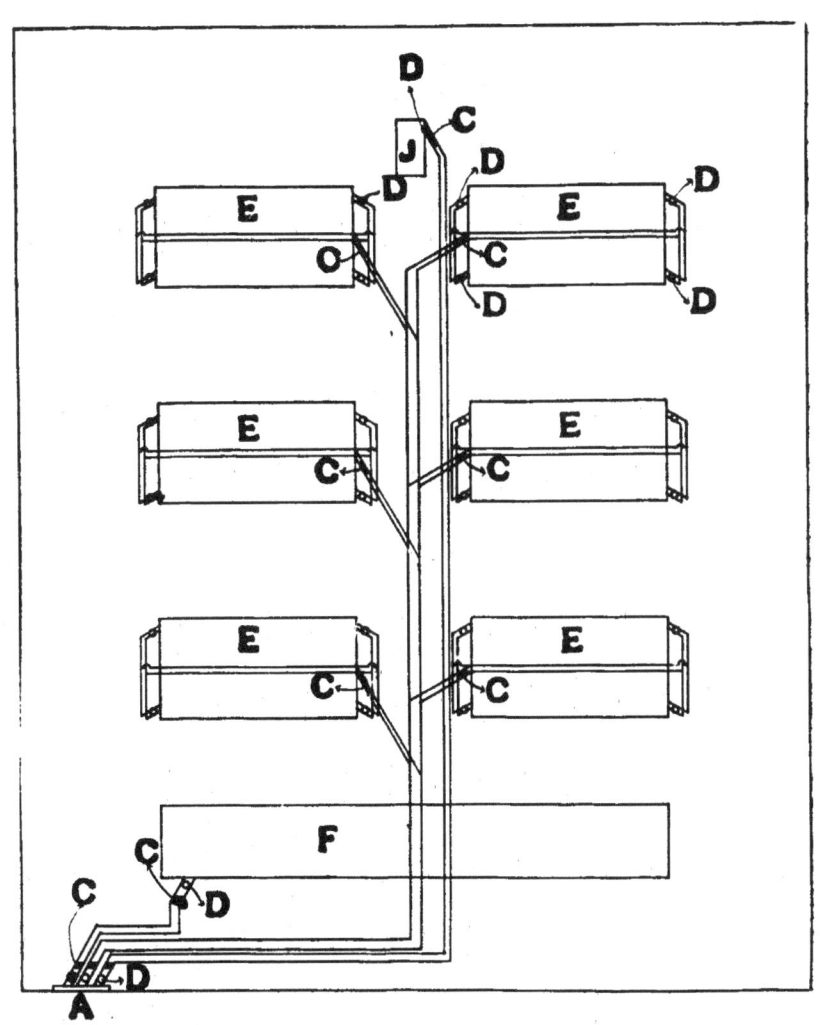

PLAN TO SHOW ELECTRICAL WIRING 111

○ Switch
● Fuse

Fig. 65.—Plan of physical laboratory to show the electrical wiring to the benches. A. Switchboard (oblique lines represent vertically running Wires). C. Fuses. D. Switches. E. Students' benches. F. Teacher's bench. J. Lantern table.

CHAPTER VI

BIOLOGICAL LABORATORY

SITUATION

WHILE good lighting is of great importance in the physical and chemical laboratories, it is still more necessary in the biological laboratory. Almost all the work consists in making the most careful examination of the details of objects which are frequently very minute, and the most perfect light possible is a necessity. It is always the light received by the pupil farthest from the windows that is to be considered. A long, narrow room with the windows on one of the long sides is probably most suitable. Consider a school having a hall running east and west and having class-rooms on each side of the hall; then a narrow room right across the east end of the building would be well situated for a biological laboratory. It would have windows on three sides. If such a position is not available, a room with windows on two sides should be selected.

SIZE

The size will be determined by a number of factors. At the present time in Ontario the classes in biology in the upper school are not large and, if used for this purpose alone, a relatively small room would be required. Much time is at present devoted to biology in the lower school, and the biological laboratory should, if possible, be constructed and equipped to accommodate these classes also. A suitable bench adequately supplied with proper apparatus is just as necessary for successful work in biology as in the other sciences. The present tendency in biological teaching is to lay stress on the study of living plants and animals, and for such teaching a special room with proper equipment is very necessary.

LIGHTING

As has been stated, adequate lighting is more important here than in any other room of the school. Microscopes and dissecting lenses are being used continually, germination of plants is carried on, museum cases are frequently on exhibition, and all of these require a good light; therefore the windows should be large and numerous. They should extend as near to the ceiling as possible, and a skylight would also be of assistance. The bases of the windows in front of the benches should be a little above the level of the pupil's eyes when he is seated at the bench, so that only reflected light will strike the eye as it examines the objects under observation on the bench. The bases of the side windows and of those used for experiments in physiological botany can be considerably lower, in order that pupils may be able to observe objects on them more readily.

FURNITURE

As is the case in the other laboratories, so here the chief piece of furniture is the pupil's working bench. There will also be a demonstration bench for the teacher. Tables for aquaria and for experiments in plant physiology will be placed near the windows. Some special arrangement is necessary for growing plants and

Fig. 66.—Pupils' individual bench for biology

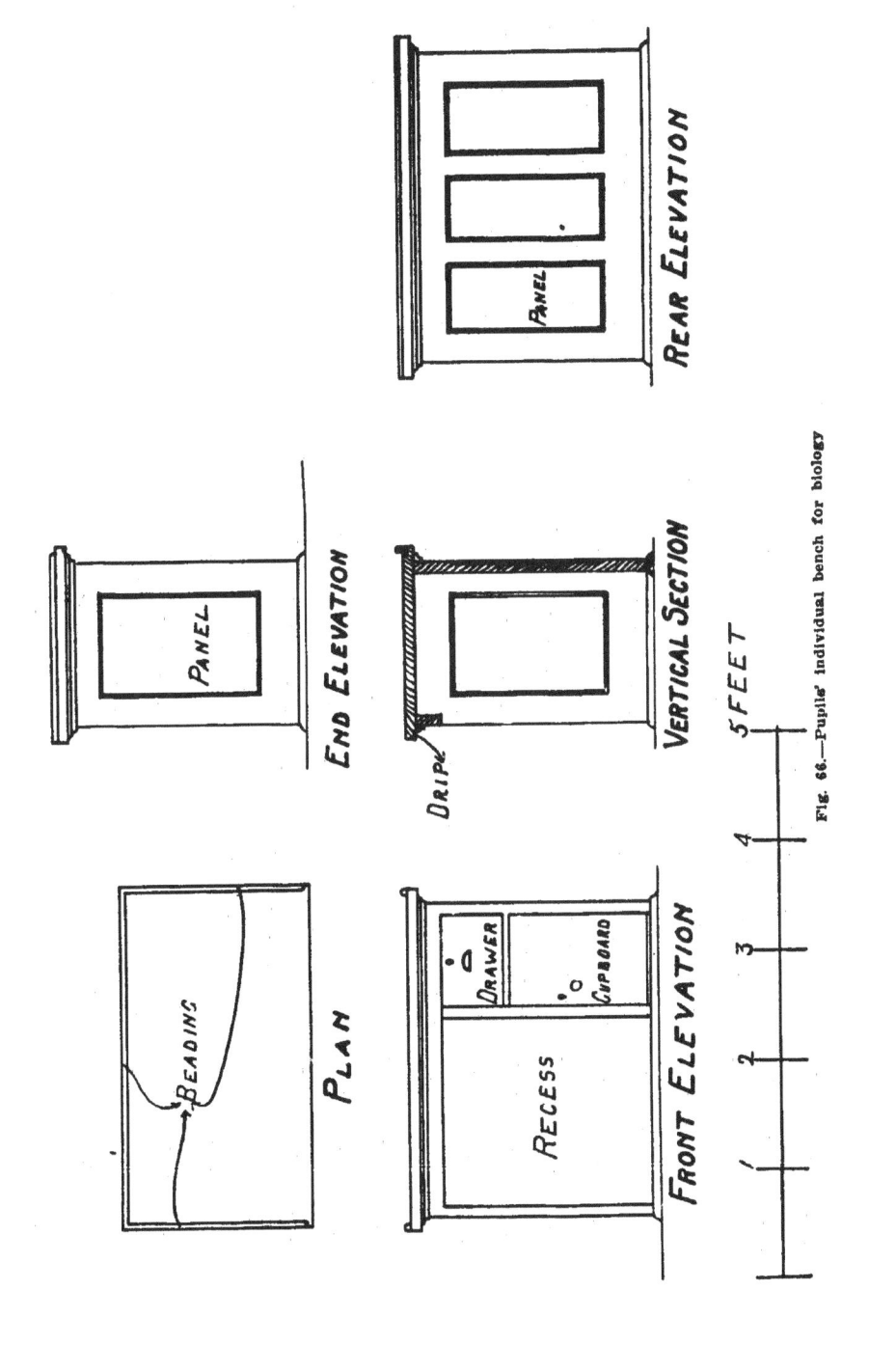

for germinating seeds; these may be grown in an ordinary window or in a special bay-window; but a small conservatory at the south or east end is by far the more effective arrangement, and there is no good reason why one should not be attached to every good secondary school. A special glazed case, in which the temperature is kept fairly constant, placed near a window, will be useful; it is called a Wardian case. If there is no separate museum, the exhibition cases for biological material should also be placed in this laboratory. Storage cabinets will also be placed either in the room itself or in the adjoining one. The structure of each of these will be taken up in turn.

Pupil's Bench

For reasons already stated in discussing the chemical laboratory (Chapter IV), the individual bench is to be preferred. However it is also the most expensive. So here both the individual bench and a multiple bench that will accommodate five or six students are described. While there is no doubt as to the superiority of the former over the latter bench, in some schools the room may be better adapted to the latter, or the cost of the former may be considered too great, and it is then necessary to select the most successful form of multiple bench. Fig. 66 shows different views of a good individual bench. It is very simple in construction and contains all the space and storage accommodation necessary for high school purposes. The top is a little over 3 ft. long and about 22 in. wide. The height will be less than that of any other laboratory bench, and it will be lower than the desk in the classroom. The reason for this is that the top must be of such a height that the pupil while seated comfortably at the bench should be high enough to look through a microscope placed vertically on the bench top. Twenty-two inches above the floor is found to be the best height for the top. The illustration shows on the left, under the top, a recess for the feet, while on the right is a cupboard below and a drawer above. The cupboard contains the compound microscope, while the drawer contains a lens and any dissecting apparatus supplied by the school for the use of the individual pupils. The cupboard has a single, hinged door. The top is made of strips 1 in. wide, glued and dowelled together, as in the case of the bench tops already described. Around the edge on three sides is a raised beading, which prevents objects from rolling off and also diminishes the danger of a microscope or other valuable apparatus being pushed over the edge. Yale cylinder locks are placed on the drawers, the keys of which are all different and are all controlled by the same master-key as is used for the drawers in the chemical laboratory benches. The material out of which the bench is constructed corresponds with that of the other laboratories, but the top should be of some hardwood, as maple or birch, which is not porous. The finish of the body has been discussed on page 10. The top is best finished with the black acid-proof finish described on page 12. This, renewed from time to time with hard oil well rubbed off, will keep a fine appearance. Under no circumstances should the top be varnished, for alcohol and other chemicals used in microscopic work dissolve varnish very readily.

The Multiple Bench

Figures 67 and 68 illustrate a form of bench used largely in the United States and originated there by the late Professor Bessey of the University of Nebraska. It is made to accommodate several pupils. Each pupil has a recess for his knees and feet and a drawer and cupboard to his right, as is the case in the individual bench already

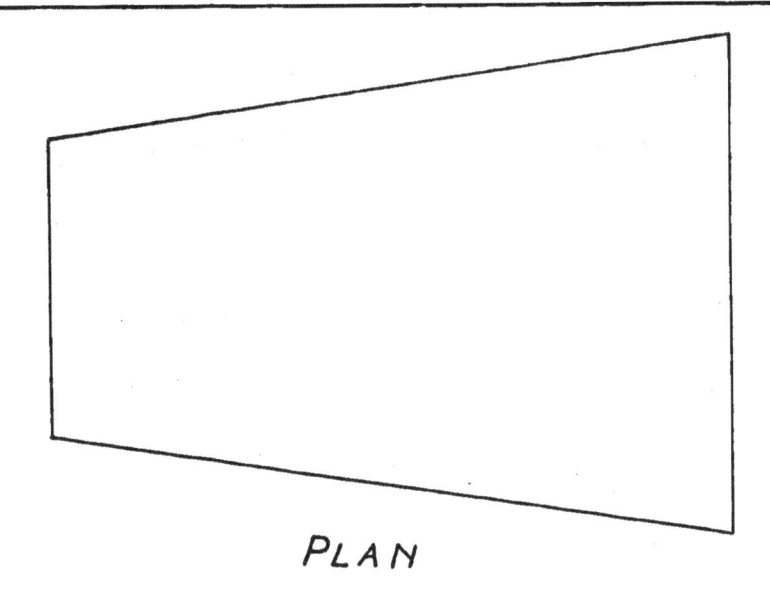

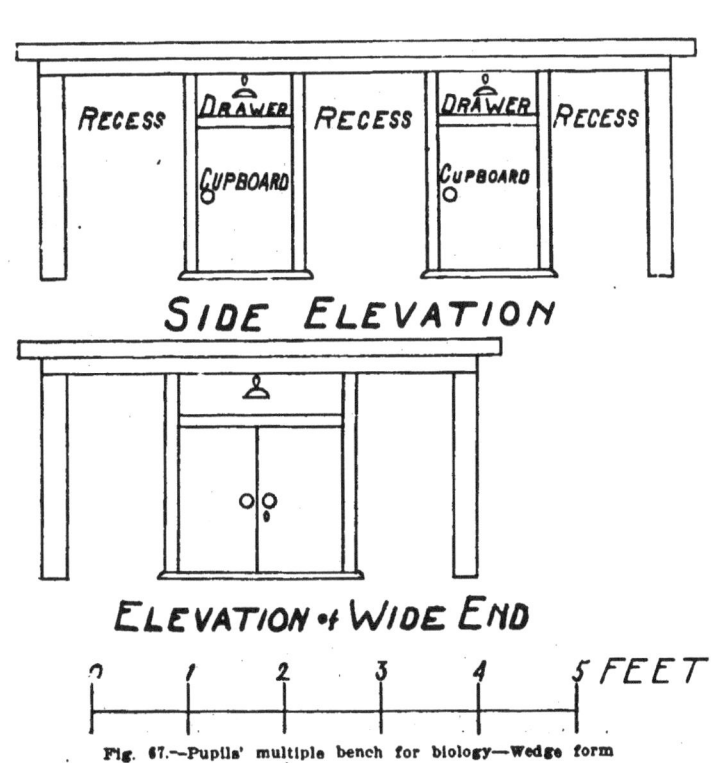

Fig. 67.—Pupils' multiple bench for biology—Wedge form

described. While in the bench first described the pupils face the light, in this one the pupils ranged at the sides receive the light laterally. In order that the one nearest the window may not obstruct the light of the pupil next him, the top of the bench is not rectangular but shaped like a trapezium, with the parallel sides running in the direction of the window. It is 5 ft. wide at the window and tapers to 3 ft. at the farthest end, and with such a shape good light is received by all the pupils. However, the pupils receive all the light from the side, and this is never so good for dissecting or for microscopic work as is the light from the front. One advantage of such benches over the small rectangular form is that they furnish more commodious spaces between the benches for the teacher when assisting members of the class. The height of the top and the amount of the bench space for each pupil will be the same as in the individual benches. The material and finish will also be the same. The drawings will make the construction and size intelligible.

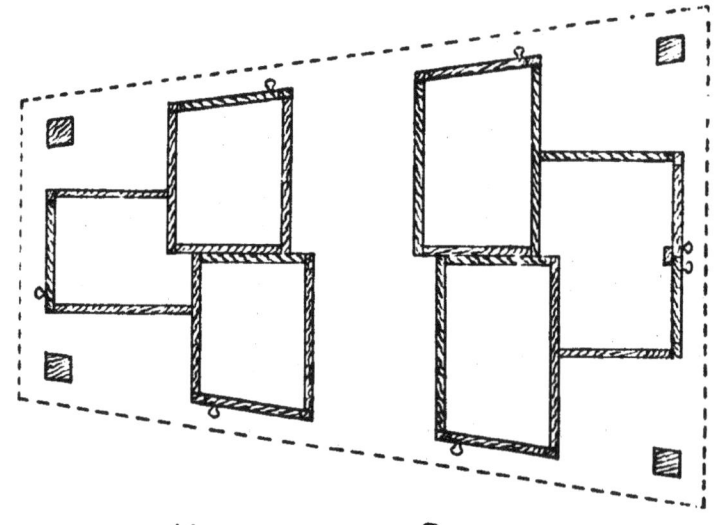

HORIZONTAL SECTION

Fig. 68.—Pupils' multiple bench for biology—Wedge form

TEACHER'S DEMONSTRATION BENCH

The structure of this bench will be in most respects the same as the corresponding benches of the physical laboratory and the lecture-room. (See Figures 59 and 60.)

It should be 3 ft. high, 2½ or 3 ft. wide, and as long as the room will admit. It should have a sink at one end and a slab of alberene stone near the centre. The latter will prove useful for many purposes. A number of gas-taps should be arranged along the edge. Drawers and cupboards should occupy all the side nearest the teacher. For complete details as to material and structures see pages 71-76, and Figures 59 and 60. While every biological laboratory must have one or more aquaria, they certainly should not occupy a large part of the demonstration bench,.

as they do in many American high schools. This bench is usually not situated in the most suitable position for an aquarium, which would be very much better on a stand of its own, so that it can be moved about. Again, such an aquarium occupies so much of the bench that there is not enough space remaining for demonstration purposes.

PLANT HOUSE

A suitable place for the growth of plants and for the carrying on of experiments in plant physiology is a prime necessity for the modern high school. Moreover, as every school should have decorative flowers in the windows, there should be some place for starting them. The ordinary school window is unsatisfactory for this purpose. The temperature is variable, and as the fire is kept low or let out at nights, on Saturdays, and on Sundays, the plants are likely to suffer. The humidity of the ordinary room is also much too low, the conditions approaching those of a desert. Moreover, the light cannot be properly regulated. In spite of all these drawbacks much can be done even in an ordinary window. However, in a conservatory, the light, heat, and humidity can be regulated to a very large extent. Nothing very elaborate is required, and it will not increase the total cost of the laboratory to any great extent. In every new high school in the Province an endeavour should be made to have a small conservatory, if it is only a bay window, fitted up in a suitable manner. Such a room should be immediately adjacent to the biological laboratory and be situated preferably on the east or south side, as this gives the most suitable light for the purpose.

THE BAY WINDOW

The simplest form of such a room is a bay window with glass on three sides and in the roof. It is divided from the biological laboratory by a glass partition and has its own source of heat. The window space is as great as possible, the walls between the windows being only wide enough to give the requisite strength. The windows will come to within two feet of the floor, and on a line with the sill is a shelf on which the germinating boxes are placed. Beneath this shelf are placed the heat coils.

THE CONSERVATORY

Suppose the biological laboratory is situated on one of the upper floors and that it consists of a long, narrow room running from north to south, and that the south end of it forms part of an outer wall (Fig. 75). The conservatory should be placed at the south end of this room. The joists under the floor of the laboratory project out beyond the wall 6 ft., and are strengthened below by brackets. On these the conservatory is supported. It is 6 ft. wide and runs along the whole end of the laboratory. It should not be more than 7 or 8 ft. high. The windows occupy the whole side and ends to the fullest possible extent. The sill is 2 ft. above the floor. The latter is made preferably of cement, and if it has a slight slope toward the outside along which is a gutter leading to a waste pipe, it will be of great assistance in carrying off spilled water. The windows in the sides and ends are of the ordinary type. The roof is sloping and is made entirely of glass supported by wooden frames. There are no cross frames of wood in the roof windows, but the several panes of glass in a row have the ends overlapping, the lower end of each overlapping the end of the one next to it. By this arrangement any moisture condensed on the roof will run out between the panes and not drip down below. Shelves (Fig 75) at the height of the window-sill are placed right around the room except opposite the door, and on these the plant boxes are supported. These shelves are preferably of slate and rest on strong iron brackets. If slate increases the cost too much, they may be of cypress wood, as it withstands dampness well. The iron brackets must be quite heavy. Near the middle of the room is a sink (D) with hot and cold water taps. The heating coils run around the room under the shelf.

Galvanized iron trays about 2 in. in depth are placed on the shelves, and these contain about 1 in. of coarse sand. On this the flower-pots and boxes are placed. The sand in the trays should always be kept quite moist, and serves the double purpose of increasing humidity of the room and of supplying a receiver into which the flower-pots drain.

The heating of such a conservatory is a matter of some difficulty under the present conditions of the smaller schools. It is about time that a protest should be entered against the prevailing custom of letting fires remain out from Friday until Monday. The school should certainly be comfortable for teachers who have work to do on Saturdays. Any saving of fuel by allowing fires to go out at the week-end is so small that it need scarcely be considered, as the extra fuel necessary to raise the temperature of a building which has become thoroughly chilled to proper room temperature, is about as much as would be required to keep it warm over the week-end. Moreover, the losses from frozen pipes, etc., may be considerable. Living plants and animals are necessities in the biology room for the most efficient teaching; they require that the rooms should never become chilled, and for that reason it should be considered imperative that they be kept throughout the winter at a suitable temperature. If the school is heated by steam or hot water and has fires over the week-end, the conservatory coils may be connected directly with the boiler. To secure the best results, however, the conservatory coils should have a separate heater, which may be located in the basement or in the biological laboratory, preferably in the latter if a gas heater is used. The heater should never be placed in the conservatory, as fumes from burning gas are injurious to plant life.

It is preferable to use gas for heating if it is at all available. The Vulcan, Ruud, or Fletcher Russell heaters, which cost from ten to twenty dollars, are suitable for this purpose. They may have attached to them an automatic gas regulator which can be set for a definite temperature, and this will keep the heating uniform. The Canadian Rector Heating Co., of Hamilton, Ontario, now have a radiator with a gas heater and thermostat attached; the heater is of the nature of a Bunsen burner, and the fumes pass out-of-doors through a flue. The thermostat is set for any temperature, and the radiator will keep the room constantly at that temperature. Such an arrangement would be most suitable for a conservatory. In order to keep the air humid there must be a large, exposed water surface to produce a sufficient amount of evaporation. The trays with the wet sand already mentioned will be of assistance for the purpose. Besides these, a set of shallow pans should extend around the room beneath the shelf and above the radiator; these are kept constantly filled with water and thus supply a large surface of water for evaporation.

The windows in the roof should open, so that the air can be rapidly changed on warm days. In the spring the windows should be frosted, so that the too great intensity of the sunlight will be softened; this can be rubbed off in the autumn if it has not already been worn away by the weather.

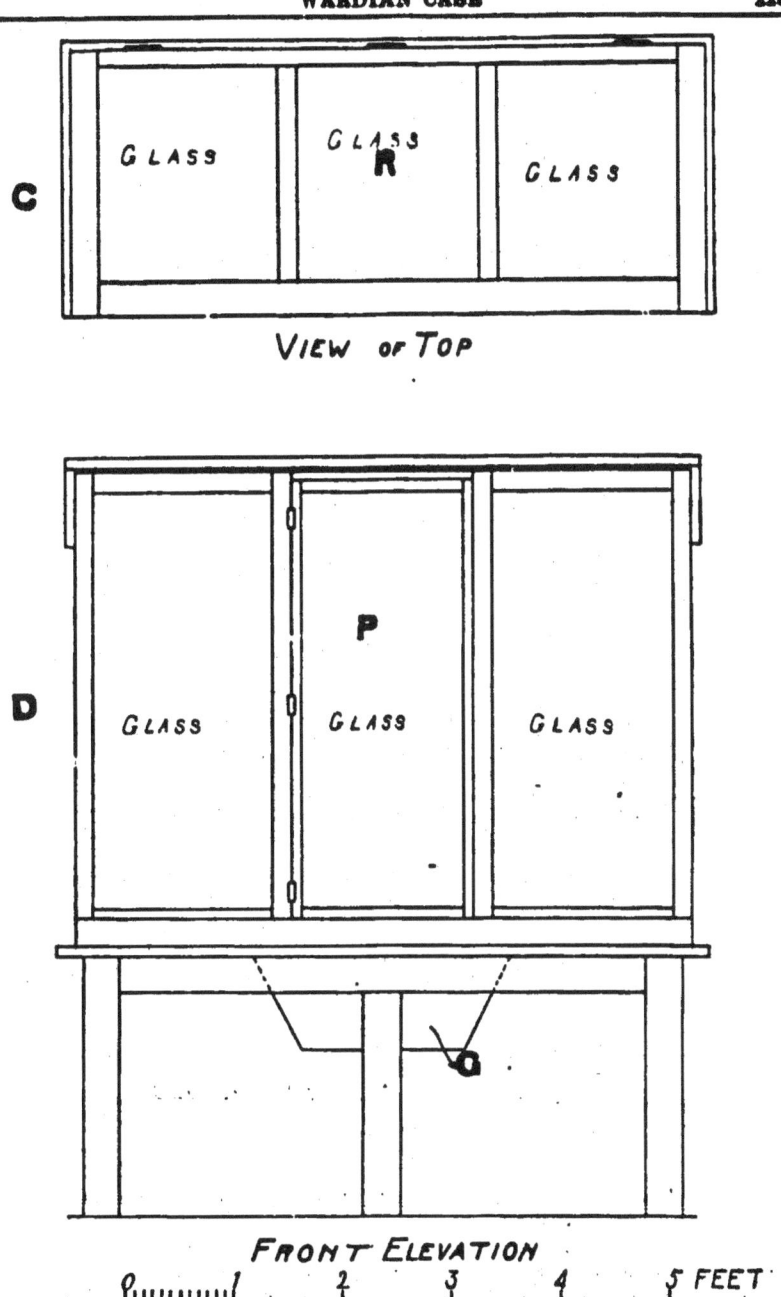

WARDIAN CASE

C

GLASS GLASS GLASS
       R

VIEW OF TOP

D

GLASS GLASS GLASS
       P

       Q

FRONT ELEVATION

0 1 2 3 4 5 FEET

The Wardian Case

While nothing will replace a small conservatory and the small expense connected with it should not prevent its construction whenever a small secondary school is being built, a Wardian case will form a fairly satisfactory substitute for it. This, Figures 69 and 70, is a large glass case standing on four legs and placed close to a large window. The floor is composed of a metal box filled with water. Under this is a source of heat. Figures 69 and 70 will make clear all the details of con-

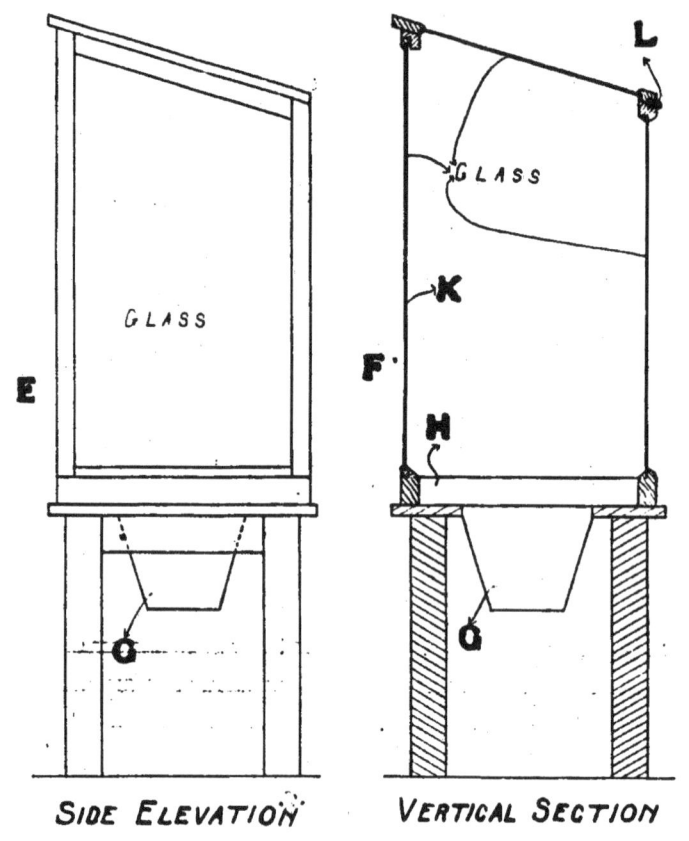

SIDE ELEVATION   VERTICAL SECTION

Fig. 70.—Wardian case. G. Inclosed shelf containing burner. H. Copper tank nearly filled with water. K. Glass side. L. Hinge of top.

struction. The size will be determined somewhat by the dimensions of the window against which it is to be placed and also by the number of plants to be grown in it. The one represented in the Figure is about 6 ft. long, 2 ft. wide, and 4 ft. high. It is not wise to make it any higher or wider than this, but the length will be determined by the available window-space. It should be constructed very tight, and the framework, while strong, should be narrow, so that the glass surface may be as large as possible in order to permit the maximum light to penetrate the case.

A tightly-fitting door (P) is placed on the side away from the window. The top (R) has a slope toward the window. This is hinged so that it can be lifted up to give good ventilation or to let the air within escape if it becomes overheated. The bottom is composed of a copper or galvanized iron tank (H) entirely closed except for a small opening through which it can be filled with water. Beneath this is a shelf protected from draughts by inclosed sides (G). On this is placed the heater. Where gas is available, a strong Bunsen burner is most suitable, but a properly constructed coal-oil lamp will serve the purpose. The heater is kept burning only when the school heat is low, as at night and during week-ends, and must be turned up so as to give the right temperature within. The height to which the Bunsen or lamp is to be turned can only be learned by practice. If it is heated by gas an automatic regulator can be introduced.

The framework of such a case will usually be of wood, though iron would be preferable if the expense of the latter was not considered too great.

Museum Case

Exhibition cases are necessary for displaying the specimens of plants and animals. Where there is an extensive collection, several cases are necessary, and these will be different for the different kinds of material; birds, mammals, fishes, minerals, and plants all require different forms. In this *Educational Pamphlet* will be described museum cases such as are suitable for a school in which one case contains all the animal specimens and in which a second case contains the systematic collection of plants of the district. These will be the conditions obtaining in all but the largest schools.

Figure 71 shows a complete plan, elevation, and sectional drawing of such an animal case. It represents one built against a wall. The first condition is to have an abundance of light, the next is to have the case so tightly constructed that it is dust- and insect-proof. The case described is 7½ ft. high, and any greater height is not to be recommended. It is about 3 ft. in depth; with such a depth shelves can be arranged on each side, and it is possible to get into the case to arrange the material. The length will be determined by the space it is to occupy and the number of specimens to be exhibited. The whole front, ends, and top are made of glass, the wooden framework being as narrow as is consistent with the requisite strength. The panes of glass are made as large as possible in order to give an unobstructed view, and plate glass is, of course, most suitable for the purpose. For panes of double diamond glass as large as those represented in the Figu. supports of wood 2 in. wide and 1 in. thick are necessary and are sufficiently large. There is no necessity to have large or numerous doors. One door occupying the lower half of the middle panel has proved quite satisfactory. The objections to large doors are that they never fit so tightly as the glass panels do, and that they diminish the amount of shelf space in front of the case. The shelves are preferably of plate glass, for wooden shelves cut off too much light from the parts below. The plate-glass shelves are polished on one edge and are from 8 to 10 in. wide. Those at the front are stationary, and are placed one well above and the other well below the eye, so that there will be little interference with the view of the shelves at the back of the case. The back shelves should be adjustable in height. The best arrangement for fastening the adjustable shelves is to fasten vertically along the back of the case metal shelf-strips with sockets into which metal brackets fit. The heights at which these shelves are placed will, of course, depend on the size of the specimens.

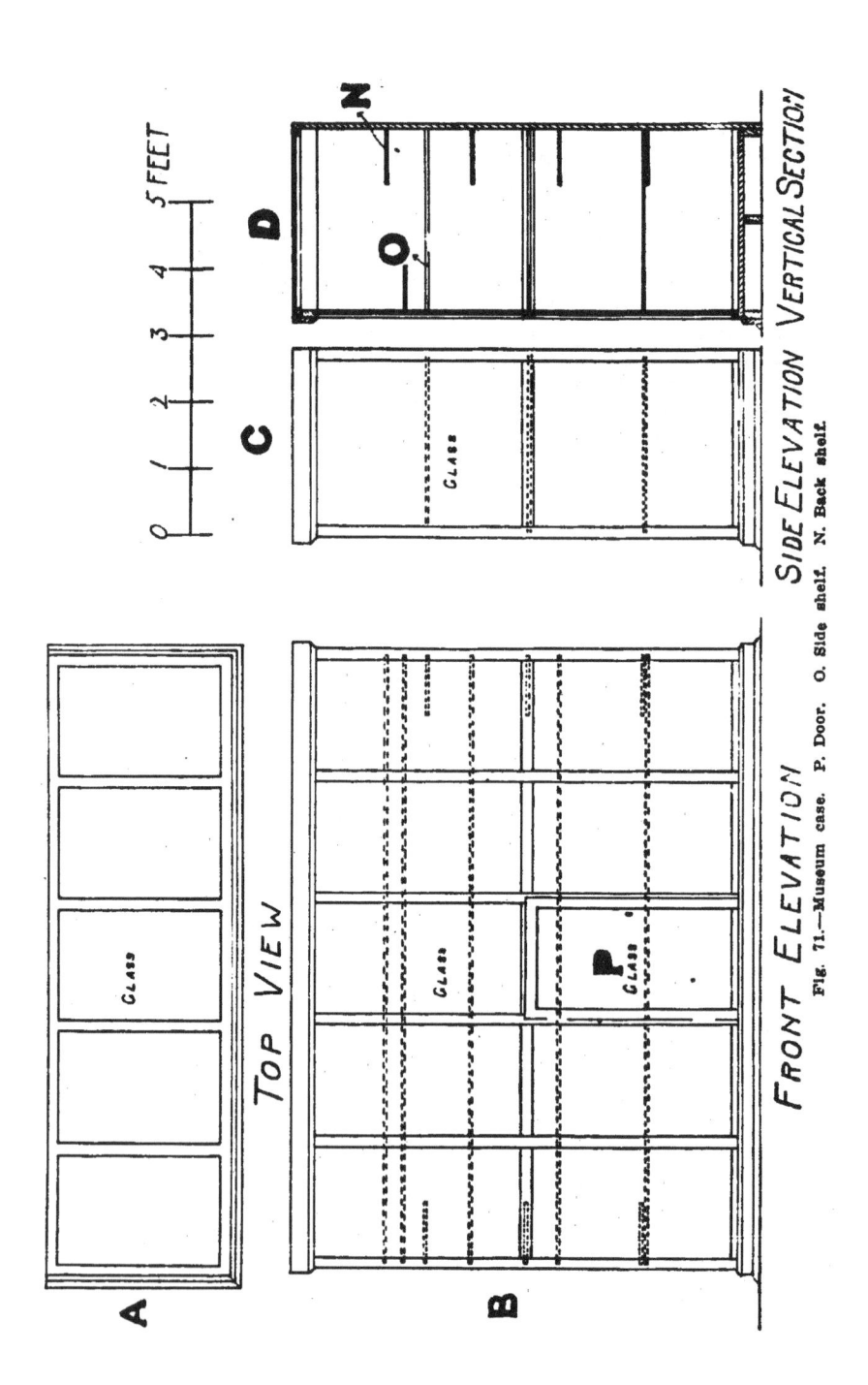

Fig. 71.—Museum case. P. Door. O. Side shelf. N. Back shelf.

Every precaution must be taken to keep dust and insects out of the case. The material for its construction should be very carefully selected, and it should be put together in the most approved method. The wooden framework must be perfectly dry and of a kind that will not warp, shrink, or crack. Teak is the best for the purpose; maple and pine are also good. The weak point is usually the back. The tendency is to put in an inferior quality of tongued and grooved material in this part, and when it shrinks in drying the tongue and groove pulls apart, knots drop out, and the dust accumulates within, through all these openings. Thoroughly dried, tongued and grooved boards at least $7/8$ in. thick and quite narrow are to be placed in this part. Much infiltration of dust takes place also in the joints between the glass and the wood. Figure 72 shows a joint which can be made dust proof. The glass (M) is not applied directly to the wood, but fits against a pad of felt which is glued to the underlying wood. The stops (K) are bevelled to an edge, and thus there are no projecting ridges to lodge dust which would gradually work through. The door should also fit tightly against a felt pad. The interior should be painted pure white with a paint containing no lead, and it should be finished with a slight egg-shell gloss.

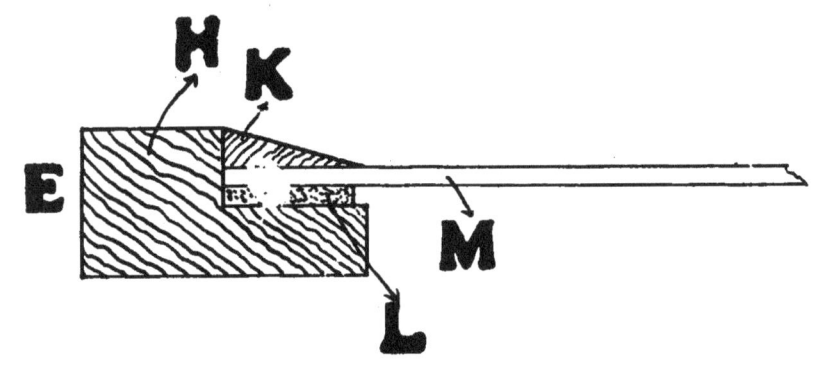

SECTION SHOWING HOW GLASS IS MADE DUST PROOF

Fig. 72.—Section through a part of sash of museum case showing the method of fixing glass that there may be a dust-proof joint. H. Sash. K. Bevelled stop. L. Pad of felt. M. Pane of glass.

HERBARIUM CABINET

The herbarium cabinet is represented in Figure 73. In every high and continuation school a collection should be made of dried and pressed specimens of all the flowering plants of the district. These will be of great assistance to the pupils in identifying the specimens they have to collect. Not only the flowering plants but also the ferns, horsetails, and the common, fleshy fungi should be pressed. The drawing represents a case with compartments for these different kinds of material. The case is 4 ft. 1 in. high, 2 ft. 11 in. wide, and 1 ft. 10 in. deep. It has a pair of doors which, when open, leave the whole front surface of the interior exposed. This consists of two rows of shelves or drawers. In the Figure they are represented as shelves, and these possess certain advantages over drawers. These shelves (R) move freely in the horizontal grooves in the uprights on each side of them, so that they can be pulled out like drawers. Each shelf gives a storage

124 LABORATORY ACCOMMODATION

space above it 18 in. by 13 in., and as the standard size for a herbarium sheet is 16½ in. by 11½ in., this space will take such a sheet with ease. At the back of the shelf is an upright, so that when the shelf is pulled out the specimens will not slide back. This shelf arrangement is much cheaper than drawers, and the specimens are much more accessible; however they are not so free from dust, but if the doors fit quite snugly against felt pads the case will be almost dust-proof. At

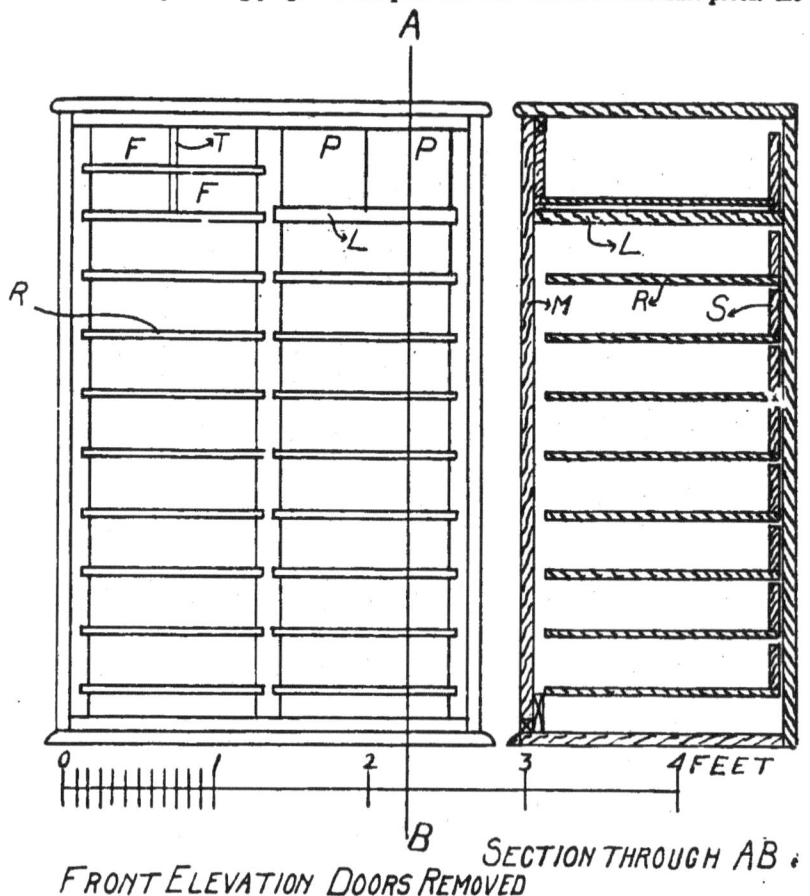

FRONT ELEVATION DOORS REMOVED   SECTION THROUGH AB.

Fig. 73.—Herbarium cabinet. F. Shelves with partitions (T) for small specimens, such as mosses and liverworts. L. A fixed shelf on which the drawers (P) rest. M. Pair of doors. P. Two drawers for storing fungi. R. Sliding shelf with upright (S) at back.

(F) are two shelves having a partition (T) running from front to back; they also have a cross partition, thus dividing them into four quarter-size pockets. These will take specimens of mosses, hepaticæ, and algæ which are usually mounted on half-size sheets. (L) is a fixed partition on which two drawers (P) rest. These are for the storage of fungi. The fleshy fungi, after being mounted on sheets, are placed in manilla envelopes, and these are placed on edge in these drawers. The ends and doors of the case may be plain or panelled. The material and finish will be similar to that of the other furniture.

AQUARIUM TABLE

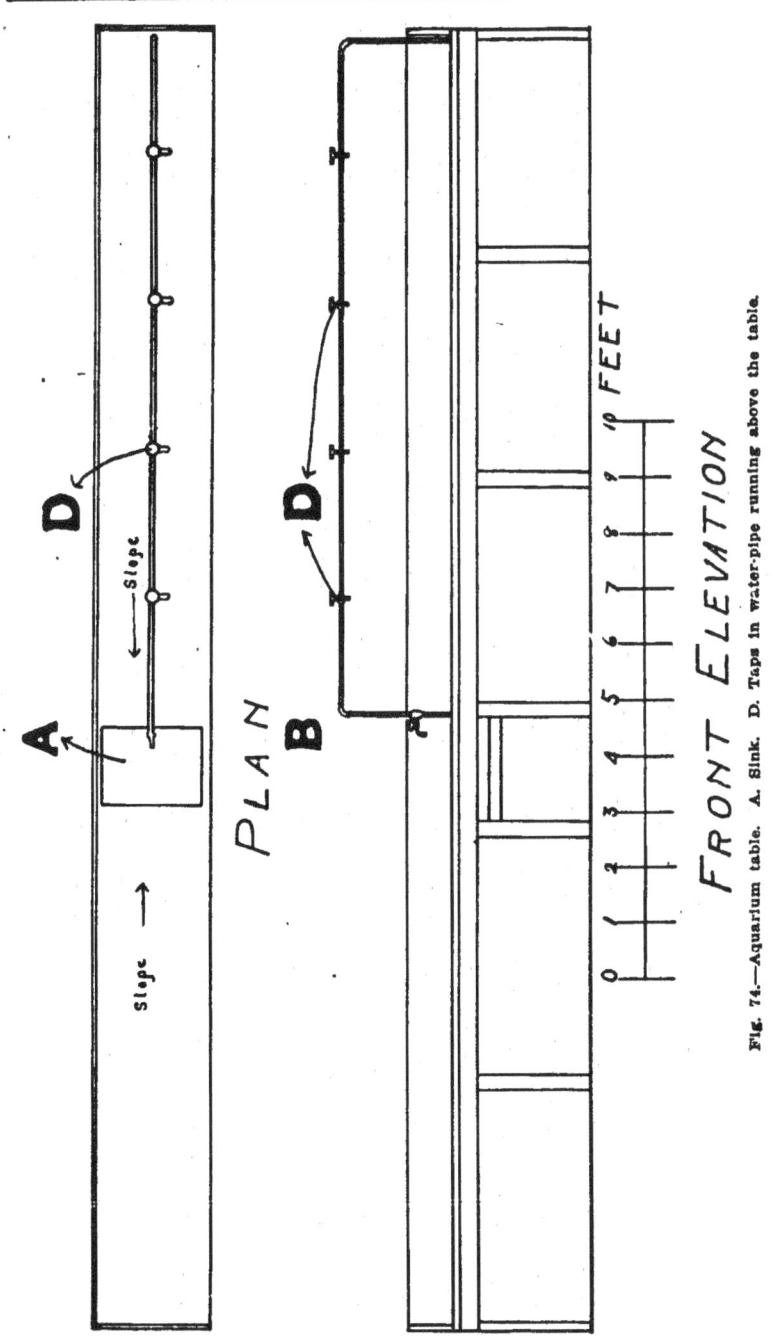

Fig. 74.—Aquarium table. A. Sink. D. Taps in water-pipe running above the table.

AQUARIUM TABLE

The high school of the future will undoubtedly spend much time in the study of living plants and animals, and then the aquarium will play a prominent part. A table that has been found particularly convenient is illustrated in Figure 74. Pupils' aquaria are placed on this table to be filled, washed, or to have the water changed. The top has a raised beading passing around the edge to prevent the water from running over. There is a sink (A) near the middle, and there is a slight slope from both ends toward the sink. On this top, aquaria can be emptied or overflowed without fear of the water running over the edge. Running above the top of the table for half its length is a water-pipe with taps (D) along it. This table will usually be placed against the wall and, in that case, an apron runs along at the back of it.

The height should be 3 ft., the width about 2 ft., and the length will be suited to the needs of the particular school. The top should be of material at least 2 in. thick at the edges and hollowed out to a depth of a little over 1 in. The best material for this is white-wood, the product of the tulip-tree. The top is to be made of narrow strips fastened firmly together by waterproof glue. The wood must be thoroughly seasoned before being used for this purpose.

OTHER TABLES

Several other tables may be used to advantage for such purposes as holding aquaria and vivaria, for setting up experiments in vegetable physiology, and for demonstrations. These may be made very simple or may have drawers and lockers under them if required.

STORAGE CABINET

A good deal of storage space is required in which to place plant and animal material for dissection, apparatus, etc. A cabinet exactly similar to the one used for chemical apparatus is quite suitable. This has been already described and illustrated on pages 79-81.

SITUATION OF ROOM

If possible a room should be chosen with windows on two or even three sides, and a room with windows on the south and east is best. One suitable position for a biological laboratory has been suggested on page 112, where the hall runs east and west. If the hall runs north and south in the building and the science rooms are on the east side of the hall, then the south-eastern room would be the one to choose for biology. Figure 75 represents a plan of a room in this position. It has one door on the west side leading into the hall. The south end of the room is completely occupied by a conservatory (A), and so will be made of glass; the east side, which is used largely for lighting the pupils' benches, will have as many and as high window as possible, except for a narrow space at the north end, which is the front of the room and occupied by the demonstrator's bench (K).

The size of the room will depend upon its uses. If it is to be utilized entirely for Upper School work and the classes are small, a room of the dimensions shown in Figure 76 will be appropriate; but if it is to be used for Lower School biology, as should be the case, or if for a large school, then a room 28 ft. by 41 ft., as represented in Figure 75, will prove more suitable.

BIOLOGICAL LABORATORY

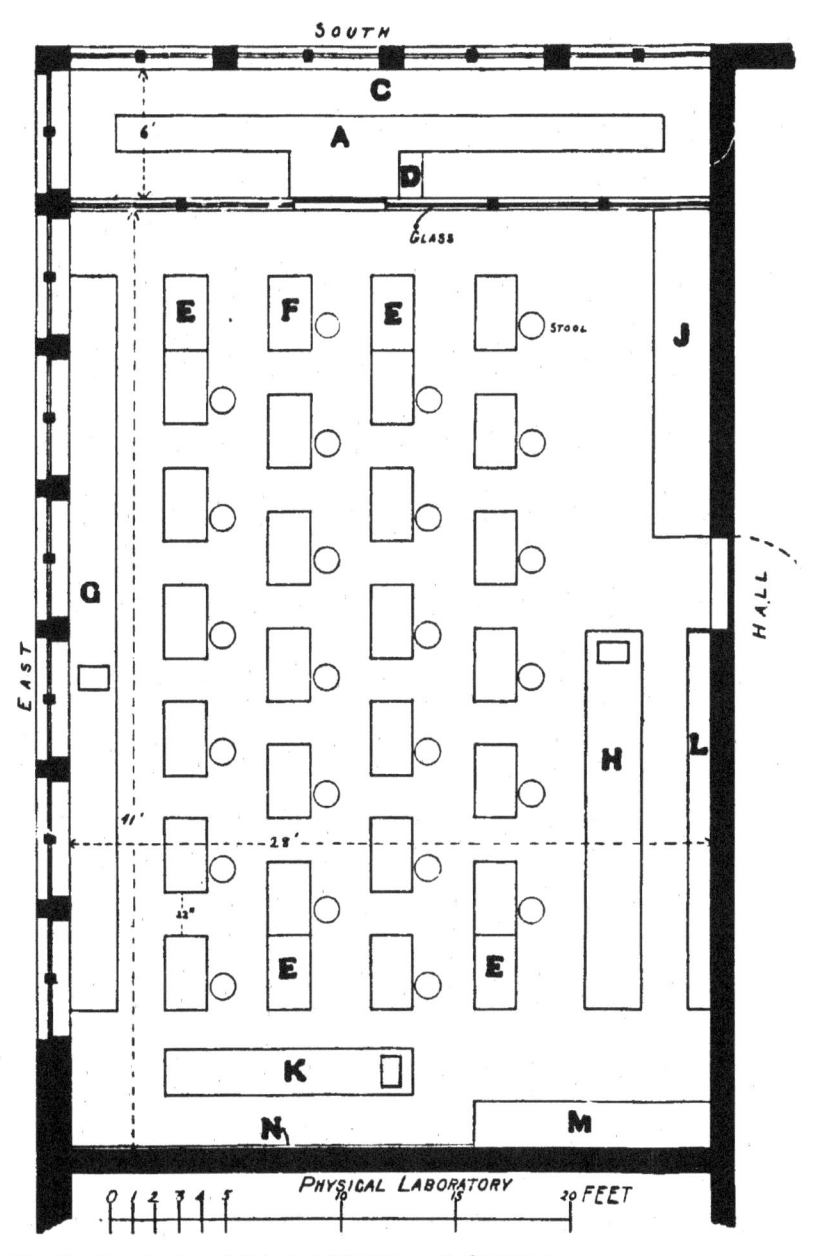

Fig. 75.—Ground plan of biological laboratory. A. Conservatory. C. Shelves in conservatory. D. Sink. E. Four simple tables for aquaria, etc. F. Pupils' bench. G. Aquarium table. H. Demonstration bench. K. Teacher's bench. J and L, Museum cases. M. Apparatus case. N. Black-board.

Figure 75 shows a room furnished with the individual benches and Figure 76 one furnished with the wedge benches. While both benches are serviceable, the individual ones are to be preferred for several reasons. The discipline will be easier, and the light will be better and from a more suitable direction, as it comes from the front rather than from the side. While in the ordinary class-room, side light is always demanded, in the biological laboratory the work is so different that a side light would usually be more trying on the eyes than one in front. The practical work in the Ontario High Schools consists almost entirely in dissecting plants and animals, and if the light is from either side the object viewed is always in the shadow of one of the hands. This is particularly irritating when working with a lens where bright lighting is required. Where the individual benches are used, as in Figure 75, they face east. The twenty-four benches (F) are arranged in four rows of six each. In order that a pupil may not be in the shadow of the one in front they are arranged in quincunx, one row being opposite the spaces between the benches in front. There is a lateral space of 22 in. between adjoining seats in the same row across the room and 3 ft. between each two rows, in order to give sufficient room for the teacher to pass freely. The natural position for the demonstrator's bench (K) is at the north end. When a pupil faces east it is a very simple matter to wheel through 90° and face north and still have the use of the bench for writing, as the latter is then to his right hand, while if one wheeled in the opposite direction the bench could only be used with great inconvenience, as it would be situated to the pupils' left. Behind the demonstrator's bench is the black-board (N), and in the corner, on his right, is a storage cabinet (M). This being so close to his bench will make the apparatus convenient for use. The museum cabinet should be in a position where adequate, though not direct, light will shine in from the front and ends. Two such cabinets are in a good position in Figure 75. The aquarium table, Figures 75 and 76, is placed along the east side under the windows. The specimens in the aquarium are thus in a good light for the pupil, and the table is in a suitable position to receive apparatus for physiological experiments with plants. The table (H) is also to be used for the same purpose, and is placed in a part of the room less brilliantly lighted. It is also in a good position for holding aquaria. E. E. E. E. represent small tables that may be used for various purposes. The conservatory is shut off by glass at the south end, and it is entered by a door in the middle.

Figure 76 shows a plan of a much smaller room. It represents the south-east corner in a school where the main hall runs east and west and has class-rooms on each side of it. It is represented as being equipped with the wedge benches (C), in order to show how they are arranged. One is placed opposite each of the large double windows with the broad end toward the light. The pupils are arranged along each side and one may be placed at the small end. The space between the benches is 3 ft. wide at the broad end and 5 ft. wide at the narrow end; this allows easy passage for the teacher between the benches. The position of the demonstrator's bench (G), the museum cabinets (J), etc., call for no comment. At the south is a bay window in which a Wardian case (B) is placed. Such a laboratory is meant to accommodate fifteen pupils.

If the wedge benches are used in a laboratory to accommodate a class of twenty-five pupils, it should be a long, narrow room with five large windows, preferably on the east. A bench is placed opposite each window, as in Figure 76. Such a room may be difficult to arrange for in a school building as ordinarily constructed. If a hall runs east and west with class-rooms on each side of it, then the biology

BIOLOGICAL LABORATORY

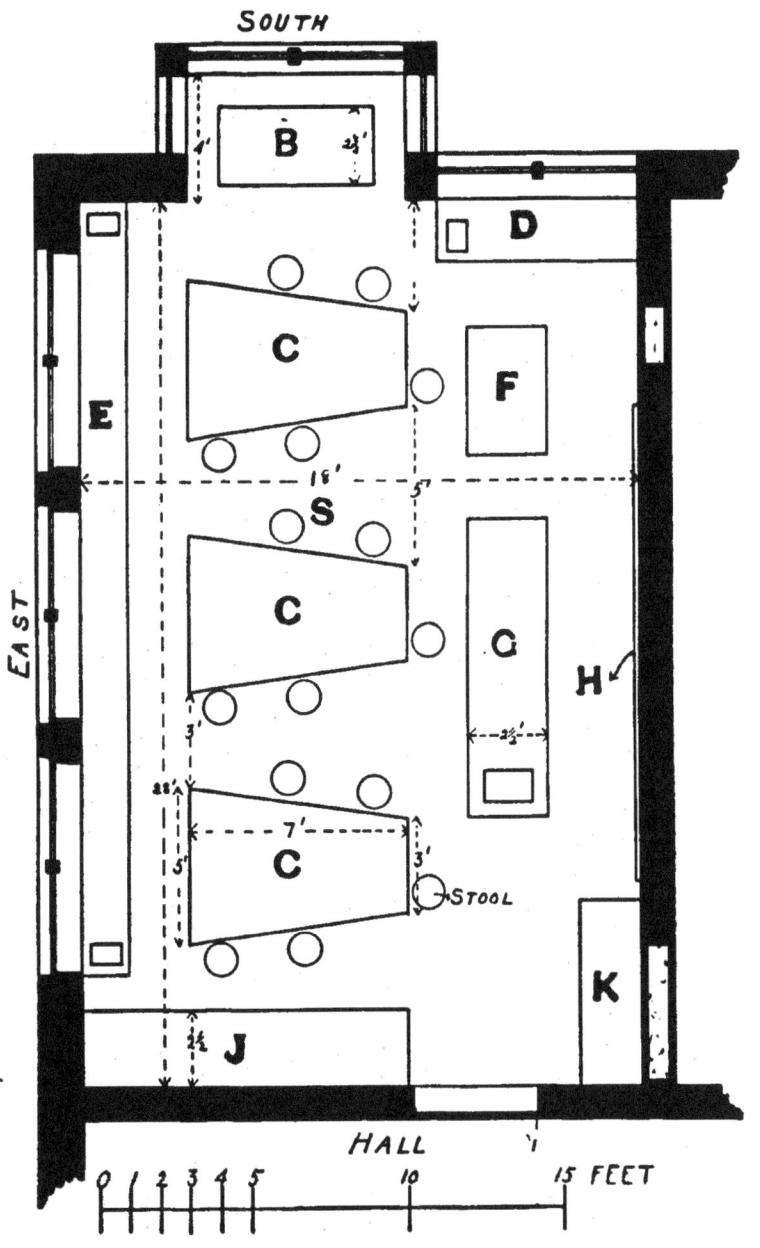

Fig. 76.—Ground plan of a small biological laboratory. B. Wardian case. C. Students' wedge benches. D. Table for botanical experiments. E. Aquarium table. G. Teachers' demonstration bench. H. Black-board. J. Museum case. K. Apparatus cabinet.

room might extend right across the east end of the school, the hall not running right to the east end, but terminating at the biology room. As the room does not require to be more than 18 or 20 ft. wide, it will only occupy a moderate amount of space.

The above description is of a biological laboratory thoroughly equipped. All of the furniture might be simplified, and some of the articles might be omitted altogether.

CHAPTER VII

LECTURE-ROOM

USES AND ADVANTAGES

THE advantages of adding a science lecture-room to the several laboratories in high schools and collegiate institutes are becoming more and more apparent. When the teacher is performing an experiment, it is necessary to have the pupils as close as possible to the bench, as the phenomena to be observed are frequently only visible at a short distance. If seated in the laboratory, those toward the back of the room probably cannot see the details as well as they should. In a lecture-room the pupils are all arranged compactly and are close to the demonstrator's bench. Such a room is also much more convenient for demonstrating with the lantern, as the light can be more effectively controlled, and the view of the screen is more perfect. A still stronger argument for the lecture-room is the fact that it leaves the laboratories free for other science classes. This is a consideration of great importance in large schools where there are several science teachers, and the classes in physics and chemistry are numerous. Such a room, equipped with a lantern, can be used, moreover, not only for science work but for other illustrated lessons in geography and history. If space can be spared to make the room capable of seating eighty pupils or more, it may be used for combined classes for lantern work as well as for meetings of the literary society, etc.

SITUATION

When there is a single lecture-room, as will usually be the case, it should be situated between the physical and the chemical laboratories and should be accessible from each. When each of these laboratories has a store-room, these latter are placed between their laboratories and the lecture-room, so that the apparatus will be handy for use in both rooms. The front of the lecture-room is situated next the store-room for physical apparatus, as this apparatus is the heaviest and most delicate and should be carried about as little as possible. In the rare cases in which there is a lecture-room connected with each laboratory, the store-room will be between the two.

LIGHTING

This should be one of the best lighted rooms in the school, as the details of apparatus and experiments on the instructor's bench have to be observed carefully even from the back of the room. The best light is that from above and, where a skylight is at all possible, it should always be utilized. A large window will be constructed in the centre of the ceiling. Where lateral light is used, either wholly or in combination with a skylight, it is placed to the left of the pupils. The side windows (Fig. 78) are made as large and as close together as possible, and should extend from 3 ft. above the floor right to the ceiling. It is a serious defect in any school window to have a large space between its top and the ceiling, as this upper light is the most useful in illuminating the far side of the room, where it is most needed. One window is placed opposite the demonstration bench, so that a flood of light will illuminate the apparatus on this. Every lecture-room should also be well lighted by electric lights. These should be suspended singly from the ceiling and distributed evenly, so that every part will be equally bright. A row of lights extends immediately above the demonstration bench. All t. e lights are controlled by switches from both the teacher's bench and the lantern table and are thrown out in sections, one small set being left shining when the lantern is in use, so that the room will be sufficiently lighted to allow the making of notes and drawings, while not being so bright as to interfere with the crispness of the picture on the screen. This set of lights has opaque shades which cut off all direct light from the lantern screen in front. These electric lights are absolutely necessary where dark blinds are used for lantern work, as it is intolerable to be raising and lowering these blinds every few minutes. There should be no glass doors or transoms with glass in the lecture-room, as these prevent it from being properly darkened for lantern work.

Dark Blinds

Besides the ordinary blinds (Fig. 80, F) on the windows, the lecture-room is fitted with opaque blinds (K) to darken the room; they are used only for this purpose and are left raised at all other times, the ordinary blinds being always utilized to soften the direct sunlight. These dark blinds are required not only for work with a lantern but also for many experiments in optics and chemistry.

There are several varieties of dark blinds. The arrangement will depend somewhat on the position of the windows. The most suitable position is that in which the windows are in one continuous series (Fig. 80) with no wall space lying between members of the series; then a single wide blind (Fig. 80, K) serves to cover all the windows. Where there are several separated windows, each requires its own blind. Dark blinds are sometimes made of wooden shutters composed of several vertical pieces hinged together so that they fold back when not in use. These are not to be recommended, for they are clumsy and unsightly, slow to adjust and, no matter how accurately they are made to fit, they will soon shrink, warp, and crack, so that they will not exclude all the light when closed. The best material is an opaque cloth made especially for the purpose, which can be purchased from regular dealers in window blinds. This material should be heavy and strong and of such a character that it will not crack. Figure 77 shows a blind complete. A wooden frame (Fig. 80, P) entirely surrounds the blind. This frame is fastened to the window frame. At the sides the two wooden slats forming the front and back of the frame have a narrow slit between them (Fig. 77) within which the blind slides; the blind should extend at least 3 in. into this slit. The bottom also has a slit within which the bottom of the blind rests when it is down. The top of this frame forms a box entirely closed except below. Into the ends of this box the roller of the blind is attached. The interior of this box as well as the faces of the lateral and lower pieces toward the slit are painted a dead black, so that there will be no leakage of light around the margin of the blind. In the lower margin of the blind is placed an iron rod, whose weight keeps the surface taut.

The mechanisms for raising and lowering the blinds are varied and depend on the number of blinds and their arrangement. The most frequent method is to have each on an ordinary spring roller by which it is raised and lowered as is an ordinary blind. In such a case a hole pierces the middle of the lower frame through which a cord attached to the lower part of the blind passes, and it is lowered by this cord. It is very difficult to get such blinds to begin moving up if

LABORATORY DARK BLINDS

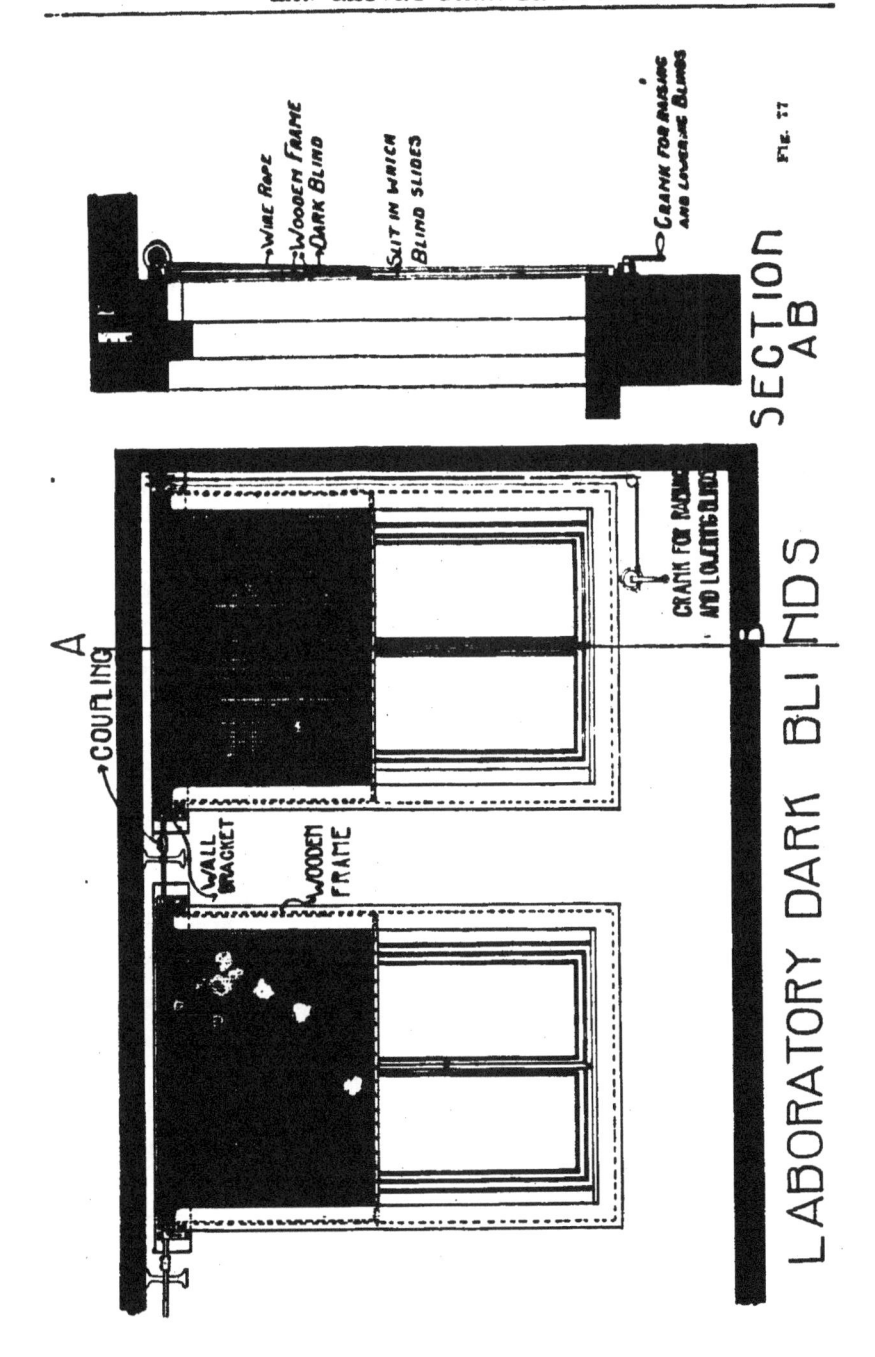

Fig. 77

they are pulled down to the bottom of the frame, and they are frequently torn during the operation. Where it is necessary to raise and lower the blinds frequently during a lesson period, the working of each blind separately is inconvenient. The ideal method is to have all the blinds working on a single shaft, which is manipulated from the front of the room near the teacher's bench (Fig. 77). Where the windows are covered by a continuous blind this is very easily arranged. A spring roller has a pulley rigidly attached to the end which is toward the front of the room. A heavy cord winds around this pulley, with one end attached to the pulley. The dogs on the end of the roller that catch it, leaving the blinds at different heights, are removed. When it is necessary to lower the blind, a pulling of the cord causes the pulley to turn and the blind lowers; when the cord is loosened, the spring will cause the blind to rise. The free end of the cord must be firmly fastened, so that the bottom of the blind will not go so high as to pass clear over the roller. Such a blind should have a heavy bar of iron in a slit at the bottom so as to give it weight. Another method by which it may be raised and lowered is by means of a second pulley and crank at the base, as illustrated in Figure 77 and Figure 80, (E); in this case no spring in the roller is necessary. Where there are several windows with intervening wall space, the best method of raising and lowering the dark blinds is illustrated in Figure 77. Each blind has its own roller; these have no springs in them but are made light and strong. Rods project from the ends of each, and these rods turn in bearings attached to the walls by brackets. The several rollers are connected by couplings, so that they all form a single shaft. A pulley is attached to the end of the shaft toward the front of the room. A wire rope fixed to the upper pulley passes vertically down and is fastened to a lower pulley to which is attached a crank for winding it up. All the blinds are thus operated by this crank at one time. When it is required to raise the blinds, the wire is wound up on the lower pulley. Each blind has an iron lath in the bottom, which has weight enough to pull the blind down, so that all that is necessary to do in order to lower the blinds is to liberate the crank and allow the pulley to turn freely. In some schools the blinds are raised and lowered by an electric motor. It is only necessary to close the switch, when the blinds lower, and to open it in order to cause them to rise again.

Where there is a skylight the manipulation of the dark blinds is not difficult. The skylight in the ceiling is always overarched by a skylight in the roof. An ordinary dark blind with its roller is placed above the skylight in the ceiling, the former sliding over the frame, its weight keeping it close to the surface of the frame. It is operated by a string sliding over pulleys. Where there are dark blinds on both side windows and a skylight, it is possible sometimes to wind the cords controlling them on the same pulley.

DEMONSTRATOR'S BENCH

The demonstrator's bench, Figure 80, is placed across the front of the room, about three or four feet from the black-board. It must not be placed too close to the pupils' seats, as the nearer it is to the front row of seats the greater the rise for the succeeding tiers. It should never be placed on a platform.

In all details it resembles the physical and chemical laboratory demonstration benches already fully described on pages 71-76, and illustrated in Figures 42, 43, 59, and 60.

Three feet is the most convenient height for this bench and three feet a convenient width, since it should not be too wide for the demonstrator to reach across it easily when standing behind it. It should be made long enough to set up on it at the same time apparatus for several demonstrations, as frequently some of this apparatus has to remain there for several days; therefore, a large top surface is required.

The top should be made of hardwood 2 in. thick. In order that there will be no warping, shrinking, or cracking, it is composed of thin strips glued and dovetailed together. The glue should be waterproof (see recipes page 11). The wood must be thoroughly seasoned. Teak is by far the best material and is used almost exclusively in English bench tops. Maple and birch are almost exclusively used in Canada and the United States and are fairly satisfactory, though not comparable with teak. Georgia pine of first-class quality is a material which gives excellent satisfaction; it is hard, non-porous, and does not shrink, warp, nor crack to any great extent. The top should have a drip on the under surface in the form of a fluted groove running completely around about 1 in. from the edge. The edges are squared and project only slightly in front, but at the ends and side toward the demonstrator they project 4 or 5 in. beyond the body of the bench. The top is perfectly flat and continuous with nothing projecting above except the water-tap; all sinks, flues, etc., are closed with flush covers. Toward the centre of the top a slab of alberene stone (Fig. 80, L) is set in the top and flush with its surface. This slab is 3 or 4 ft. long and almost as wide as the bench. It has openings for a small sink and a fume flue as shown in Figure 80. These can both be covered with flush tops. A depression (Fig. 80, M) to be used as a mercury tray is sometimes inserted in the top. This depression is quite shallow and has a gentle slope to one edge, and along this edge is a furrow which deepens toward the back, where there is a glass or iron tube leading into a vessel on a shelf below. A 3- or 5-ply cover fits into this depression when it is not in use. If an experiment is to be performed in which there is any danger of spilling mercury, it will be performed over this tray, then any mercury that is spilled runs at once into the receptacle beneath.

Gas-taps should be placed every 2 ft. along the back of the bench. The gas-pipe runs along beneath the top of the bench and taps project up through circular openings in the top as shown in Figure 43. These openings are about 3 in. in diameter, slightly bevelled on the upper surface, and the top of the gas tube is almost flush with the surface of the bench.

Several electrical terminals are placed along the back edge of the top as in Figure 43. It will be found convenient to have one or more of these in the form of sockets into which a plug is fitted. Several plugs attached to free wires are kept on hand. Some terminals of ordinary binding posts are also convenient. The switches may be of the knife or button varieties. The mains leading to the bench should be connected to the switchboard in such a manner that all the kinds of current available can be connected with them.

A sink 12 in. by 16 in. is placed toward one end of the bench. Five or six inches is of quite sufficient depth. This should be of earthenware, white glazed inside, cane-glazed outside. (See page 19 for full description of sinks.) A cover placed on this sink gives a larger surface for demonstration, but it is difficult to know where to place the cover when not in use. This sink should have two taps laid on with hot and cold water. One of these should be of the swan-neck variety to allow large vessels to be placed under it, and the other should be a lower tap (Fig. 44), springing from the pipe on a level slightly above the top of the bench, to serve as a convenience for running water into the sink and to obviate the splashing which the use of the tall tap would cause. One of the water-taps should have a narrow, corrugated nozzle, in order that rubber tubing may be easily slipped over it to use with a filter pump and in many other operations. A water-pipe runs along just under the top of the bench at the back and to it several taps are attached. These have narrow, corrugated nozzles and are used chiefly for the attachment of rubber tubing passing to condensers, etc. The small sink (Fig. 43, D) is merely for carrying off running water required for cooling or other purposes during an experiment, and may be dispensed with.

The fume vent (Fig. 43, C) in the alberene stone is of great importance, particularly if the room is used for chemical experiments. It is a round, funnel-shaped opening about 8 or 10 in. in diameter, covered by a perforated metal screen, and connected with the fan used for ventilating the fume closets in the chemical laboratory (page 75). If the apparatus is placed near this opening when an experiment is being performed in which irritating or evil-smelling gases are generated, these gases will not escape into the room but will be sucked down through this vent. Some use for a fume vent a large funnel and tube above the bench, the funnel considerably elevated and with the mouth facing down, but experience with both would lead to a preference for the former contrivance. Of course it is an advantage to have both for then the lighter gases will be caught in the funnel and the heavier ones in the vent below. All the openings have closely fitting covers with flush ring handles.

The body of the bench is constructed according to the requirements of the teacher in respect to drawers, cupboards, and recesses. The panelled front is put together in one or two pieces according to its length and is screwed on to the body; so that when it is removed the plumbing, which runs along just behind it, is exposed and easily accessible. Several tiers of drawers of varying depths are placed in the body. Some drawers are shallow, others as deep as 10 in. Some of the shallow drawers are divided by partitions running from front to back, giving long, narrow sections suitable for holding glass tubes, pipettes, and other long, narrow pieces. Others are divided by two sets of partitions at right angles to one another into square compartments, which are used for storing corks and a great variety of other material. Some cupboards occupy part of the space and a recess is left under the middle in which a crock is placed for receiving waste material. Two uprights with a cross-piece may be attached to the top, as in the physical laboratory demonstration bench Figures 59 and 60. These are used for suspensions and are not permanently fixed to the bench but are placed there only when required for use.

All drawer pulls, handles, taps, and other exposed metal work should not be bright, but oxidized or of gun-metal, as nickel and brass rapidly become tarnished by chemicals.

The bench top is finished either with paraffin or any acid-proof stain. The composition and the method of application have been fully discussed already on pages 11, 12. The finish of the exposed parts below will be in keeping with the rest of the furniture.

PUPILS' SEATS

Fig. 78 shows the best arrangement of the pupils' seats. There is an aisle 3 ft. wide on each side, and the individual seats are arranged in a continuous row across the room. It is preferable to have these rows curved, so that the pupils seated toward the ends will face toward the demonstrator at the middle of the teacher's bench. The circular arrangement is particularly necessary where the room is wide. The rows are arranged on platforms each higher than the one in front, so that all pupils are able to see over the heads of those in front. It is of great importance that the heights of these platforms should be accurately known, for the rise is not regular and varies for different rooms. The front row of seats should be not less than 5 ft. from the demonstration bench. If the front row is placed nearer, the tiers of seats will increase in height very rapidly. In

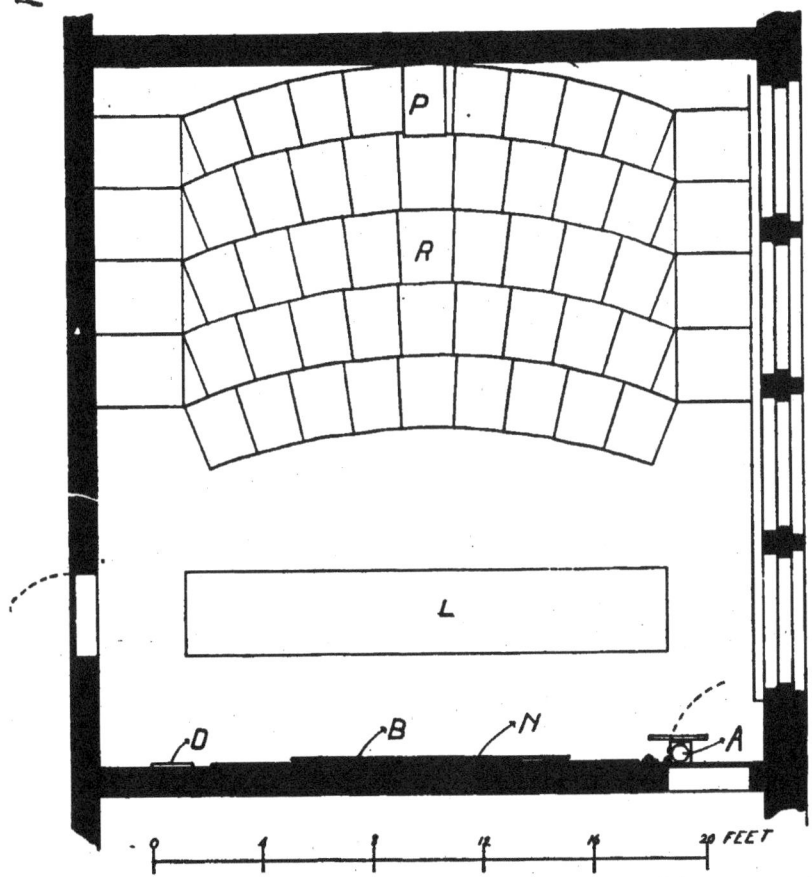

Fig. 78.—Ground plan of science lecture-room for forty pupils. A. Galvanometer and stand. B. Lantern screen. D. Water air-pump and blast. L. Demonstration bench. N. Black-board. P. Lantern stand. R. Pupils' seats.

order to get the heights of the platforms make a sectional drawing of the room, Figure 79. The demonstrator's bench (A) and the pupils' seats (C) must be drawn to scale. Draw vertical lines to represent the backs of the seats. On the front seat measure off 4 ft. 4 in. (1 ft. 4 in. from the floor to the seat and 3 ft. from the seat to the top of the pupil's head (D) when he is seated). From a point (B) above the middle of the teacher's bench draw a line through the point (D) in the front row of seats at the level of the top of the head, and produce it to the second seat (F). This will be the position of the eye of the pupil in the second row. Measure 8 in. above this point in the second row to represent a position 2 in. above the top of the head, and draw a line from the point (B) on the teacher's bench through this point above the head in the second row and produce it to cut the third row. By continuing this the level of the top of the head in each row is found and by measuring down 4 ft. 10 in. the level of the floor of each platform is at once ascertained. It is found that the height increases rapidly toward the back. The platforms (E) are constructed in relation to the seats as represented in Figure 79, each row of seats being placed at the back of the platform. Each platform is 2 ft. 8 in. wide and a lateral space of 2 ft. is devoted to each seat. The aisle on each side will consist of a series of steps. Instead of these steps being the same heights as the platforms it is better to have all of them as nearly as possible of the same height, for nothing is more likely to cause stumbling than to have a series of steps of varying heights.

The seats are of the opera-house type. They have iron frames and wooden backs and seats, the wood being made of several ply to give strength and avoid warping. The seat folds up. The seat is 1 ft. 4 in. above the floor and the back is 1 ft. 3 in. high. A support for a note-book is necessary. This is fixed on the right arm of each desk and is about 10 in. long and 6 or 8 in. wide. It is best to have these supports fixed rigidly, provided platforms can be supplied of sufficient width to allow easy passage between the support and the back of the seat in front. Book supports are supplied that fold in a vertical position and then can be dropped down between two seats. These are noisy and liable to get out of working order, and it is advisable only to use the folding support when so pressed for room that the rows of seats are placed very close together. Of course the seats are screwed to the floor, and numbers on the back of each will be found useful.

The Black-board

Figures 78 and 80 show the position of the black-board. A black-board suspended by pulleys and counterbalanced by weights is most serviceable. As the board in a lecture-room is generally restricted in length, it should be made as wide as possible. The height of the room and other factors may determine to a certain extent the width. When the bottom of the board is a foot above the floor the top should be as high as can be easily reached. As the upper part is written upon it is pushed up and the lower part utilized. Such a board may be suspended in two ways. Two cords pass up from near the ends and have counterweights suspended over pulleys; this is the same method that is used for hanging a window sash. The second is what is known as the Kelvin suspension method. In this method there is a single continuous cord with the two ends attached to the black-board about one fourth of the distance from the ends. On a beam above the black-board are four pulleys; two of them are situated directly above the points of attachment of the cord, the other two are placed above the centre of the black-board and so close together that there is just room for a loop of the cord to hang between them. The cord on each side passes vertically up from its point of attachment to the black-board, over the outer pulley, then over the inner pulley, and hangs in a loop between the inner pulleys. A weight is suspended from the loop. Sash-cord is not strong enough for these suspensions and a socket chain or wire cord should be used. The sides of the black-board run in grooves. Such a movable black-board is always to be recommended, and is quite necessary where

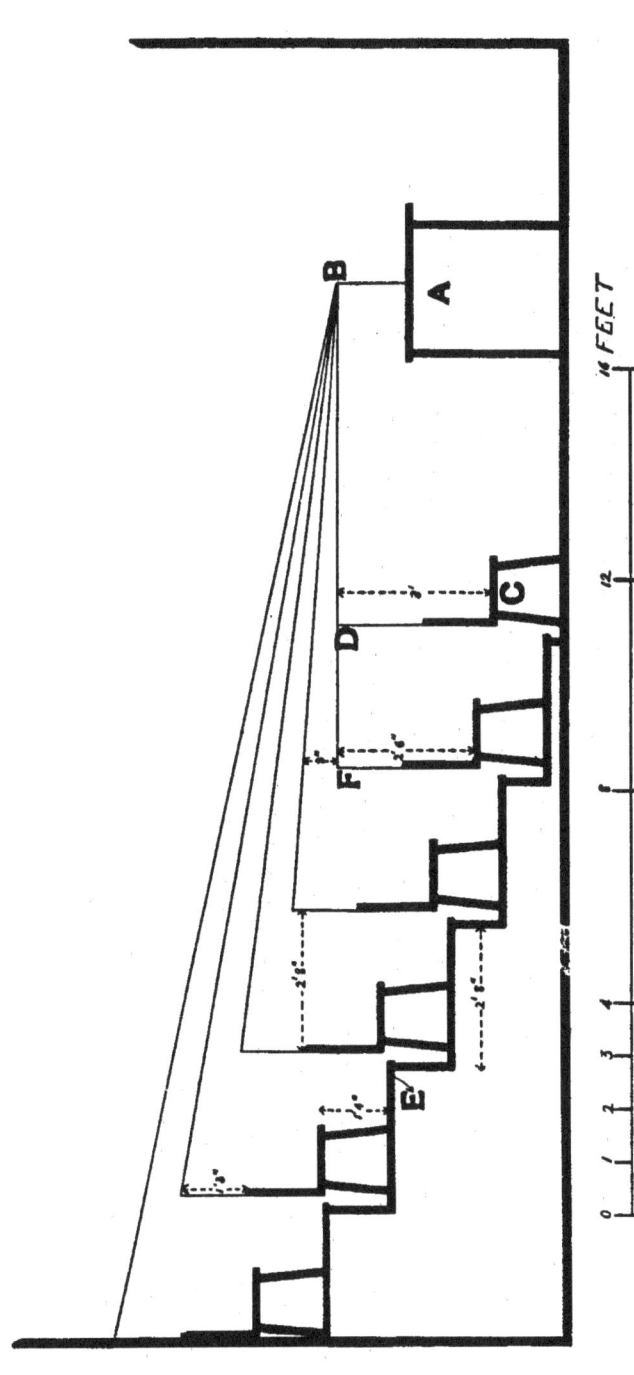

Fig. 79.—Sectional diagram of lecture-room to show how the heights of the platforms for the successive rows are estimated. A. Demonstrator's bench. B. Point above centre of bench. C. Pupils' lecture-room chair. D. Position of top of head of pupil in first row. F. Position of eye of pupil in second row. E. Platform.

there is a fume cupboard in the wall behind the demonstrator's bench. A stationary black-board is sometimes placed behind the movable one; this adds still more to the available black-board surface. If the black-board is stationary, the top of it is fixed at the highest point to which a person can conveniently reach when writing; this will not be more than 6 ft. 9 in. The bottom of a stationary board is placed 3 ft. 6 in. above the floor, as this is about as low as well can be seen from the pupils' seats; this gives a board 3 ft. 3 in. wide. There are only two materials which are found to be satisfactory for black-boards—ground glass and slate. Painted boards are entirely unsuitable, as is also any plaster composition. The black wears off and the board becomes shiny. A sheet of plate glass with the front surface ground rough and the back painted black makes the most pleasing surface to write upon, while a good quality of fine-grained slate is excellent also. The slate is if anything superior to the glass.

Demonstration Galvanometer

There are two special pieces of apparatus that have proven so useful and are so little known in Canada that it is proposed to describe them briefly. It is of great convenience to have some quick method of demonstrating the presence and direction of an electric current. The ordinary lecture-room galvanometer requires much adjustment and then is not sensitive enough to be of great value. Figure 80, (A) shows a galvanometer that is always ready for use and indicates the slightest current in a manner that is plainly visible to the whole room. A sensitive, deadbeat mirror galvanometer is placed on the upper platform. Two or three cells are placed in the box at the bottom. These run a small incandescent lamp in the base of the telescopic tube, which has a lens in the top and a cross wire near the lamp. The film in the lamp is a single, straight thread. The light from the film passes up and is reflected by the mirror into the galvanometer, the mirror on it sends the light back, and the mirror again reflects it down upon the scale. By adjusting the telescope both in position and in direction and by drawing the lens out or in, an image of the cross wire in front of the glowing film of the lamp is thrown on the scale. The galvanometer is adjusted until the image falls on the centre of the scale. Two wires pass from the galvanometer and terminate in binding posts on the demonstration bench. When it is desired to use it, whatever circuit is to be tested for the presence of a current is connected to the binding posts and the current from the dry cells is thrown through the lamp to illuminate it. Then the image on the scale moves either to the right or to the left. The whole apparatus is placed high on the wall of the room facing the class.

Combined Air-pump and Air-blast

The second piece is one much used in Germany but not at all, as far as is known, in Canada. It is a combined water blast and water air-pump. In Figure 80 it is shown at D. This piece of apparatus is purchased complete and already attached to the board, so that it has merely to be connected with the water-pipes, and the outlets from it lead to taps on the demonstration bench. It is used as an air-pump and for producing an air-blast. As an air-pump it will rapidly give a vacuum that is sufficient for all high school experiments. The blast is sufficiently strong to run a strong blast lamp, to blow an organ-pipe, or to demonstrate some of the experiments used to illustrate Bernoulli's principle. It has one pipe connected to the water-works main, one to the waste, and two terminating in taps on

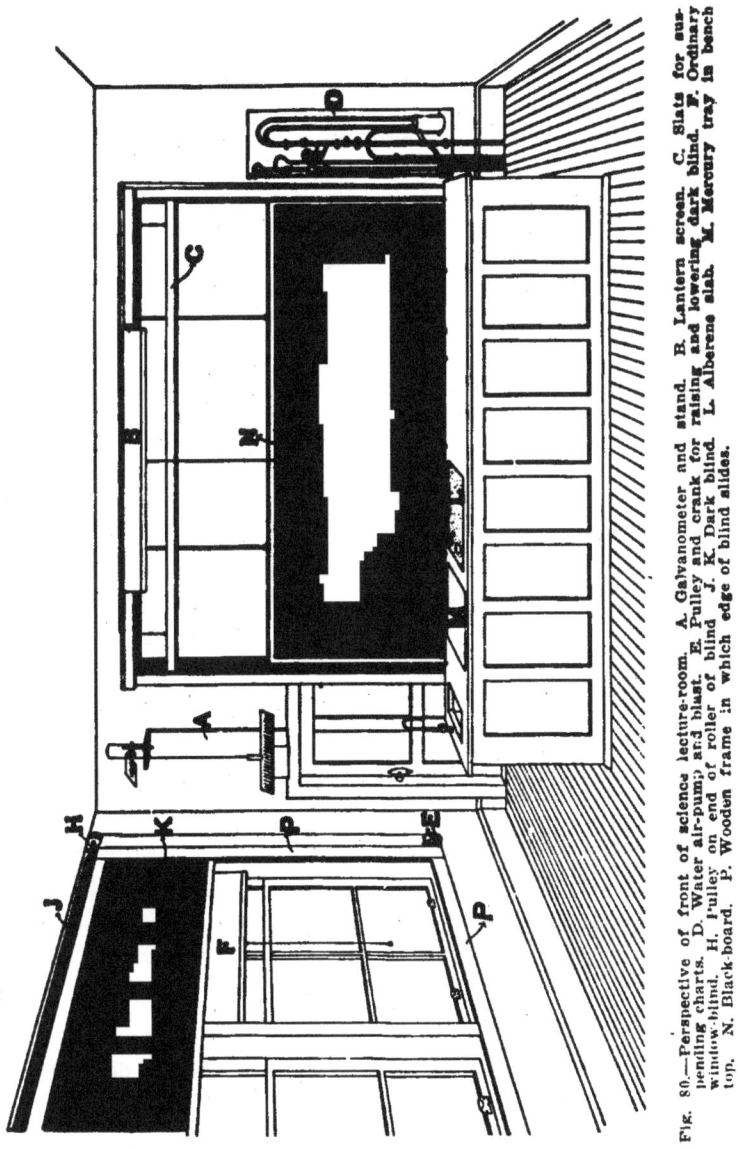

Fig. 80.—Perspective of front of science lecture-room. A. Galvanometer and stand. B. Lantern screen. C. Slats for suspending charts. D. Water air-pump and blast. E. Pulley and crank for raising and lowering dark blind. F. Ordinary window-blind. H. Pulley on end of roller of blind. J. K. Dark blind. L. Alberene slab. M. Mercury tray in bench top. N. Blackboard. P. Wooden frame in which edge of blind slides.

the demonstration bench. In order to get a vacuum or a blast one or the other of the taps is connected by tubing with the bell-jar, organ-pipe, or other apparatus. Of course such a piece of apparatus can be installed only where there is a water-works system, and the stronger the water pressure the more rapid and effective the result. There are two gauges on the board, one to register the vacuum the other to indicate the water pressure. As the whole apparatus costs less than forty dollars it is not so expensive as a moderate priced air-pump, and yet it will do all the work of an air-pump and much else besides, as indicated above and, unlike the air-pump, is not likely to get out of order.

A CHART HANGER

In the lecture-room the chart is a more valuable means of illustration than even the lantern slide. It can be shown in colours, and several can be arranged side by side for comparison. Several devices to serve for exhibition of these charts have been described, the simplest and most effective one being that described by Ganong. A wooden slat, Figure 80 (C), extends horizontally, and the ends run in grooves on two vertical uprights. The horizontal bar is raised and lowered by means of two cords attached near the ends of it. These pass vertically over two pulleys and pass down at one end over a third pulley. Two or three of these bars may be made one in front of the other, each sliding in its own groove and raised and lowered by its own set of cords. The charts are suspended from this by card-holders consisting of a bulldog clip with a hook above it. The board from which they are suspended is 4 in. wide, ⅞ in. thick, and as long as the available space will permit. The upper edge is rounded to fit the hooks of the card-holders. These boards should be thoroughly seasoned, so that where there are several of them, they will not curve and warp and thus interfere with one another in passing up or down.

SUSPENSIONS

There should be a means of suspension over the demonstration bench. This may be achieved in several ways. Metal uprights with an adjustable horizontal cross-bar, such as is shown in Figures 59 and 60, are valuable. These can be removed when not in use. But a support attached to the ceiling is also useful as supplementary to these. This may be a wooden scantling immediately over the middle of the demonstration bench and suspended rigidly from the ceiling at such a height that it can be reached when standing on this bench. It has a set of hooks attached to the lower side of it, and from these pendulums, wire springs, etc., can be suspended.

ARRANGEMENT OF LABORATORIES

It will only be necessary in concluding this *Educational Pamphlet* to state a few facts in regard to the arrangement of the several laboratories in relation to one another. It should scarcely be necessary to say that all should be situated on the same floor. Much of the apparatus is used in all the laboratories, and to have to carry it from one floor to another is an unnecessary waste of time. They should be placed as compactly as possible. They may be in a row on one side of the hall or on opposite sides of it. Store-rooms are placed preferably between laboratories, so that the stored material is accessible to both.

Fig. 81.—Ground plan of science rooms in a medium-sized school. The furniture in the chemical and physical laboratories is arranged the same as in the ground plans shown in Figs. 54 and 64, where each article is named.

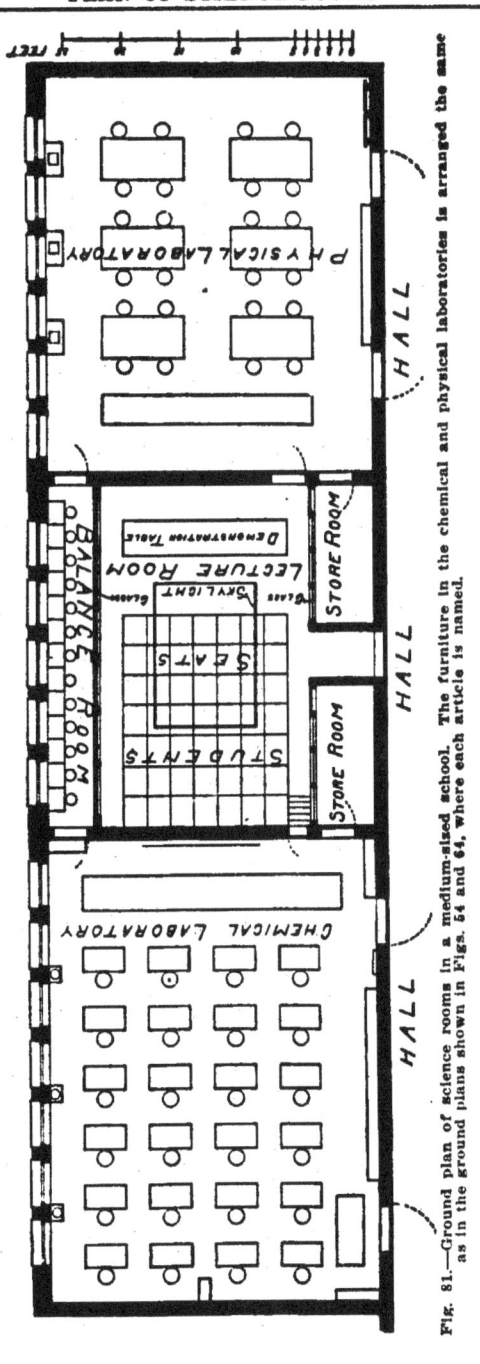

In Figure 81 is shown a plan of a set of rooms for science work which can be recommended strongly to the moderate-sized high school and collegiate institute. It consists of physical and chemical laboratories, a lecture-room, and two store-rooms, with a well-lighted balance-room that is adjacent to both laboratories. These are all placed compactly and do not occupy an excessive amount of space. The lecture-room is placed between the two laboratories, so that it may be easily reached by doors from both. After pupils have finished their experiments in the laboratory, they can pass into the lecture-room for explanations. The lecture-room also has a door leading into the hall, so that it is accessible from the hall without any interruption to the laboratory classes. There are two store-rooms, one for chemistry and one for physics, with doors leading directly into the respective laboratories. As the apparatus from each laboratory will be continually used for demonstration work in the lecture-room, both store-rooms have doors into the lecture-room as well, so that their apparatus is just as convenient to the lecture-room as it is to the laboratory. The store-rooms should have their sides that are toward the lecture-room made of glass partitions that extend right to the ceiling, in order that they may have good light. The partition between the balance-room and the lecture-room consists of prismatic glass right to the ceiling, so that the latter will be excellently lighted from the lateral windows. The drawing represents a skylight as being in the lecture-room. Such a light is a great advantage, but is possible, of course, only when the science rooms are located on the top floor.

The balance-room is long and narrow, and is equally accessible from both laboratories, so that the same set of balances can be used for both physics and chemistry. The doors leading into it from each laboratory should be made largely of glass, so that the teacher in the laboratory has complete observation of the pupils while they are at work in the balance-room. It has a balance shelf 24 ft. long, which is sufficient for twelve balances.

The furniture of the physical and chemical laboratories is the same in character and arrangement as is represented in Figures 54 and 64, and the explanations given there can be used to interpret the meaning of the drawing. It is necessary to call the attention to one detail in the arrangement. The demonstrator's bench in each laboratory is placed preferably at the end nearest to the store-room; this makes the apparatus convenient for the teacher. For the complete arrangements of the furniture in the physical and chemical laboratories, Chapters IV and V should be consulted, and also Figures 54 and 64.

This plan of laboratories is suitable for large high schools and small collegiate institutes. The larger collegiate institutes will have in addition at least a biological laboratory, and perhaps an elementary laboratory. A suitable place for the biological laboratory would be on the opposite side of the hall directly across from the lecture-room, so that the latter would be accessible to it also. However, much will depend on the direction in which the hall runs, as the biological laboratory requires eastern or southern light or both, and it might be better to put it at the end of the physical or chemical laboratory where it would probably have windows on two sides.

CPSIA information can be obtained
at www.ICGtesting.com
Printed in the USA
BVHW041024170119
538079BV00004B/55/P